INSIGNIA

of

WORLD

WAR II

INSIGNIA

of

WORLD WAR II

◆

LESLIE McDONNELL

SILVERDALE BOOKS

Published by Silverdale Books
an imprint of Bookmart Ltd
Registered Number 2372865
Trading as Bookmart Ltd
Desford Road
Enderby
Leicester LE9 5AD

ISBN: 1-85605-463-2

Editorial and design by
Amber Books Ltd
Bradley's Close
74–77 White Lion Street
London N1 9PF

Design: Hawes Design

Artwork credits:
Mainline Design: 10(r), 11 (r), 13(l), 14, 17(r), 18(l), 29(l), 32(l),
35(r), 38(r), 40(r), 42(l), 50, 51(l), 52(r), 54, 55, 56(l), 57, 58, 59(l),
60(l), 61, 62, 63, 70(l), 71, 72, 73, 74, 75, 76(r), 78, 79(l), 80, 82(r),
83, 84, 85, 86, 87, 88, 89, 90, 91, 92(r), 93(r), 104, 105, 106, 107,
108, 109, 110, 111, 119, 120, 121, 122, 123, 128, 129, 130, 131,
132, 133, 142, 144, 145, 146, 147(r), 148, 149(r), 150, 151, 161(l),
163, 187, 188(r), 189
All other artworks © Orbis Publishing Ltd

Picture credits:
TRH Pictures

Printed in Singapore

Contents

INTRODUCTION

Insignia has always played an integral part in warfare. Flags, banners and regimental crests have been an effective way of binding soldiers' allegiances to individual units. Though fighting formations in World War II did not go into combat with battle standards, unit identification and loyalty was just as strong as in preceding conflicts. This book contains the badges and emblems of the most famous units that participated in World War II, such as the German Waffen-SS divisions, the British Parachute Regiment and Grenadier Guards, the Italian *Bersaglieri*, the US Marine Corps, and the French Foreign Legion. Each badge is accompanied by text that details the unit's history and its most notable engagements in the war.

As well as individual units, this book also features the rank insignia of the armed forces of all the nations that participated in the most destructive conflict mankind has known. The superb full-colour rank insignia spreads show all the braiding, piping, cap badges, shoulder boards and sleeve stripes to full effect, and also allow the reader to appreciate the subtle differences in rank differentiation between the armed forces of the warring countries. Because there were a plethora of idiosyncratic rules and regulations regarding the wearing of rank insignia, in both Allied and Axis formations alike, the art-works are accompanied by text that explains how and where rank badges were worn on uniforms.

Nations have always rewarded the bravest of their soldiers, sailors and air-men, and so the medals and awards of the major belligerent nations are cov-ered in full. As well as the more famous gallantry awards, such as the Iron Cross, Knight's Cross, Victoria Cross, Purple Heart and Congressional Medal of Honor, the book also includes lesser-known medals, such as the Order of Ushakov, Medal of Aeronautical Valour, Military Order of William and the Order of the Grunwald Cross. Many of these awards were given posthu-mously, for let it not be forgotten that millions of servicemen gave their lives in the service of their country between 1939 and 1945.

Leslie McDonnell

Germany

By the end of World War II some 9,400,000 Germans had been called to the colours: Army 6,500,000; Air Force 2,100,000; and Navy 800,000. They served in dozens of regiments, squadrons and flotillas, and wore a plethora of rank and unit insignia, plus, for those who earned them, there were a host of military awards.

Germany

Knight's Cross of the Iron Cross

Reintroduced on the order of Adolf Hitler on 1 September 1939 as an award for Germans and citizens and her allies displaying exceptional bravery and/or leadership in the face of the enemy, the Knight's Cross was among the most prestigious of Nazi Germany's combat awards. When awarded, it was worn at the neck from the ribbon.

The number of grades of the Iron Cross was expanded to eight, which, listed in ascending order, were: second class; first class; Knight's Cross; Knight's Cross with oak leaves; with oak leaves and swords; with oak leaves, swords and diamonds; with golden oak leaves, swords and diamonds (awarded only once) and a larger Grand Cross (awarded only once, to Hermann Göring for the Luftwaffe's part in the 1940 French campaign).

During World War II, approximately 7300 Knight's Crosses were bestowed, a total of eight with oak leaves, 158 with oak leaves and diamonds, and 27 with oak leaves, swords and diamonds.

Badge	A Maltese Cross 48mm (1.89in) wide of cast iron edged with silver. Reverse: silver. Front: the swastika centred
Ribbon	Red with white and black outer edge stripes

The Iron Cross, 1939

Introduced by Frederick William III in 1813 as a Prussian Military Decoration for distinguished service in the Prussian War of Liberation, it was revived by William I for the Franco-Prussian War of 1870, recreated in 1914 and last revived by Adolf Hitler on 1 September 1939, on the outbreak of World War II.

The symbols of the crown and royal cypher, which adorned the centre of the original Crosses, was replaced by a swastika in 1939. The original Cross had three classes, in ascending order; second class, first class and Grand Cross, the latter being awarded 19 times during World War I. A special class, the Grand Cross on a radiant star, was created especially for Field Marshal Blucher after the Battle of Waterloo. It was awarded on one other occasion, to Field Marshal Paul von Hindenburg in 1918. Since 1957, a Federal German statute permits the Iron Cross to be worn only if the swastika is removed.

Badge	A black cross of cast iron within a silver frame. Front: the swastika centred, the date 1939 on the lower arm. Reverse: plain save for the original inception date of 1813 on the lower arm
Ribbon	Red with white and black outer edge stripes

4th Panzer Division

Pour le Mérite

A distinguished Prussian order established in 1740 by Frederick the Great. The original order had individual classes for the military and for scientific and artistic achievement. Frederick III limited the award to the military in 1810, but in 1842 Frederick William IV created a civilian division for the arts and sciences.

During the Franco-Prussian War and World War I, the military division was the highest individual reward for gallantry in action. The award went into a period of stagnation in 1935 but was revived by the Federal Republic of Germany in 1952. The order is currently awarded for outstanding achievements in either the arts or sciences. Membership is limited to 30 German citizens, and up to 30 foreigners.

In the German Army, divisional signs existed only after October 1940 when the High Command decreed that the existing 18 panzer divisions then extant should display allotted symbols. Therefore, in 1941 every German division adopted a sign, which was painted on its vehicles.

The 4th Panzer Division was formed in November 1938 at Würzburg, being based at Nuremberg as part of XIII Military District. Its first action was in Poland, when it formed part of Army Group South. At this time it was composed of the 35th and 36th Panzer Regiments, the 12th Schutzen Regiment, the 103rd Artillery Regiment, the 7th Reconnaissance Battalion, the 49th Anti-tank Battalion, and the standard support services.

During the campaign in Poland the division took part in the assault on Warsaw, and it later went on to fight in France and central Russia. At the beginning of the war its main armour component consisted of Panzer II tanks, though as the conflict went on it took delivery of better armoured and armed Panzer IV and Panther tanks.

Badge	Originally a Maltese Cross in blue enamel edged with gold, with four gold eagles between the arms of the cross. The crowned letter 'F' appeared on the top arm of the cross, and the legend POUR LE MERITE on the three lower arms. The ribbon was held by a top suspension clip.
Ribbon	Black with edge stripes of silver-white

Battle Honours

- *Poland, 1939*
- *France, 1940*
- *Central Russia, 1941–44*
- *Germany, 1945*

369th Croat Infantry Division

The 'Free and Independent State of Croatia' was declared by the pro-Nazi Ante Pavelic on 10 April 1941. Within days of the German invasion of Russia, Pavelic appealed for volunteers to form a Croat Legion. Three battalions were raised, and at Dollersheim in Austria they were formed into the 369th Reinforced (Croat) Infantry Regiment. The Regiment, or Croat Legion, as it became known, had an effective strength of 5000 officers and men serving in three battalions with machine-gun, anti-tank and field artillery support.

The Regiment joined the German 100th Light Division on 22 August 1941. Posted to the southern sector of the Russian front, it saw action at Valki, Kharkov, Kalatch and along the River Don, and took part in the battle for Stalingrad, where all but 1000 of its members were killed or captured when von Paulus was forced to surrender. Between September and December 1942 the Germans raised two new Croatian regiments, designated the 369th Infantry Division.

15th Panzer Division

The 15th Panzer Division was equipped with powerful PzKpfw Mark III and IV tanks. In addition to an artillery regiment of three battalions with 24 105mm and 12 150mm guns, the core of the Division was provided by two battalions of 8th Panzer Regiment, each comprising three companies with 20 tanks, further divided into four troops of five tanks each.

Support for the tanks was found by the 15th Infantry Brigade (Motorised), with its two regiments, the 115th and 200th, each with three battalions of three companies, plus a machine-gun company of 150 men with 18 guns and six mortars, an engineer platoon and a signal section. An additional company within each regiment was armed with a highly potent combination of nine 75mm, 105mm and 150mm guns.

Battle Honours

- *North Africa, 1941*
- *Battle of El Alamein, October 1942*
- *Tunisia, 1943*
- *Sicily, 1943*

Battle Honours

- *Eastern Front, 1941*
- *Southern Russia, 1942*
- *Stalingrad, 1942–43*
- *Yugoslavia, 1943–44*

Afrika Corps

General Rommel landed in North Africa on 12 February 1941, and on 14 February was joined by the first elements of the Afrika Corps. Within days the 5th Light Division, supported by two Italian divisions, launched an attack against the British positions. Over the coming 18 months, the Afrika Corps built up a fearsome reputation for professionalism.

Despite Rommel's success, Hitler regarded North Africa as a side-show and denied the Corps crucial personnel and equipment. It was never more than two German panzer divisions and a light division supported by two Italian divisions. The build up of British and Commonwealth forces in Egypt meant that defeat for the Afrika Corps was simply a matter of time. The Afrika Corps' palm-and-swastika sign, which was painted on vehicles, is shown above.

Belt Buckle

The SS (*Schutzstaffel* – Protection Squad) was formed as a body guard to Adolf Hitler in April 1925 shortly after his release from Landsberg Prison. By the end of 1944, it had grown to a strength of some 910,000 men in 38 divisions – an army in itself. Originally the SS was seen as a paramilitary police force, but after the 'Night of the Long Knives' it began to develop along different lines, and in March 1935 its full-time armed units were redesignated SS-*Verfügungstruppen* (SS-VT – special purpose troops).

The first unit to be formed was the *SS Leibstandarte Adolf Hitler*, followed in October 1933 by the SS-Standarte *Deutschland*. Many factors played a role in motivating volunteers to join the SS, not all of them evil: political ideology, a belief that Germany had been betrayed by her politicians in 1918, and the hope of advancement, all played their roles.

The SS swore an oath to Adolf Hitler. The Waffen-SS belt buckle, which was worn by all members of the organisation, is shown above. It carries the motto of the SS, 'Loyalty is my Honour', in German.

Battle Honours
● *Agedabia, March 1941*
● *Tobruk, June 1942*
● *First Battle of El Alamein, July 1942*
● *Second Battle of El Alamein, October 1942*

Battle Honours
● *Poland, 1939*
● *France, 1940*
● *The Balkans, 1941*
● *Eastern Front, 1941–45*

Condor Legion

The Condor Legion was formed in November 1936, four months after the outbreak of the Spanish Civil war. Under the command of General-Major Hugo Sperrle the force quickly grew to incorporate fighter, bomber and reconnaissance gruppen (wings), with a supporting coastal element, flak and administrative units.

Each Group was identified by the number '88'; thus the bomber element became Kampfgruppe 88, the fighters Jagdgruppe 88, and the reconnaissance group Aufklarungsgruppe 88. The fighter group initially comprised three Staffeln, each with 12 He 51 fighter aircraft, but was soon expanded to a fourth, again flying He 51 fighters together with other 'volunteer' German units fighting in Spain. The Condor Legion was used as an ideal opportunity to train Luftwaffe pilots in the art of war, a factor which was to prove crucial in the years ahead.

By the beginning of 1938 the Legion was a rather battered force: its crews were flying up to seven misions a day. Worse, some of its aircraft, such as the He 51, were becoming dangerously obsolete even in the ground-attack role, and the flak guns were all but worn out. Between July and October 1938, the Legion could field only 70 aircraft, and the last missions were flown on 6 February 1938. In total the Legion had destroyed 386 enemy aircraft in Spain.

Das Reich *Division*

The 2nd SS Panzer Division *Das Reich* was formed as the SS-VT (*SS-Verfügungstruppen* - Special Purpose Troops) in 1935. Its two principle regiments, the *Germania* and *Deutschland*, were each expanded to three battalions in 1936, before the Division obtained its own general staff. A third regiment, *Der Führer*, was added in 1938. In 1939, the Division was expanded to incorporate artillery, reconnaissance and communications support units.

After seeing action in Poland, it reformed in Neidenburg. In 1940 the *Der Führer* Regiment spearheaded the assault on Holland; the rest of the Division fought its way through France. Badly mauled at Arras, it undertook a forced march south to secure the Maginot Line. Later that year, the *Germania* Regiment was transferred to the newly formed *Wiking* Division and *Das Reich* fought through the Balkans and played a major part in Operation 'Barbarossa'. The divisional insignia is shown above. Such markings were usually painted in white, yellow, grey or black on the front and rear of the division's vehicles.

Battle Honours

- *Durango, April 1937*
- *Guernica, April 1937*
- *Madrid, July 1937*
- *Aragon, June 1938*

Battle Honours

- *France, 1940*
- *The Balkans, 1941*
- *Eastern Front, 1941–45*
- *The West, 1944*

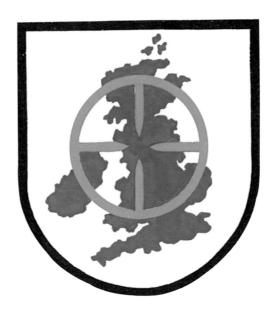

Estonian Legion

The 'Estonian Legion' was formed to assist in the overthrow of Bolshevism on 28 August 1942, the first anniversary of the liberation of the capital, Talin, by German forces. The hatred of Russia was so strong that recruitment was highly successful, permitting the formation of three battalions, designated the 1st Estonian SS Volunteer Grenadier Regiment.

In March 1943 the 1st Battalion was detached for service with SS Division *Wiking* on the Eastern Front, where it was redesignated the Estnische Freiwilligen-Bataillon *Narwa*. Recruitment remained so solid that within two months the residue of the Regiment had expanded to brigade strength, and on 5 May was redesignated the 3rd Estonian SS Volunteer Brigade.

The Brigade was first employed on anti-partisan operations in Estonia, but was later rushed to the front to help repel an imminent Russian breakout. Despite its losses the Brigade was steadily expanded, and on 24 January 1944 was officially designated the 20th Armed Grenadier Division. The Division fought to the end, most of the Estonians being captured by the Soviets, and summarily executed, in May 1945. A few escaped and gave themselves up to the Anglo-American forces.

Experimental Group 210

Luftwaffe Erpobunsgruppe (Experimental Group) 210, which bore the motto 'England in a Bombsight', was formed in June 1940. The Group was equipped with 24 Messerschmitt Bf 109Es and 110s, all of which retained their standard armament and were equipped to carry 500lb and 1000lb bombs. Once they had dropped their bomb load, they could return to their fighter role and defend themselves.

During the early stages of the Battle of Britain the Group conducted large-scale raids, but transferred to hit-and-run sorties flown in pairs. In June 1941 it was assigned to the Eastern Front, where in Operation 'Barbarossa' it flew in support of Army Group Centre. Having flown almost non-stop strafing actions against Soviet airfields in the Minsk area it moved in support of the panaceas advancing through the Pripet marshes towards Smolensk. It was finally disbanded in 1942.

Battle Honours

- *Eastern Front, 1943*
- *Battle of Narwa, 1944*
- *Czechoslovakia, 1944–45*
- *Eastern Germany, 1945*

Battle Honours

- *Battle of France, 1940*
- *Battle of Britain, 1940*
- *Invasion of Russia, June 1941*
- *Eastern Front, 1942*

Finnish Volunteer Legion

Finland was never occupied by Germany, yet her nationals volunteered for service with the Waffen-SS in sufficient numbers to form a Volunteer Battalion which paraded on 5 June 1941 in Germany. Originally, its 125 officers, 109 NCOs, and 850 other ranks were to be designated Jager Battalion, after the 27 Jager Battailon of World War I. However, the title was ultimately rejected in favour of SS-Volunteer Battalion Northeast.

Some 400 members of the Battalion, all with combat experience from the 1939–40 Winter War against the Soviets, were attached to the SS-Division *Wiking*, taking part in the German invasion of Russia in 1941. The remainder were joined by fresh drafts, and in September 1941 redesignated the Finnish Volunteer Battalion of the SS.

Flemish Legion

While most Flemish and Dutch citizens remained totally loyal to their governments in exile, some elected for service with the German occupiers. The SS-Regiment *Westland*, formed shortly after the invasion, was brought up to strength within weeks. Although theoretically trained for domestic 'police duties', the Regiment was absorbed into the Waffen-SS as part of the *Wiking* Division during the winter of 1940–41, and was eventually transferred to the Eastern Front.

A second unit, the Volunteer Regiment *Northwest*, comprising volunteers from Belgium, Holland and Denmark, was formed in April 1941. When Hitler invaded Russia in June, it was broken up, and its Flemish recruits transferred to the newly formed Flemish Legion. Membership was open to those aged 17–40, and preference given to Belgian ex-regular soldiers. The Legion received its Colours (shown above) in August 1941.

Battle Honours

- *Operation 'Barbarossa', 1941*
- *Eastern Front, 1941*
- *Southern Russia, 1942*
- *Southern Russia, 1943*

Battle Honours

- *Leningrad, 1941*
- *Leningrad, January 1942*
- *Northern Russia, January–July 1942*
- *Northern Russia, 1943–44*

Grossdeutschland Division

Cuff bands were an important aspect of German military dress, and thus a large number existed during the Third Reich period. The *Grossdeutschland* cuff band was introduced on 7 October 1940 to replace the Infantry Regiment *Grossdeutschland* cuff band which had been issued six months previously. It was worn on the right forearm.

The *Grossdeutschland* Panzergrenadier Division was formed from the regiment of the same name in 1942, and as such fought mostly on the Eastern Front. As a regiment of four battalions it had seen action in France in 1940 as part of Guderian's XIX Army Corps. In 1941 it received substantial artillery, flak and pioneer reinforcements. As part of the 10th Panzer Division it spearheaded the invasion of the Soviet Union in June 1941, but suffered severe casualties in the process.

Panzer Corps *Grossdeutschland* was formed in November 1944, and for the rest of the war it fought a valiant rearguard campaign in the face of overwhelming Russian forces, giving ground grudgingly. The *Grossdeutschland* was an élite unit of the German Army, and as such it had SS-style entry requirements. With the exception of the *Grossdeutschland* Guards Battalion, which was annihilated in Berlin, the corps fought its last action in northern Germany, in the Schleswig-Holstein area.

High Seas Fleet Badge

During World War II eight badges were introduced by the German Navy as a reward for individuals or crews who had achieved special merits in action. All these badges were worn on the left breast.

The High Seas Fleet War badge was instituted in April 1941 to reward the crews of battleships and cruisers for 13 weeks of active service at sea, or single successful actions. There was a high award, in diamonds.

The High Seas Fleet had a chequered career, but it was viewed with suspicion by Hitler, who believed it tied down valuable resources for very little in return. This was rather unfortunate, because the fleet had seen hard service against the superior Royal Navy.

Battle Honours

- *France, 1940*
- *Yugoslavia, 1941*
- *Eastern Front, 1941–44*
- *Germany, 1945*

Battle Honours

- *Norway, April–May 1940*
- *North Atlantic, May 1941*
- *English Channel, 1941–43*
- *Baltic, 1945*

SS-Leibstandarte 'Adolf Hitler'

The Leibstandarte 'Adolf Hitler', Hitler's SS body guard, represented the élite of the Waffen-SS. During the early stages of the war, before wartime demands forced a relaxation of standards, its Commanding Officer, 'Sepp' Dietrich, recruited exclusively from those who were aged 23–35, at least 1.8m (5ft 11in) tall, and in peak physical condition. No man was accepted if he had a criminal record, or unless able to prove pure Aryan ancestry. Initially, Dietrich would not even accept a man if he had a single tooth filled.

The Regiment, which was based in Berlin, received its first standard during the Party Congress at Nuremburg in September 1933. It was committed to battle from the onset of World War II, forming part of the second echelon during the invasion of Poland. It quickly gained a reputation for brutality, being responsible in June 1940 for the massacre of some 70 British prisoners-of-war at Wormhoudt.

The unit took part in the invasions of Greece and Yugoslavia in 1941, and later also joined the invasion of Russia. In 1942 it was transformed into a Panzergrenadier division, remaining on the Eastern Front throughout the year after that. It was decimated in the months following the Allied landings at Normandy, having to be pulled out in order that it could be reformed.

Leibstandarte Division Waffen-SS

In almost every campaign in which the German armed forces fought during World War II, the armed SS made a significant contribution. It could trace its origins back to 1923, when a special guard element was formed from within the Nazi Party to act as a bodyguard for Hitler. The power of the SS grew under its Reichsführer, Himmler, and in 1934 it became omnipotent when its rival, the SA, was ruthlessly suppressed.

The Waffen-SS quickly gained a reputation for brutality, as well as dependability and steadfastness. As the war progressed it was rushed from crisis to crisis as the German armies struggled to hold back the weight of numbers on the Allied side. Officially entitled the Waffen-SS from spring 1940, by 1945 it had grown into a force of 910,000 officers and men. Shown above is the formation sign of the *Leibstandarte*.

Battle Honours

- *Poland, 1939*
- *France and The Low Countries, 1940*
- *Eastern Front, 1941–45*
- *The West, 1944–45*

Battle Honours

- *Poland, 1939*
- *France and The Low Countries, 1940*
- *Eastern Front, 1941–45*
- *The West, 1944–45*

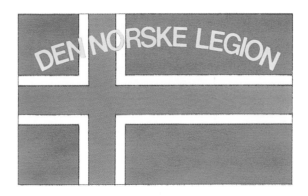

Mountain Troops

The Mountain Troops were formed during World War I, and went on to earn a reputation as tough fighting soldiers during World War II. During the invasion of Poland, the 1st, 2nd, and 3rd Mountain Divisions, which were deployed on the southern flank of the German advance, moved forward at such speed that they out-flanked the defenders. Later the force fought with distinction in several campaigns.

In Norway the 2nd and 3rd Mountain Divisions linked up to fight their way to Narvik, seeing action at Trofors, Eisford and Rognan. In 1941, the newly formed 5th and 6th Divisions deployed to the Balkans where they helped to open up the route into Greece. The 5th Mountain Division went on to further distinguish itself during the invasion of Crete. The woven white metal edelweiss insignia, shown above, was worn on the right upper sleeve.

Norwegian Legion

The formation of the Norwegian Legion commenced on 29 June 1941, exactly one week after the German invasion of the Soviet Union. The SS who carried out the formation intended the legion to be manned exclusively by nationals and organised on Norwegian Army lines. Two regiments were formed as a result; the *Viken* Regiment and *Viking* Regiment.

The first 300 officers and men travelled to Germany on 29 July 1941, followed in mid-August by a further 700 volunteers. The Legion saw its first service in February 1942, as part of the 2nd SS Motorised Infantry Brigade on the Leningrad front.

Further vigorous recruiting in the middle months of 1942 resulted in the raising of two further companies, one largely from the Norwegian Labour Service, which was called the Arbeidstjenesten, the other from the Police. The latter, the Politikompaniet, joined the Legion on the outskirts of Leningrad in September 1942.

The survivors were withdrawn from the front in March 1943, and on 20 May the Legion was officially dissolved. The Norwegian flag insignia of the Legion was worn on the right upper sleeve.

Battle Honours

- *Poland, 1939*
- *Norway, 1940*
- *The Balkans and Crete, 1941*
- *Eastern Front, 1941–45*

Battle Honours

- *Leningrad, February 1942*
- *Leningrad, July 1942*
- *Leningrad, September 1942*
- *Northern Russia, early 1943*

Schalburg *Corps*

The first Danes to be recruited into the German forces were enlisted into the SS-Verfügungstruppen Standarte *Nordland*. By the spring of 1941 recruitment had slowed to a trickle; Himmler ordered the formation of a new volunteer regiment, named *Nordwest*, to be organised by, but not belonging to, the Waffen-SS. Within a week of the Russian invasion, the Danish Government announced the formation of a such a group, the Free Corps.

A second battalion was raised in August, and the unit first saw action in May 1942, fighting as part of the *Wiking* Division. Reorganisation of the Waffen-SS in 1943 demanded that those Danish volunteers still serving were transferred to the *Nordland* Regiment of the *Wiking* Division. After the disbandment of the Free Corps in 1943, survivors were enlisted into the *Schalburg* Corps, bearing the name of the previous Free Corps commander, SS-Obersturmbannführer Christian von Schalburg. The Corps was divided into two distinct groups, one active and the other in support. It was disbanded in February 1945.

Stuka 2

StG2, which could trace its origins to the Luftwaffe's first dive-bomber unit formed in 1935, was the most successful German unit employed in the tank-killing (Panzerknacker) role. The unit, which was equipped with the Ju 87A Stuka, was evaluated during the Spanish Civil War, but underwent its first real test in September 1939 when it was heavily involved in the Blitzkrieg attack on Poland. In June 1940, as part of the Luftwaffe's VIII Flierkorps, it was equally successful in the Low Countries and France.

The unit was markedly less successful against the RAF during the Battle of Britain, to the extent that the Luftwaffe was forced to withdraw its entire Stuka fleet from the front. Nevertheless, the aircraft remained a potent weapon, and was again used successfully in the invasion of Greece and in the Mediterranean. It was transferred to the Eastern Front, where it remained until 1945.

Battle Honours

- *Demyansk Pocket, 1942*
- *Northern Russia, 1943*
- *Yugoslavia, 1943*
- *Eastern Front, 1943–45*

Battle Honours

- *Spanish Civil War, 1935–38*
- *Poland, 1939*
- *The West, 1940*
- *Eastern Front, 1941–45*

Totenkopf *Division*

The Totenkopf, the Death's Head, with the crossed bones positioned directly behind the skull, was originally worn by the Prussian 1st and 2nd Bodyguard Hussars.

The *Totenkopf* Division, commanded by Theodore Eicke, originated from the so-called Death's Head Unit formed as a police unit for concentration camp duties. The members of the Division wore the Death's Head on their left collar patches, while the badge was also worn throughout the Waffen-SS as a whole on various headgear.

The *Totenkopf* Division was moulded by Eicke into a fearsome fighting machine, and on the Eastern Front showed it was among the best units in the German war machine. However, Eicke also instilled into his men a hatred of the enemies of National Socialism and total contempt for so-called 'lower' races. This resulted in countless atrocities against prisoners and civilians alike, especially in Russia.

Wiking *Division*

During World War II, and particularly after the invasion of Russia, the German propaganda machine attempted to depict Germany as a bastion against democratic excesses and the canker of communism.

Essential ingredients in this propaganda were the non-German volunteer contingents, variously known as Legions and Free Corps, which were organised by the SS and served alongside the German forces, mainly on the Eastern Front. From the outset these Legion and Free Corps volunteer units were mere tokens, comparatively insignificant in numbers, and maintained largely for their propaganda value. However, as Germany's pressing need for troops increased throughout World War II, and especially in view of her impending defeat, earlier Nazi principles of an inherent racial hierarchy were gradually bending. Replacing battle casualties had made lifting other recruiting restrictions amongst the German population also necessary.

To facilitate recruitment, most volunteers from Finland and the occupied Baltic fought collectively in the *Wiking* Division. As the war turned against Hitler, the Finnish Government, mindful of the possibility of Soviet retaliation, actively discouraged membership whilst recruitment in Denmark and Norway virtually ceased. Most battalions within the *Wiking* Division were disbanded in 1943, although the overall strength of the SS by the autumn of that year was 350,000. The Division was one of the Waffen-SS crack units.

Battle Honours

- *France, 1940*
- *Demyansk Pocket, 1942*
- *Kharkov, March 1943*
- *Battle of Kursk, July 1943*

Battle Honours

- *Southern Russia, 1941*
- *Ukraine and the Caucasus, 1943–44*
- *Cherkassy Pocket, 1944*
- *Hungary, 1945*

Collar Patches

Shoulder

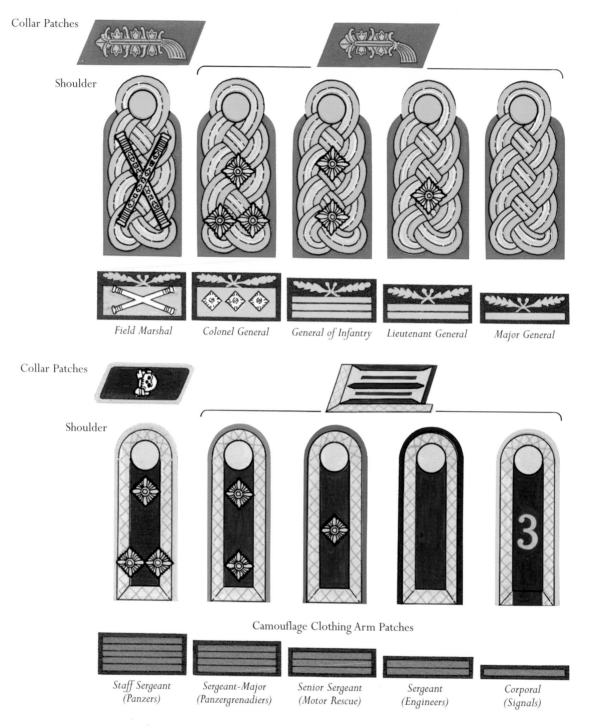

Field Marshal   *Colonel General*   *General of Infantry*   *Lieutenant General*   *Major General*

Collar Patches

Shoulder

Camouflage Clothing Arm Patches

Staff Sergeant (Panzers)   *Sergeant-Major (Panzergrenadiers)*   *Senior Sergeant (Motor Rescue)*   *Sergeant (Engineers)*   *Corporal (Signals)*

German Army

The uniform of the German Army was a development of the field-grey dress of World War I. From 1933 onwards, the final version was introduced in stages. Rank was identified primarily by shoulder straps which also denoted the wearer's arm of service, forma-tion and status. Officers were further identified by their headdress (peaked cap with silver chin cords and side cap with silver piping) and leather equipment.

The shoulder straps for officers of General rank comprised three cords, two gold and one silver, inter-

Colonel
(Infantry)

Lieutenant Colonel
(Mtn Troops)

Major
(Cavalry)

Captain
(Panzers)

Lieutenant
(Transport Supply)

2nd Lieutenant
(Artillery)

Arm Patches

Infantryman

Lance Corporal

Senior Lance
Corporal

Lance Corporal

Private 1st Class

Artillery Senior
Sergeant

laced; senior officers wore two silver double cords interlaced, and junior officers the same cords but straight. Initially, Generals had gold buttons and silver pips, and all other officers silver buttons and gold pips. However, in 1941 Field Marshal's shoulder straps were changed to gold cords, onto which were pinned the traditional silver batons.

Non-commissioned officers wore the same basic uniform as the private soldier, but were identified by silver lace on their tunic collar and shoulder straps. Ensigns and specialist warrant officers of the Artillery, Medical and Veterinary Corps, and Paymasters were entitled to wear officers' headdress. All wore the same badges as officers on their peaked cap, with a cockade and oak wreath of white metal. Corporals and senior privates wore their badges on the left sleeve.

The arm of service was indicated by various colours which appeared as piping on the peaked cap, chevrons on the front of the side cap, stripes on the collar badges patches, and as piping and underlay on the shoulder straps.

Medals and decorations were comparatively rare and were often worn in action, although this singled the wearer out as a target for snipers.

Germany

Collar Patches

Shoulder

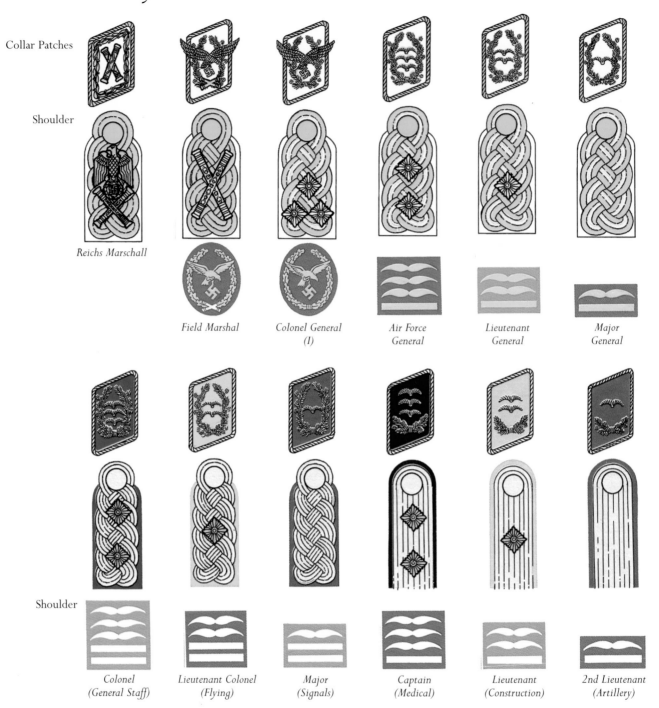

Reichs Marschall

Field Marshal

Colonel General (I)

Air Force General

Lieutenant General

Major General

Shoulder

Colonel (General Staff)

Lieutenant Colonel (Flying)

Major (Signals)

Captain (Medical)

Lieutenant (Construction)

2nd Lieutenant (Artillery)

German Air Force

The primary means of identifying Luftwaffe rank were collar patches and shoulder straps. Army rank titles and rank badges in the form of Army shoulder straps were retained, while two new systems of badges for wear on the collar patches and flying suits were introduced.

General officers wore white lapels on their dress jacket and greatcoat, and white stripes on their breeches and trousers. Their parade and service dress buttons and badges were gold. During the early stages of the war aiguillettes and full dress belts with sword were worn, but this habit was quickly discontinued, the sword being replaced by a pistol.

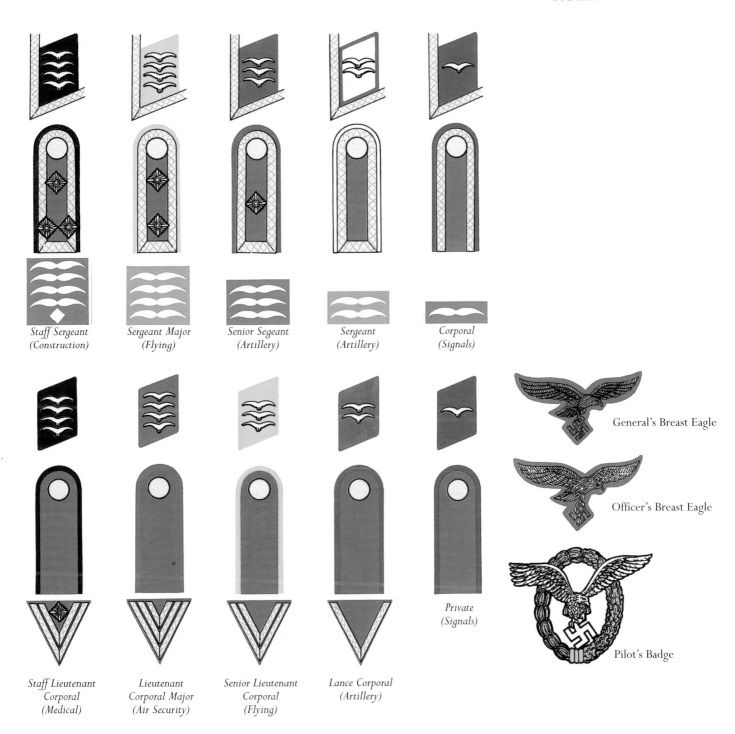

Staff Sergeant
(Construction)

Sergeant Major
(Flying)

Senior Segeant
(Artillery)

Sergeant
(Artillery)

Corporal
(Signals)

General's Breast Eagle

Officer's Breast Eagle

Private
(Signals)

Pilot's Badge

Staff Lieutenant
Corporal
(Medical)

Lieutenant
Corporal Major
(Air Security)

Senior Lieutenant
Corporal
(Flying)

Lance Corporal
(Artillery)

Air crew rank was denoted by a special flying uniform badge worn on the upper sleeve of flying uniforms and overalls.

Arm of service was indicated by colours worn on the headdress, collar patches, shoulder straps, and collar piping.

Before World War II, during the summer months officers and non-commissioned officers were permitted to wear caps with white tops, white trousers and shoes, while officers could also wear a white tunic. After the start of hostilities the white cap continued to be worn in Italy, the Mediterranean, southern Russia and occasionally Germany.

The large number of skilled tradesmen in the Luftwaffe wore a badge on the lower left sleeve. This badge was winged for air-crew but was circular for ground crew, with an emblem to indicate each person's particular skill.

Germany

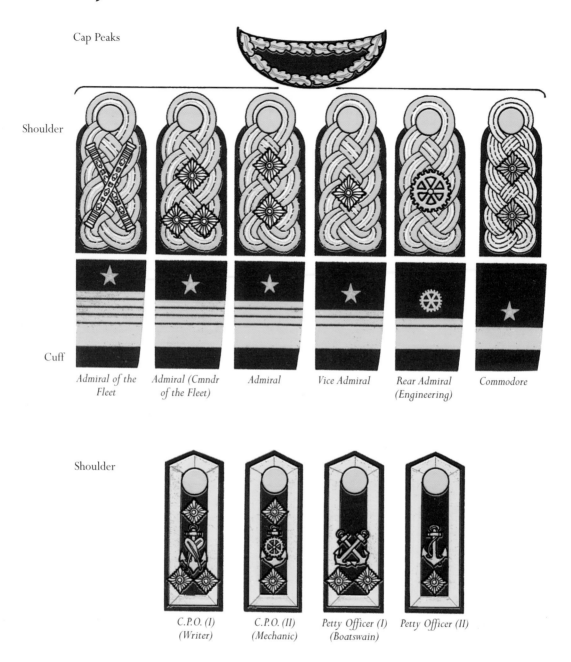

Cap Peaks

Shoulder

Cuff

| Admiral of the Fleet | Admiral (Cmndr of the Fleet) | Admiral | Vice Admiral | Rear Admiral (Engineering) | Commodore |

Shoulder

C.P.O. (I)
(Writer)   *C.P.O. (II)*
(Mechanic)   *Petty Officer (I)*
(Boatswain)   *Petty Officer (II)*

German Navy

The German Navy uniform of World War II was based on that of the Prussian Navy from 1848 and the British Royal Navy. The three main types of uniform were: navy-blue; white for summer and tropical wear and field-grey for land-based personnel. A range of protective clothing was provided for extreme conditions ranging from the heat of the Mediterranean to the frozen temperatures of the Arctic.

Officers were identified by the pattern of embroidery on the peaked cap, the number and width of the gold lace rings on the reefer cuffs, or by the shoulder straps on the greatcoat and field-grey uniform. Admirals wore a greatcoat with blue lapels and a double row of gold-embroidered oak leaves on their peak caps, other officers a single row. Land-based officers, when wearing field-grey uniform, displayed their branch-of-service colour and badge on Army-pattern shoulder straps.

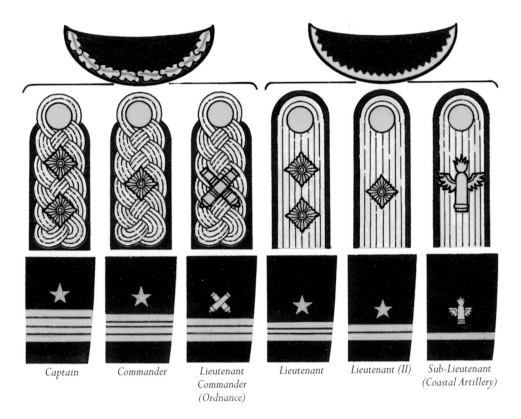

| Captain | Commander | Lieutenant Commander (Ordnance) | Lieutenant | Lieutenant (II) | Sub-Lieutenant (Coastal Artillery) |

Collar Patches

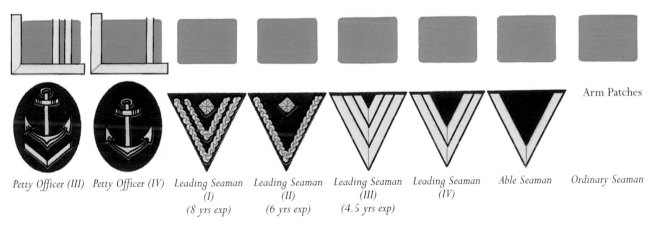

Arm Patches

| Petty Officer (III) | Petty Officer (IV) | Leading Seaman (I) (8 yrs exp) | Leading Seaman (II) (6 yrs exp) | Leading Seaman (III) (4.5 yrs exp) | Leading Seaman (IV) | Able Seaman | Ordinary Seaman |

In 1944, to facilitate inter-service rank identification, Naval officers serving on the Atlantic Wall began to wear shoulder straps which denoted their rank on the reefer in addition to the cuffs.

Petty officers and cadets wore their rank badges on shoulder straps on their reefers and greatcoats. Before walking-out dress was abandoned in 1941, Petty Officers rank was indicated on it by a gilt metal badge on the left sleeve and gold rank distinction lace on the cuff.

White covers were often worn on their peaked caps by U-boat commanders. White cap covers and white shirts were not officially worn by others during the war, although petty officers and ratings occasionally ignored regulations when on leave. The cap tally with the name of the ship was quickly replaced by a standardised model, bearing the word *Kriegsmarine*.

There were no arm of service designations as such in the Navy, although ratings skills and trades were identified by badges worn on the upper left sleeve.

Germany

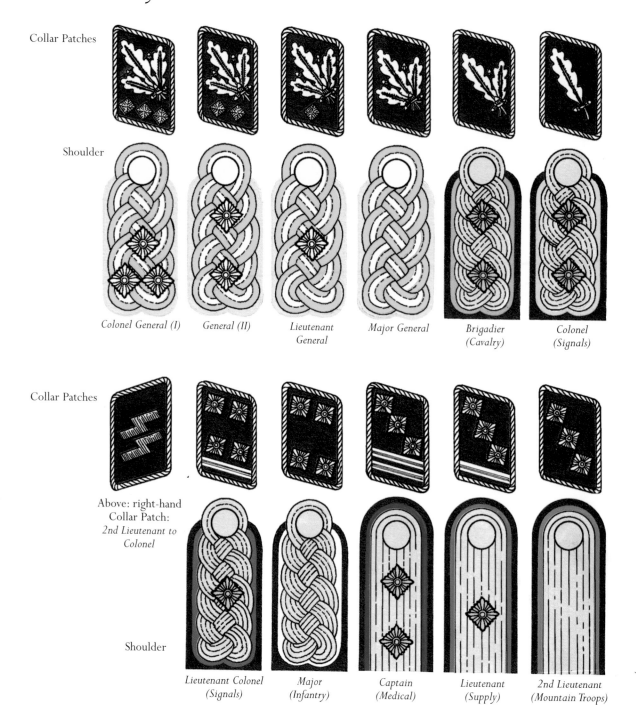

Collar Patches

Shoulder

Colonel General (I)   General (II)   Lieutenant General   Major General   Brigadier (Cavalry)   Colonel (Signals)

Collar Patches

Above: right-hand
Collar Patch:
*2nd Lieutenant to
Colonel*

Shoulder

Lieutenant Colonel (Signals)   Major (Infantry)   Captain (Medical)   Lieutenant (Supply)   2nd Lieutenant (Mountain Troops)

Waffen-SS

The pre-war uniform of the SS was black but after 1935 a grey uniform was introduced for active service. Although commissioned and non-commissioned ranks within the Waffen-SS were wholly independent of the Army, they relied increasingly on the Army for training. Rank badges were worn on the left collar patch by all ranks up to and including Lieutenant-Colonel, and on both collar patches by more senior officers.

Army rank badges were worn on the shoulder straps. After 1943, a new type of rank insignia, worn on the upper left sleeve, and comprising a combination of bars and oak leaves on a black rectangular or

Rank

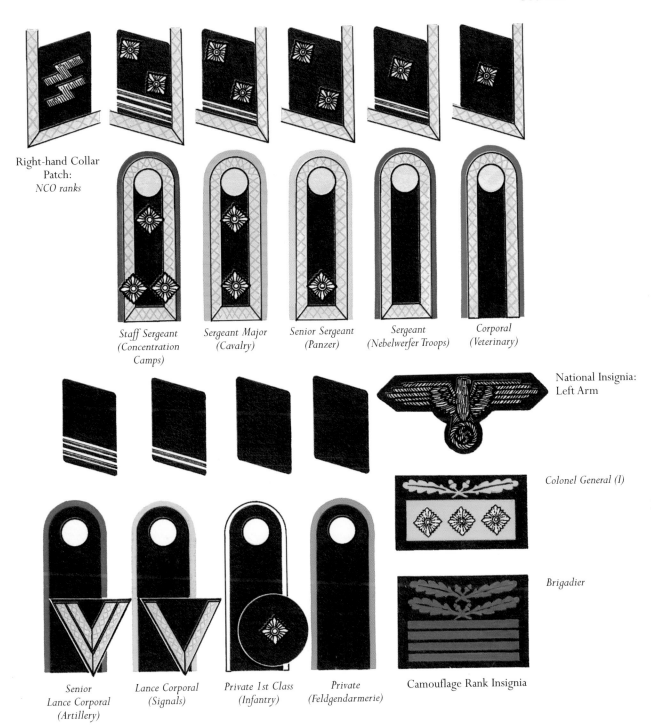

Right-hand Collar
Patch:
NCO ranks

*Staff Sergeant
(Concentration
Camps)*

*Sergeant Major
(Cavalry)*

*Senior Sergeant
(Panzer)*

*Sergeant
(Nebelwerfer Troops)*

*Corporal
(Veterinary)*

National Insignia:
Left Arm

Colonel General (I)

Brigadier

*Senior
Lance Corporal
(Artillery)*

*Lance Corporal
(Signals)*

*Private 1st Class
(Infantry)*

*Private
(Feldgendarmerie)*

Camouflage Rank Insignia

square background, was adopted for uniforms without shoulder straps. The bars and oak leaves were yellow for Generals and green for subordinate ranks. Corporals continued to wear the traditional triangular chevrons. Generals wore silver piping on their head-dress, with grey lapels on their greatcoats. Regulations stated that all other officers should wear white piping

on their head-dress, including side cap. Nonetheless, a number informally wore arm-of-service coloured piping on their peaked caps.

During the early stages of the war, arm-of-service colours were worn as piping on the shoulder straps, and as a chevron on the side cap. Specialists wore a diamond-shaped badge on the left cuff.

27

Bomber Badge

Officially constituted in 1935, the Luftwaffe was never, in reality, as powerful as it appeared. Although it gained a series of major successes in the first year of the war, it was unable to defeat the Royal Air Force, and by 1943 was slowly but inexorably bleeding to death in a war on two fronts.

The role of the Luftwaffe was not to defend Germany, nor to launch strategic attacks from fixed home bases, but to support large and mobile ground forces. Crucially, it therefore lacked four-engine heavy bombers. The medium bombers which it did possess at the beginning of the war, Junkers 88s, Dornier 17s and Heinkel 111s, were too lightly armed, short-ranged, and carried too small a bomb-load to be truly effective without supporting ground forces.

The bomber badge was worn by aircrew on the left breast, above service ribbons. At the beginning of the war, the Germans were far ahead of their rivals when it came to dive-bombing techniques. Indeed, Luftwaffe 'flying artillery' was crucial in the early war campaigns in Poland, France and the Balkans, when Ju 87 Stukas provided support for ground units, cutting off the enemy from his supply sources and destroying opposition infantry, artillery and tank formations. Precision bombing against bridges and railways was particularly effective.

Badge	Qualification Clasp, Bomber Aircrew, Luftwaffe (Frontflugspange). Either bronze, silver or gold; it was awarded for a specific number of operational sorties.

Day Interceptor's Badge

When the US Eighth Air Force introduced a policy of 'round-the-clock' bombing in 1943, the Luftwaffe fighter squadrons came into their own. It was not until December 1943 that the P-51 Mustang fighter entered service in sufficient numbers to protect Allied bombers.

The number of Luftwaffe interceptors in the West rose steadily to 900 by October 1943. Most were armed with one or more 20mm (0.78in) or 30mm (1.18in) cannon, which caused devastation and took a heavy toll of enemy aircraft. The Luftwaffe also experimented with air-to-air bombing, the use of 210mm (8.26in) rockets and reinforced fighters for ramming.

By 1944, the Luftwaffe had introduced a complex fighter control system. The major organ of command was the *Jagddivision* (JD), five of which were spread around Germany. But the introduction of the P-51 Mustang turned the tables in favour of the Allies. By mid-1944, a chronic shortage of fuel caused the Luftwaffe interceptors to curtail their activities, leaving the skies relatively free for the Allied bombers.

Badge	A central device surrounded by a wreath, with a spray of oak leaves on either side. Bronze, silver and gold identified the class of the clasp, parts of which were made of bronze or were black according to qualification. A gold pendant was added in June 1942.

General Assault Badge

The white metal General Assault Badge was instituted on 1 June 1940. It was awarded for three assault actions on three different days. Originally, only assault engineers were eligible for this award.

On 22 June 1940, two more types of the same badge were introduced, with the number of assaults added on a tablet at the base of the badge. The General Assault Badge was worn on the left breast pocket, by personnel not eligible for the Infantry Assault Badge or the Tank Battle Badge. Many of these badges were won on the Eastern Front, where the fighting was invariably intense and often hand-to-hand or at close quarters.

Badge	*Constructed of white metal. The 25 and 50 Assault Badge has the eagle, crossed bayonet and grenade in black, with the wreath in silver, while the 75 and 100 Assault Badge has a gilt wreath.*

Infantry Assault Badge

The Infantry Assault Badge, together with the Tank Battle Badge, was instituted on 20 December 1939, and worn on the left breast pocket. The award was originally in silver, but a later bronze variant was introduced for motorised infantry troops. It was awarded for three assault actions on three different days, although subsequently the number of assaults was added on a tablet at the base of the badge.

Other combat badges awarded by the Germans in World War II were the Army Parachutists Badge instituted on 15 June 1937, the Army Balloon Observer's Badge instituted on 8 July 1944, and the Army Anti-Aircraft Badge, instituted on 18 June 1941.

Badge	*Silver badge (Infanterie-Sturmabzeichen) awarded to infantry personnel; later a bronze variant for motorised infantry was issued. Worn on the left breast pocket above any ribbons.*

Germany

Night Interceptor Badge

Qualification clasps were introduced in January 1941 and were worn on the left breast above service ribbons. Clasps, which were awarded for a specific number of operational flights, originally consisted of a central device surrounded by a wreath, with a spray of oak leaves on either side. Both cloth and metal versions were issued; in the latter, bronze, silver or gold identified the class.

In June 1942 a gold pendant was added to the gold clasp in recognition of the execution of over 500 operational flights. In late 1944, the pendant was replaced by a tablet with the appropriate number of operations (with a minimum of 200 increasing in denominations of 100), inscribed in its centre.

On 3 November 1944, the Ground Combat clasp was instituted for Luftwaffe personnel who had taken part in close combat (German Air Force personnel performed a host of ground duties, and towards the end of the war were formed into army infantry divisions, with varying results). This consisted of a central device made of silver, with the rest of the badge being bronze, silver or gold for 15, 30 or 50 days respectively of close combat with the enemy. Those wounded in action received the badge for shorter periods of combat with the enemy.

Tank Battle Badge

Instituted on 20 December 1939, it was worn on the left breast pocket. The badge was awarded in silver to tank crews and bronze to support troops. On 22 June 1940, two further classes were instituted: the 25 and 50 Battles badge in black and silver for tank crews and bronze for panzergrenadiers in supporting divisions; and the 75 and 100 Battles badge in gilt and silver for tank crews and bronze with a guilt wreath for panzergrenadiers. The number of assaults undertaken was added in a tablet at the base of the badge up to a maximum of 100.

Badge	A central device surrounded by a wreath, with a spray of oak leaves on either side. Bronze, silver and gold identified the class of the clasp, with gold or black identifying class of qualification.

Badge	Tank Battle Badge (Panzerkampfabzeichen) in silver and bronze, with gilt wreath. Issued to tank crews, crews of support armoured fighting vehicles and panzergrenadiers.

30

United States of America

Animals featured greatly on American insignia and awards, the American bald-headed eagle holding a sprig of laurel in its right claw and a bundle of arrows in the other being the most notable. On the other hand, other insignia could be very plain: US Army Air Force badges were often simply wings with the number of the unit in the middle.

Congressional Medal of Honor

Established by Congress in July 1862 as the United States' supreme award for bravery and awarded on behalf of the Congress to an officer or enlisted soldier 'who shall in action involving actual conflict with the enemy, distinguish himself conspicuously by gallantry and intrepidity at the risk of his life above and beyond the call of duty.'

Between 1904 and 1944, the medal was worn with a chest ribbon of light blue charged with 13 white stars.

Badge	*A bronze five-pointed star sits on a laurel wreath, a bust of Minerva facing right within the circumscription UNITED STATES OF AMERICA. The star hangs from a bar inscribed VALOR, above which an American eagle spreads its wings. Reverse: THE CONGRESS TO, followed by the recipient's name and details of action.*
Ribbon	*Pale blue silk with 13 white stars, worn as a neck ribbon.*

Purple Heart

The first United States military decoration, instituted by George Washington in 1782, and originally awarded for bravery in action. Only three men received the Purple Heart during the Revolutionary War, all of them non-commissioned officers. The original medal, a piece of purple, heart-shaped cloth with silver braid, was sewn onto the coat.

The medal lay dormant for about 150 years, but was revived on 22 February 1932, the 200th anniversary of Washington's birth. It is currently awarded to those wounded or killed (when awarded posthumously).

Badge	*A purple, heart-shaped bronze-edged badge depicting a profile of George Washington in the uniform of a General in the Continental Army. Reverse: the inscription FOR MILITARY MERIT with the recipient's name inscribed below.*

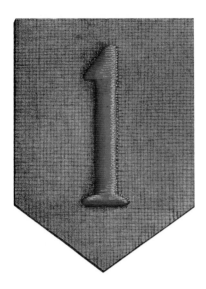

1st Infantry Division

A red figure '1' on an olive drab shield-shaped background. Shown above is the divisional shoulder patch, which was worn on the left shoulder by soldiers assigned to the division. If they had been assigned during a period when the division was in combat, then on transferring to a new unit they were allowed to retain their old patch on the right shoulder, with the new patch on the left.

The 1st American Division, known as 'Big Red One', saw considerable combat throughout the war. It served in Algeria and Tunisia, took part in the invasion of Sicily, named Operation 'Husky', assaulted Omaha Beach in Normandy on D-Day, and took part in the Battle of the Bulge in the Ardennes. It was one of the units which spearheaded the Allied advance into Germany. At the beginning of the war the division consisted of three infantry regiments: the 16th, 18th and 26th. The 16th and 18th were formed in the spring of 1861, and had fought in the American Civil War, the Spanish American War and World War I.

1st Marine Aircraft Wing

US Marine Corps aviation personnel wore special patches based on the design of an aircraft fuselage insignia with yellow stars, wings and the wing's number depicted by a Roman numeral below. The headquarter's emblem displayed a Spanish crown. As the war progressed, the shield badges were replicated by a kite-shaped design, somewhat simplified in their symbolism, which depicted a winged Marine Corps emblem with the unit designation below.

The original units of the 1st Marine Aircraft Wing arrived on Guadalcanal on 20 August 1942. They were VMF-223, an F4F Wildcat squadron, and VMSB-232, an SBD Dauntless squadron. Later they were joined by 67th Pursuit Squadron, VMF-224 and VMSB-231. These units combined became known as the Cactus Air Force. Individual units served with this formation for periods varying from three days to more than six weeks. Operating from Henderson Field on the island, the Cactus Air Force fought gallantly to ensure that Guadalcanal remained in American hands in the face of repeated Japanese attacks.

Battle Honours

● *North Africa, 1942–43*
● *Sicily, 1943*
● *D-Day, 6 June 1944*
● *Northwest Europe, 1944–45*

Battle Honours

● *Henderson Field, 12 August 1942*
● *Guadalcanal, October 1942*
● *Henderson Field, November 1942*
● *Japanese withdrawal, January 1943*

1st Raider Regiment

In the 1930s the US Marine Corps experimented with the concept of using raider forces behind enemy lines. The first of such units were the 1st and 2nd Raider Battalions, each of which was made up of over 850 officers and men divided between six rifle companies and a headquarters staff.

The raiders were formed to carry out three specific types of operation: spearheading amphibious landings; undertaking hit-and-run attacks on enemy held islands; and launching long-term guerrilla-style operations behind enemy lines. As well as standard infantry hardware, the raiders were equipped with shotguns, chainsaws and bangalore torpedoes. By mid-1942 both battalions were in the field, and other similar units were formed.

The badge of the 1st Raider Regiment is in the style of other US Marine cloth badges, with a blue background sporting five five-pointed stars and a red and white badge in the centre.

2nd Ranger Battalion

The 2nd Ranger Battalion was activated on 1 April 1943 at Camp Forrest, and on 1 August was redesignated Ranger Infantry. It moved to Fort Pierce, Florida, in September to learn small boat drill, and in November deployed to Britain. It trained closely with No 4 Commando, specialising in cliff climbing, reconnaissance and prisoner snatching, but did not see action until D-Day.

On the morning of 6 June 1944 elements of Coys D, E and F, under the command of Lt Col Rudder, were landed at the foot of Pointe du Hoc, a rocky feature some 30.5m (100ft) above sea level which they succeeded in climbing under heavy enemy fire. Gaining the position, they quickly moved to an enemy gun position which they had been ordered to destroy, only to find it empty. The Rangers fought off persistent counter-attacks throughout the next 48 hours before being relieved by 5th Rangers advancing from Omaha Beach.

After a short period of consolidation 2nd Rangers redeployed to Brittany where their expertise was found to be invaluable in the taking of a number of defensive positions. The unit joined the advance into Belgium and Luxembourg, and ultimately into Germany, before moving to Czechoslovakia in May 1945. The Battalion was reduced to zero strength in June 1945 and formally deactivated in October of that year.

Battle Honours

- *Makin Island, August 1942*
- *Guadalcanal, November 1943*
- *Solomon Islands, 1942–43*
- *Central Pacific, 1945*

Battle Honours

- *D-Day, 6 June 1944*
- *Normandy, August–September 1944*
- *Huertgen Forest, November 1944*
- *Germany, February–March 1945*

5th Army Air Force

Based in Australia, the US 5th Army Air Force initially found itself severely stretched in its struggle to repel the Japanese in New Guinea. Its P-39s and P-40s coped well with their ground-support requirements, but the limited number of heavy bombers available, the long distances over which they had to operate, and the long escort missions which only the P-38s could manage, together with the shortages of spares and arduous operating conditions, made its task all but impossible.

By late 1943, the increase in aircraft production, coupled with the introduction of the long-range B-24, considerably eased matters. The 5th Army Air Force absorbed the 13th Air Force on Luzon, and in November 1944 took part in the assault on Leyte Gulf in the Philippines. A few weeks later it supported the Marines landing on Mindoro and later Lingaye Gulf. The conditions under which the 5th Air Force operated were unrelenting in the Pacific theatre, but without its endeavours the island assaults of 1943–45 would have been far bloodier.

5th Rangers

The number '5' in black within an orange diamond superimposed on a white stripe.

The 5th Ranger Infantry Battalion was activated on 1 September 1943, and undertook training at the Scouts and Raiders School in Florida before embarking for England in January 1944. Having honed their skills at the Commando Training Centre and British Assault Training Centre in April, the Rangers undertook a series of amphibious exercises prior to D-Day.

The 5th Rangers landed on the western end of Omaha Beach, from where they fought their way through to the heights above Pointe du Hoc. They consolidated before moving along the coast to assault German strong points in the Brest area. During October and November, the unit provided security for the Twelfth Army Group Headquarters in Belgium.

In February 1945, the unit undertook the most difficult operation in its short history: it infiltrated the German lines prior to the breakout from the bridgehead on the Saar River. Ranger casualties were so great that the unit had to be withdrawn to rebuild. The unit was in Austria when Germany surrendered.

Battle Honours

- *New Guinea, January 1943*
- *Hollandia, April 1944*
- *Leyte Gulf, October 1944*
- *Luzon, December 1944–July 1945*

Battle Honours

- *D-Day, 6 June 1944*
- *Belgium, October–November 1944*
- *Saar River, February 1945*
- *Germany, 1945*

8th Air Force

A golden '8', the white five-pointed star with central red circle and golden wings, set on a blue circular background.

Originally a tactical force, the 8th Air Force began to concentrate on heavy bombing missions when transferred to Britain. Initially it concentrated on daylight precision raids against coastal targets, but after the Casablanca Conference in January 1943, joined the RAF in attacking Germany itself.

The 8th Air Force reached its peak in June 1944, when it had 40 bomber groups and a mixed Pathfinder group under command. Losses were high until mid-1944, at which time the Allies were able to field sufficient long-range fighters to establish air superiority over the more distant targets.

In total the 8th Air Force flew just over one million sorties, losing 11,687 aircraft in the process, 5548 of them heavy bombers. It dropped a total of 634,158 tonnes (624,141 tons) of bombs, destroying an estimated 20,419 enemy aircraft, 6098 of which fell victim to the bombers' own guns.

Battle Honours

- *Northwest Europe, 1942*
- *Schweinfurt, October 1943*
- *Germany, 1944–45*
- *Dresden, February 1945*

9th Air Force

A red '9' on a golden circle below a white five-pointed star, with a central red circle flanked with white wings. The whole design was on a blue shield.

The 9th U.S. Air Force was originally based in North Africa where it flew missions in the Western Desert, and later in support of the invasions of Sicily and Italy.

When the Italian Government surrendered and fighting in that theatre moved further north, the 9th Air Force was transferred to England, and with the 8th U.S. Air Force was responsible for the American contribution to the bombing offensive against Germany and occupied Europe. Before the United States entered the war, Americans had been engaged in the war only as part of the British or Canadian forces.

By 1944 the 9th Air Force comprised of a troop-carrying command with 15 groups, a bomber command with 11 groups, and two tactical air commands disposing 18 fighter groups.

Battle Honours

- *North Africa, 1942*
- *Sicily, 1943*
- *Italy, 1943*
- *Northwest Europe, 1944–45*

10th Mountain Division

When the United States entered the war, she quickly realised the need for troops capable of operating in mountainous conditions. The 87th Mountain Infantry Regiment was raised with National Ski Patrol assistance, and in June 1943 was expanded into the 10th Mountain Division, comprising some 14,000 skiers, mountaineers and winter sportsmen.

By now fully trained and acclimatised, the Division joined the Fifth Army in the mountains of Northern Italy in January 1945. It was here that is took part in a successful attack on Monte Belvedere before spearheading the advance into the Po Valley. In 114 days of continuous action the unit suffered losses of 4000 killed and wounded. The division was deactivated on 1 December 1945.

15th Air Force

The five-pointed star with a round red centre set on a round blue background was the fuselage marking of American aircraft from 1921 to 1942. The star with the red centre remained the main insignia of US Army Air Forces (USAAFs). The main exception was the earlier patch of the USAAF authorised on 20 July 1937 for wear by personnel of GHQ Air Force. This badge symbolised a spinning propeller and was in the colours of the Air Corps: ultramarine blue and orange.

The 15th Air Force was one of the formations that carried out the strategic bombing campaign against the cities and industrial capacity of Nazi Germany. It was activated on 1 November 1943 in the Mediterranean area for strategic operations. Together with the Royal Air Force (RAF) and the 8th Air Force, the USAAF and RAF were able to achieve a good balance of tactical and strategic air power against the Axis, the 8th striking from the west and the 15th from the south against Italy and southern Germany.

Battle Honours

- *Monte Belvedere, February 1945*
- *Po Valley, March–April 1945*

Battle Honours

- *Southern Italy, 1943*
- *Monte Cassino, February 1944*
- *Northern Italy, 1944*
- *Southern Germany, 1945*

16th Infantry Division

The 16th Infantry Regiment was one of the oldest in the United States Army, having been formed in 1861. Garrisoned in New York the Regiment gained the nickname the 'Subway Soldiers'. In 1939, together with the 18th and 26th Infantry Regiments, 1st Division it was formed into a 'combat team' of 3300 men with supporting artillery, engineer, signal and reconnaissance.

The Regiment sustained heavy losses in Normandy, being landed on Omaha Beach. As the men poured ashore they were met by a hail of machine-gun and artillery fire. It was on D-Day that the regiment's commander, Colonel George Taylor, issued his famous words: 'Two kinds of people are staying on this beach, the dead and those who are going to die – now let's get the hell out of here.' The Regiment ended the war in Czechoslovakia.

Battle Honours

- D-Day, 6 June 1944
- Normandy, June 1944
- Northwest Europe, 1944
- Germany, 1945

29th Rangers

Blue and white circular motif within a green edge, the whole beneath a shoulder flash depicting 29th Rangers in blue on a red background.

The 29th Provisional Ranger Battalion was raised at Tidworth, England, on 20 December 1942 to replace 1st Rangers then due for service abroad. The unit – volunteers from the 29th Infantry Division supplemented by 18 members of the 1st Rangers – undertook British Commando training, then amphibious assault training at Bridge Spean in February 1943. They were then attached for six weeks to No 4 Commando, elements of which executed three small raids on the Norwegian coast.

The unit moved to Bude, Cornwall, and then to Scotland, from where it undertook a raid on Ushant Island off the tip of Brittany. Despite attempts to retain it, the unit was disbanded in October 1943 and its personnel returned to the 29th Infantry Division.

Battle Honours

- Norway, April 1943
- Ushant Island, July 1943
- Dover, August 1943
- Disbanded, 15 October 1943

101st Airborne Division

The cloth insignia of the division depicts an American Eagle's head in white with a yellow beak. It is set on a black shield, above it the word 'Airborne' in an arc in yellow on a black background.

Formed on 15 August 1942 at Camp Clairborne, Louisiana, the 101st Airborne Division became well known in Britain, where it undertook much of its training. It saw action at Normandy during the D-Day landings, won fame for its stubborn defence at Bastogne in the Ardennes, and fought in Holland and near Berchtesgaden.

By 1945, the 'Screaming Eagles' had been awarded the Distinguished Unit Citation, the French and Belgian Croix de Guerre and the Dutch Orange Lanyard. The Division was deactivated in 1945.

354th Fighter Group

The 354th Fighter Group was activated in November 1942. Comprising three Squadrons, the 353rd, 355th and 356th, it was transferred to England as part of the 9th Army Air Force in the autumn of 1943. It was re-equipped with P-51B Mustang fighters, and for the next few months escorted the bombers of the 8th Army Air Force on long-range missions over Germany.

After D-Day the Group moved to a series of landing strips in France, from where it deployed in a multitude of roles, including ground strafing and air interdiction, as well as more conventional escort duties. By the end of the war the 354th had claimed a staggering 701 enemy aircraft destroyed, and although this figure was later revised, the 'Pioneer Mustang Group' enjoyed unparalleled success.

As well as the enemy aircraft it shot down, the 354th's achievements on the ground included the following: 1543 military vehicles destroyed, 96 armoured vehicles destroyed, 532 trains destroyed, 1465 rail wagons and coaches destroyed, 26 bridges blown up, 75 gun emplacements silenced, 69 roads obstructed, and nine airfields attacked. Its own losses were minimal: from the Group's first mission in December 1943 to the end of the war, 187 aircraft went missing in action and 92 pilots were killed in combat duty.

Battle Honours

- *D-Day, 6 June 1944*
- *Normandy, June 1944*
- *Bastogne, December 1944*
- *Germany, 1945*

Battle Honours

- *Escort duties, Germany 1943*
- *D-Day, 6 June 1944*
- *Escort duties, France 1944*
- *Ground targets, Germany, 1945*

504th Parachute Infantry Regiment

The 504th PIR, in conjunction with the 509th Parachute Infantry Battalion (PIB), formed the 504th Parachute Combat Team (PCT). The 509th PIB jumped into Algeria in 1942, and at once gained a reputation for aggression and tenacity. In September 1943, it parachuted into the hills around the Salerno beachhead. When the bulk of the 82nd Airborne Division was withdrawn from Italy, the 504th PCT remained, and was resting in the Naples area after a period of hard combat when ordered to Anzio.

In conjunction with the 367th Parachute Artillery Battalion and Company, the 307th Parachute Engineer Battalion fought tenaciously. The PCT landed by boat in the centre of the bridgehead and initially advanced against little opposition. However, the 504th had to endure 63 days of continuous combat before it was withdrawn, during which time it lost half its men.

Alamo Scouts

The Alamo Scouts Training Centre was established on Fergusson Island on 28 November 1943. It was formed by Lt Gen Krueger to train selected volunteers from the Sixth Army for reconnaissance and raider work and was so named after the town of San Antonio, the site of the Alamo and the home town of Krueger, who became its commanding officer. After a gruelling six-week course, most personnel were returned to their units to pass on their new skills.

A contingent of 21 officers and 117 enlisted men were, however, retained or on assignment to the Alamo Scouts, a specialist long-range intelligence-gathering unit. The Scouts conducted over 80 missions throughout the Southwest Pacific, including two prisoner-of-war camp rescues and a number of combat sorties.

The unit was disbanded at Kyoto, Japan in November 1945, having survived two years of continuous combat without sustaining the loss of a single life.

Battle Honours

- *Algeria, 1942*
- *Salerno, September 1943*
- *Anzio, January–March 1944*
- *Nijmegen, September 1944*

Battle Honours

- *Southwest Pacific, 1943–45*

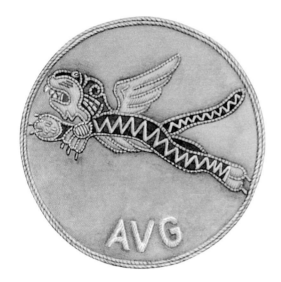

Flying Tigers

The cloth insignia is of the American Volunteer Group, the 'Flying Tigers', hence the letters 'AVG' and the tiger motif. The AVG were a group of 90 American mercenaries who fought for China against Japan before America's entry into the war.

The Tigers' leader, Colonel Claire Lee Chennault, drilled his men endlessly in a number of tactics, which enabled them to down nearly 300 Japanese aircraft between 20 December 1941 and 4 July 1942, when the Tigers became part of the US China Air Task Force. The airmen flew obsolete P-40B fighters which sported vicious-looking shark's teeth painted on the lower nose-cone. Although the P-40Bs suffered poor manoeuvrability, limited range and had inadequate gunsights, the combination of excellent training and high-quality support from their American ground crews enabled them to play a crucial part in this often forgotten campaign. The pay for the pilots was reasonable: US$600 per month, with a bonus of US$500 for every Japanese aircraft shot down.

Battle Honours

- *South China, 1941*
- *Manchuria, 1941*
- *Burma, 1942*

Merrill's Marauders

The 5307th Composite Unit (Provisional), named Merrill's Marauders, was raised for irregular warfare in the jungles of northern Burma. In August 1943 Lieutenant General 'Vinegar Joe' Stilwell requested a specialist force of jungle fighters for a proposed attack; he was sent a mixture of the bored, the restless and the indifferent. The force was organised into three battalions, each comprising two regimental combat teams and a headquarters.

Major General Frank Merrill assumed command in January 1944 and began to discipline the troops. Later that year the Marauders spearheaded the drive for northern Burma, and in May captured the critical airfield at Myitkyina. Lacking logistical support, especially medicine, many fell victim to disease. They were kept in the jungle beyond the limits of their effectiveness until 10 August 1944, when the unit was inactivated and awarded the Presidential Unit Citation.

Battle Honours

- *Northern Burma, January 1944*
- *Nhpum Ga, March–April 1944*
- *Burma, April–July 1944*
- *Battle of Myityina, 1944*

Tank Destroyer Units

Arms of service badges were introduced into the United States Army in the 1880s, but did not take the form of shoulder sleeve insignia such as this until the beginning of World War II. Originally all badges were circular, but as the Army expanded a number of triangular divisional badges were also introduced.

Theatre badges, each of which was designed as a representation of the area, were worn by troops posted to a combat zone. Other badges, such as the Tank Destroyer Units, were worn by personnel on general, often holding, duties, frequently prior to posting to active service.

The Tank Destroyer Units were part of the US Army Ground Forces, which trained men in colleges and provided services and supplies for all army units. In addition, it also trained its own men. Based predominantly in the United States, with the deployment of US units across the world during the war, its personnel went overseas as well.

US Marine Corps

The emblem of the Marine Corps is worn on ceremonial headgear. Made of brass, it comprises the American Eagle above the globe, which is superimposed upon a foul anchor.

The US Marine Corps fought a long and hard campaign throughout World War II. At the beginning of the war the Corps was made up of the 1st and 2nd Marine Divisions, though both formations were well below strength. The Corps numbered 20,000 men in 1939, though by the war's end this number had increased to a staggering 450,000.

The Corps performed two basic functions in the war: to carry out amphibious operations on its own, and to act as land troops on behalf of the US Navy. In the Pacific the Marines had to clear Japanese-held islands one by one, resulting in a series of vicious battles against fanatical defenders, the names of which have gone down in Marine history: Tarawa, Iwo Jima and Okinawa.

Battle Honours

- *Continental United States, 1941–45*
- *North Africa, 1942*
- *Europe, 1942–45*
- *Pacific, 1941–45*

Battle Honours

- *Philippines, 1942*
- *Solomon Islands, 1943*
- *New Georgia Group, 1943–44*
- *Treasury/Bougainville, 1944–45*

US Navy

All US Navy officers wore the same cap badge, which was produced in metal or embroidered versions. Initially, until May 1941, the eagle faced to the left, later to the right, towards the wearer's sword arm. The warrant officer's cap badge depicted two crossed foul anchors, the Midshipman wore one gold anchor and the petty officers had the initials 'U.S.N.' in silver superimposed upon the anchor.

The US Coast Guard had different cap badges, with the United States Shield in prominence, super-imposed on the anchors of the warrant officers and petty officers and in the centre of the cap badge worn by Shore Establishment personnel.

The US Navy performed valuable service throughout the war, both in the Pacific and European theatres, not least in transporting hundreds of thousands of troops to Britain to take part in the Allied liberation of Nazi-held Europe.

VMF-214

Most US Marine Corps aviation units were designated 'VM' to indicate Marine aircraft, with one or two letters following to designate the type of aircraft: VMF for fighters, VMB for bombers and VMA for attack aircraft.

Marine Fighter Squadron 214 was nicknamed the 'Black Sheep Squadron' and was commanded by Colonel Gregory Boyington, the top US Marine Corps air ace of World War II, with 28 kills to his name. The units nickname stemmed from the fact that the unit was reputedly manned by misfits who found it difficult to fit into other units. The bar on the insignia signified illegitimacy, hence the squadrons other name of 'Boyington's bastards'. The squadron flew the Corsair, which also appeared on the insignia.

Despite its nicknames, the squadron fought well: on Guadalcanal, for example, in its first month of combat it shot down 57 enemy aircraft, Boyington shooting down 22 of them, making him the Corps' leading ace.

Battle Honours
● *Eastern Pacific, 1942*
● *Mediterranean, 1942*
● *New Georgia, 1943–44*
● *Western Pacific, 1945*

Battle Honours
● *Guadalcanal, November 1942*
● *Rabaul, June 1943*
● *Kahili, October 1943*
● *Solomon Islands, March 1944*

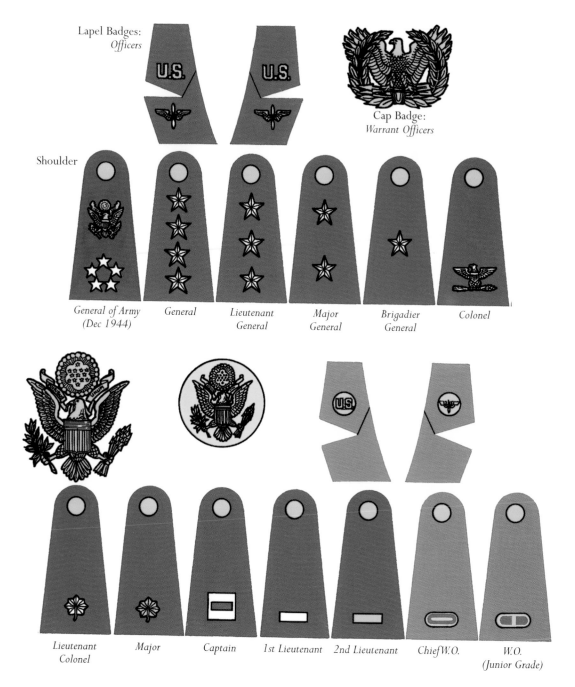

Lapel Badges:
Officers

Cap Badge:
Warrant Officers

Shoulder

General of Army
(Dec 1944)   General   Lieutenant
General   Major
General   Brigadier
General   Colonel

Lieutenant
Colonel   Major   Captain   1st Lieutenant   2nd Lieutenant   Chief W.O.   W.O.
(Junior Grade)

United States Army

United States Army uniform, outdated and untried in 1941, developed steadily throughout the war. The coat of arms depicting an American eagle, the stars and stripes set on a shield on its chest, its right claw holding a sprig of laurel, and the other a bundle of arrows, represented the badge worn by all ranks on their peaked caps. Officers' badges were of brass or gilded brass manufacture; other ranks were attached on a brass disc and were approximately half the size.

Uniquely, officers' rank insignia was represented by a combination of silver or gold eagles, leaves and bars worn on the shoulders or right side (both sides for generals) of the shirt collar, on the left front of the overseas cap, and sometimes painted on the front and

44

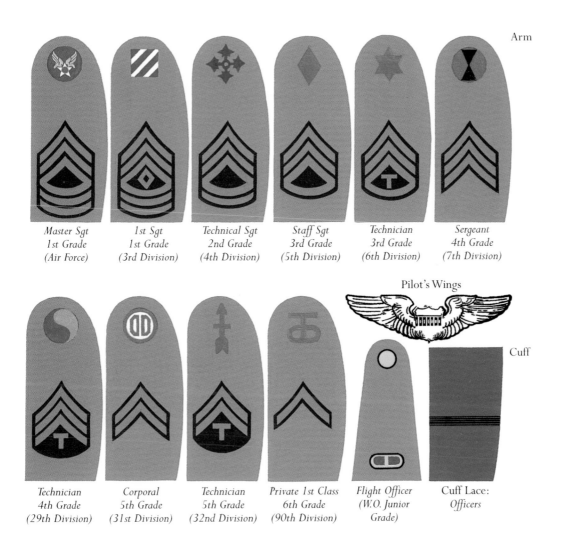

Arm

Master Sgt *1st Grade* *(Air Force)*	*1st Sgt* *1st Grade* *(3rd Division)*	*Technical Sgt* *2nd Grade* *(4th Division)*	*Staff Sgt* *3rd Grade* *(5th Division)*	*Technician* *3rd Grade* *(6th Division)*	*Sergeant* *4th Grade* *(7th Division)*

Pilot's Wings

Cuff

Technician *4th Grade* *(29th Division)*	*Corporal* *5th Grade* *(31st Division)*	*Technician* *5th Grade* *(32nd Division)*	*Private 1st Class* *6th Grade* *(90th Division)*	*Flight Officer* *(W.O. Junior Grade)*

Cuff Lace: Officers

rear of the steel helmet. Due to an historical anomaly caused when the rank of lieutenant-colonel had been introduced, silver badges were senior to identical badges in gold.

Officers wore their arm-of-service insignia in the form of collar badges on their jackets, the U.S. national insignia on top and service branch badges below. Aides-de-camp wore an eagle clutching a shield with the 'stars and stripes' engraved in coloured enamels, the number of stars corresponding to the rank of the general to whom they were responsible.

Warrant officers wore rank badges of brass and red or brown enamel, non-commissioned officers chevrons, the peak pointing upwards, on both upper sleeves. Technicians displayed a small 'T' within the chevrons. During the war first sergeants and master sergeants were of equal status; the title held, and chevron worn, being determined by the individuals' assignment.

Other ranks wore the letters 'U.S.' on their right lapels and their arm-of-service badges on the left, as well as on the left side of their overseas caps.

Formation signs in the form of coloured patches were worn on the sleeves at shoulder height, and were occasionally painted on the helmet.

As a branch of the Army, the United States Air Force did not have its own distinctive uniforms, although many airmen attempted to personalise their equipment.

Badges of rank were identical to those of the Army, although the new rank of Flight Officer was introduced in 1942. Arm-of-service badges with the image of winged propellers were worn on both lapels by officers, and on their left lapels and their overseas cap by other ranks.

Formation signs, which were predominantly ultramarine, white, red or yellow in colour, were worn on the upper-left sleeve.

45

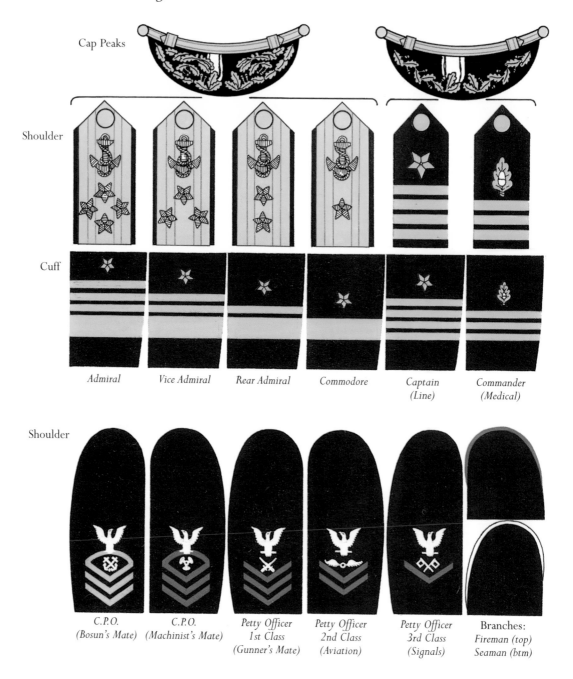

Cap Peaks

Shoulder

Cuff

| *Admiral* | *Vice Admiral* | *Rear Admiral* | *Commodore* | *Captain (Line)* | *Commander (Medical)* |

Shoulder

| *C.P.O. (Bosun's Mate)* | *C.P.O. (Machinist's Mate)* | *Petty Officer 1st Class (Gunner's Mate)* | *Petty Officer 2nd Class (Aviation)* | *Petty Officer 3rd Class (Signals)* | *Branches: Fireman (top) Seaman (btm)* |

United States Navy

United States Navy uniforms underwent a complete review in 1941. Officers' basic uniform comprised a peaked cap with a blue or white top, an overseas cap, a reefer jacket over a white shirt, with matching trousers and black shoes. Double-breasted greatcoats and raincoats were issued, both with twin rows of four buttons. A light Army-style khaki working dress was introduced for warm climates.

Officers could be identified by the rank distinction lace worn on their cuffs and shoulder straps, and by metal Army rank badges worn on their overseas caps and khaki shirt collars. Line officers wore five-pointed stars above their rank distinction lace, and rank badges on both sides of their shirt collars; officers in other corps wore their arm-of-service insignia above their rank laces and on their right collars only, and on the left side of their overseas caps.

46

Lieutenant Commander

Lieutenant (Supply)

Lieutenant Junior Grade (Civil Engineer)

Ensign (Line)

Chief W.O. (Gunnery)

Warrant Officer (Electrician)

Seaman 1st Class (3 Good Conduct Stripes)

Seaman 2nd Class (2 Active Service Stripes)

Apprentice Seaman (1 A. S. Stripe)

Cap Badges: C.P.O. (top) W.O. (btm)

Cap Badge: *Officers*

Chief petty officers and petty officers' uniforms were virtually identical to the officers', save for their different cap badges and rank badges worn on the left sleeves for corps members, and right sleeves if in the executive.

The three seamen classes wore one, two, or three stripes on the cuffs of their dress jumper. In cold weather ratings wore a shortened overcoat or pea-coat with two rows of large plastic buttons bearing the American Eagle. Their working dress in warm climates comprised a white cap, blue shirt and blue jeans, or a roll-neck pullover worn under a blue jean jacket.

The seamen classes were also provided with a working dress for cold weather: padded blue cloth helmets, navy blue tanker's jackets with knitted collars and matching lined trousers. A white fatigue cap was worn when overseas.

United States of America

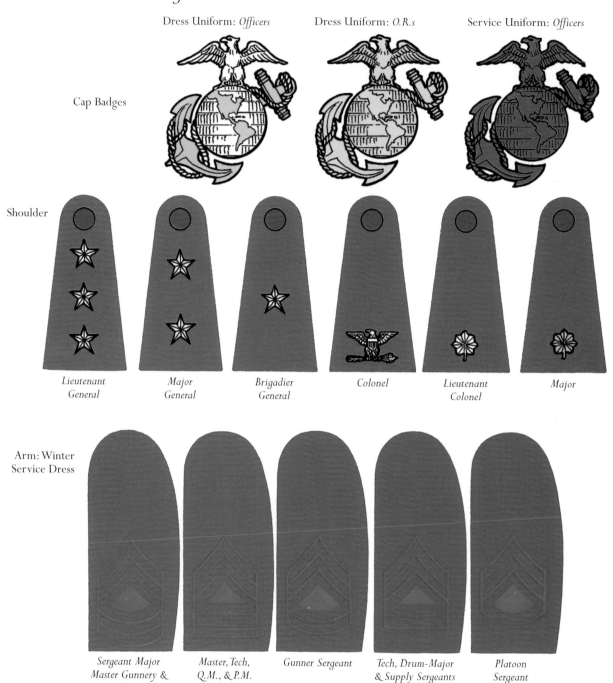

Cap Badges

Dress Uniform: *Officers* Dress Uniform: *O.R.s* Service Uniform: *Officers*

Shoulder

| Lieutenant General | Major General | Brigadier General | Colonel | Lieutenant Colonel | Major |

Arm: Winter Service Dress

| Sergeant Major Master Gunnery & 1st Sergeants | Master, Tech, Q.M., & P.M. Sergeants | Gunner Sergeant | Tech, Drum-Major & Supply Sergeants | Platoon Sergeant |

United States Marine Corps

The Marine Corps, or 'leather necks', probably the most famous of America's fighting units, had its own traditions, uniform, and organisation. The basic green service dress went with the typical head-dress, the felt campaign hat with red cords. At the beginning of the war an olive-drab service dress was worn, the letters USMC stencilled in black above the corps emblem on the left breast pocket.

A variety of head-dress was worn, as well as the felt campaign hat with red cords: a side or overseas cap, and a peaked service cap. The bronzed metal Marine Corps cap badge was worn on the front of the

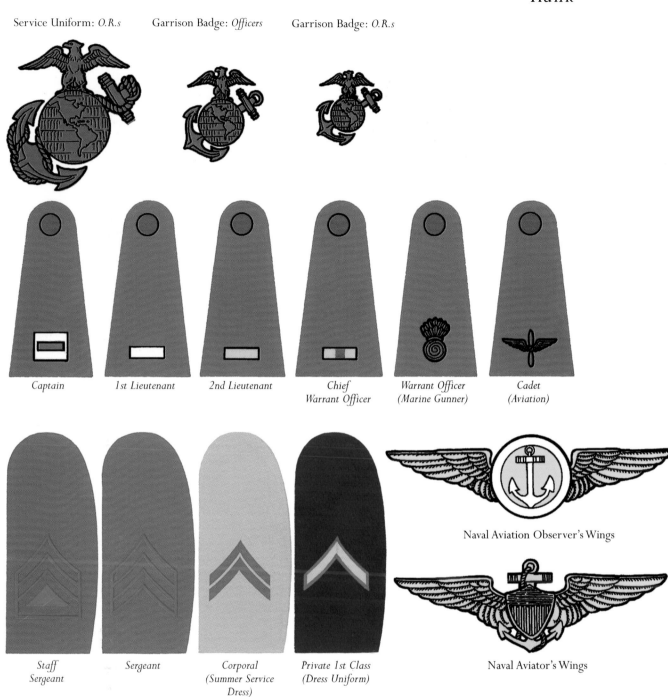

Service Uniform: *O.R.s*   Garrison Badge: *Officers*   Garrison Badge: *O.R.s*

Captain   *1st Lieutenant*   *2nd Lieutenant*   *Chief Warrant Officer*   *Warrant Officer (Marine Gunner)*   *Cadet (Aviation)*

Staff Sergeant   *Sergeant*   *Corporal (Summer Service Dress)*   *Private 1st Class (Dress Uniform)*

Naval Aviation Observer's Wings

Naval Aviator's Wings

peaked cap and pith helmet, and on the left front of the side cap.

Officers wore their metal Army-style badges of rank on their shirt collars. Non-commissioned officers wore their chevrons on their left sleeve; in fact, in 1942 it was ordered that the left sleeve was the only place for them. Chevrons were coloured yellow upon red in dress uniform, red upon green on the standard green uniform, and khaki upon khaki in camouflage uniform.

Certain officers, such as paymasters, quartermasters, aides-de-camp and band leaders, distinguished themselves by wearing special Marine branch badges on the collar in place of their corps badge.

Air Crew Member

Specialist United States Naval Aviator insignia was adopted shortly after the end of World War I, and was worn by air crews from the Navy, Marine Corps and Coast Guard. The Air Crew Insignia itself, however, was not introduced until 1944. Up to three stars were worn in a scroll above the insignia, each representing the number of engagements in which the wearer had participated, whether air combat, action against enemy shipping, or against fortified positions on the ground.

Unusually, the badge was worn by all flight personnel, whether officers or enlisted men. The badge shown above is a US Navy insignia. Wings were only adopted by the Navy at the beginning of 1919, though official approval for the project was stated in Change 12 to Uniform Regulations, which was issued in September 1917.

A gold metal badge with a pin at the back was finally chosen as the Naval Aviator's device, and the badge did not change a great deal, the only major difference being that the original pattern was solid, whereas later versions were not. In addition, later versions did vary slightly in style, though not significantly in design.

Badge	*Gold, as laid down in regulations issued on 16 March 1938. The appearance of the actual wings was standardised to a design by Herbert Adams, adopted in 1919.*

Flight Surgeon

The Navy Flight Surgeon's qualification badge was introduced when the United States entered the war. The Naval Aviator wings themselves were adopted at the beginning of 1919 and were used during World War II by pilots of the US Navy, Marine Corps and US Coast Guard.

In the US Air Force there were two Flight Surgeon badges. The first had wings that were gold plated, though later these were changed to silver in September 1944. Smaller gold wings, 50mm (2in) in diameter, were adopted in 1943 for the Flight Nurse. These were also subsequently changed to silver.

In general, the US Marine Corps and US Coast Guard used the same qualification badges as the US Navy. Some smaller wings, approximately half the size of the normal ones, were worn by officers on the evening dress and the white mess jacket.

The personnel of the Air Carrier Contract organisation wore army uniforms with special bronze badges and one, two or three stripes on the sleeves of the service jacket, or short bars on the shoulder straps of the trench coat. There was no Flight Surgeon badge for the personnel of this organisation, just air crew badges and insignia.

Badge	*Of gold texture and slightly more intricate than the earlier crew badges. A smaller version, about half the size of the original, was worn by officers on their evening dress or white mesw jacket.*

Navigator

Surprisingly, this most important qualification was only recognised by a qualification badge in the final stages of the war. Aviation Observers were recognised with a one-wing badge as early as 1922, developed into the Balloon Observers' Badge in 1927 and later designated the Balloon Pilot Badge. Naval Aviator Observers, the predecessors of the true Navigator, received their winged badge in 1929.

In the US Air Force, the winged balloon was reinstated to the Balloon Pilot and a new badge was authorised for Balloon Observer, with an additional 'O' on the balloon. Balloon pilots with 10 years of service, who had piloted military airships or motorised balloons for 100 hours, were granted a new badge with star and the qualification of Senior Balloon Observer.

More badges appeared in 1942, and that of Navigator had an armillary in its centre. The Liaison Pilot wings were worn regardless of rank by men assigned to organic air observation of the field artillery. The granting of this badge to enlisted men was later discontinued. Naval aviators, who were often tasked with getting aircraft back to carriers after a sortie, were arguably the most important air crew members.

Submarine Combat Insignia

The Combat Insignia badge was awarded to officers and men who completed one or more missions in which the submarine sank at least one enemy vessel or accomplished a combat mission of equal importance.

US submarines in the Pacific carried out a number of missions, their prime targets being aircraft carriers, tankers, other warships and mercantile vessels. As the war progressed American submarines sank a large number of Japanese ships. By the end of 1943, for example, the total shipping sunk was 3,048,150 tonnes (nearly three million tons). In 1944, nearly 1,016, 050 tonnes (1,000,000 tons) was sunk in the first five months. Ironically, as the Japanese were forced to rely more and more on small junks and coasters for moving cargoes, the big American submarines found themselves short of targets. The American submarines' greatest military successes were the sinking of the new carrier *Taiho* and the giant ex-battleship carrier conversion, the *Shinano*, both in 1944. By the end of World War II only 231 Japanese merchant ships were still afloat, out of a pre-war total of 2337 vessels.

Badge	*The badges of the Tactical Observer, Navigator and Radar Observer were adopted during World War II. Smaller wings, about half the size of the normal ones, were worn by officers on evening dress.*

Badge	*Silver badges denoting a submarine on the surface of the ocean, with three gold stars below. Awarded to both officers and men, the officers wearing it below their ribbons.*

Navy Aviator's Badge

The Naval Aviator wings were adopted at the beginning of 1919, and were used during World War II by pilots of the US Navy, US Marine Corps and US Coast Guard. The Aviation Observer badge appeared in 1922 as a one-winged device, which, in 1927, developed into the Balloon Observer badge, which was later redesignated Balloon Pilot Badge.

Naval aviators played a crucial part in securing victory for the United States in the Pacific. During the Battle of Midway in June 1942, for example, aircraft from the heavy carriers *Yorktown*, *Enterprise* and *Hornet* sank the Japanese carriers *Akagi*, *Kaga* and *Soryu*, together with their aircraft. In addition, the Japanese carrier *Hiryu* was also sunk. These victories were not bought at a cheap price: the Americans lost 150 aircraft, 307 men. However, the Japanese lost 275 aircraft and around 5000 men. Midway was the turning point of the war in the Pacific and paved the way for an American counteroffensive.

During this and many subsequent battles at sea, the Americans lost aircraft when they ran out of fuel after after a sortie. This may seem surprising, but the distances covered by aircraft were great, and it was invariably dark when the aircraft returned to their carrier. Many crews had to bale out or ditch in the sea after failing to find their ship.

Badge	*Gold badge, comprising wings and shield over a foul anchor. Originally badge was a gold embroidered fouled anchor badge. Naval Aviator wings were adopted in 1919.*

Submarine Officer

US Naval personnel attached to the submarine fleet wore one of three insignia badges; for officers, for surgeons and the Combat Insignia. The last was worn by the entire crew of a vessel which had successfully completed one or more missions in which the submarine had sunk one or more enemy ships, or had accomplished a combat mission of equal importance.

The officers wore the badge below their ribbons. Enlisted men wore an embroidered badge of similar design on their right forearms.

US submarines in the Pacific initially suffered from a major drawback: the magnetic pistols on their torpedoes were faulty. That said, this was rectified and the submariners found to their delight that their enemy believed that commerce protection was less honourable than engaging warships.

At first the Americans had only the old 'S' class boats, which were not suited to the Pacific theatre. However, these were soon supplemented by the latest 'Gato' class. These were formidable long-range boats with a heavy armament of six bow tubes and four stern tubes. The design proved well suited to the Pacific, and only minor improvements were made in the light of war experiences. They were still cramped and uncomfortable, though.

Badge	*Gold badge, comprising two fish facing each other with waves below. The badge was usually worn on the left breast, above ribbons. It was worn by officers only. It was one of three submarine badges.*

Great Britain

Many of the British regiments that went to war in 1939 had a long and prestigious history, such as the Coldstream Guards, first raised in 1650. Similarly, many Royal Navy ships carried proud names, such as Ark Royal, Glorious and Nelson. The Royal Air Force, though the youngest service, would soon contain famous squadrons.

Distinguished Flying Cross

This cross was introduced in June 1918. It was originally awarded to Royal Air Force officers and warrant officers, and subsequently to Fleet Air Arm and Army air-crew members, 'for an act or acts of valour, courage or devotion to duty performed whilst flying on active operations against the enemy'.

During World War II 20,354 Crosses, 1550 first Bars, and 42 second Bars were awarded. The completion of 40 bombing operations against the enemy was considered sufficient for the award.

Distinguished Flying Medal

The medal was introduced in June 1918 for non-commissioned officers and Royal Air Force men for an act of valour, courage, or devotion to duty whilst flying in active operations against the enemy. During World War II the completion of 40 bombing operations was considered sufficient for the award.

Badge	*A silver cross with a laurel wreath containing the RAF monogram. The royal crown sits above. The cross arms are decorated with bombs, propeller and wings. Reverse: the Royal cypher above the date 1918. Since World War II and after, the award's year has been engraved on the lower arm of the cross. The suspender is a straight silver bar.*
Ribbon	*Violet and white diagonal stripes.*

Badge	*Of silver oval design with a laurel wreath. Front: the Monarch's head and title. Reverse: the inscription FOR COURAGE, with the figures 1918, and Athena Nike, her extended right palm holding a hawk. The suspender comprises two rosettes, obverse and reverse. The recipient's name, rank, and number are inscribed on the medal edge.*
Ribbon	*Violet and white diagonal stripes.*

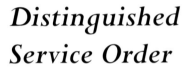

Distinguished Service Order

Established November 1886. Awarded to military and naval officers 'for distinguished services under fire or under conditions equivalent to service in actual combat with the enemy'. It was extended to Royal Air Force officers in 1918, to the Home Guard in 1942, and to the Merchant Navy under Royal Navy command in 1943. During World War II 4880 were awarded. The award may only be made to someone who has previously been Mentioned in Despatches.

Badge	*A white enamelled cross with curved arms, originally of gold, but later silver gilt. Front: the Monarch's crown within a laurel wreath; reverse, the crowned Royal cypher set within a laurel wreath whose centre is finished in red translucent enamel. Since 1939 the year of the award has appeared on the reverse of the suspender.*
Ribbon	*Red with dark blue borders.*

Military Cross

The Cross was established on 28 December 1914 to award officers up to the rank of substantive major and warrant officers 'for gallant and distinguished services in action'. It was later extended to Royal Navy and Royal Air Force officers and warrant officers engaged in ground duties, and to Allies of similar status fighting with the British.

The Prince of Wales, later King Edward VIII, gained the Military Cross for services in France during World War I.

During World War II, 10,386 Crosses, 482 first Bars, and 24 second Bars were awarded.

Badge	*A Greek cross of silver with splayed arms, their ends decorated by a raised king's crown, the orb breaking the straight line. The royal cypher of the reigning monarch appears at the centre. During World War II the date of the award was engraved on the lower arm of the cross. Reverse: plain and flat.*
Ribbon	*White with one central wide purple stripe.*

Military Medal

The medal was originally introduced on 25 March 1916 as a reward for N.C.Os. and below 'for individual or associated acts of bravery on the recommendation of a Commander-in-Chief in the Field'. Although basically an Army medal, it could be awarded to members of the Royal Navy and RAF of equivalent rank for ground actions, and was later extended to Allied forces.

During World War II, 15,225 Medals, 164 first Bars, and two second Bars were awarded.

Badge	*Silver. Front: the crowned George VI with the letters 'PM' for the designer Percy Metcalfe. Reverse: a laurel wreath tied at base with a pair of bows, its apex open and between the two arms, the Victorian crown. Beneath is the royal cypher of George VI and the inscription FOR BRAVERY IN THE FIELD. The recipient's name, serial number and unit are inscribed around the edge of the medal.*
Ribbon	*Dark blue with three white and two crimson stripes down the centre.*

Victoria Cross

Possibly the most renowned of any decoration in the world, the Victoria Cross was introduced by Queen Victoria on 29 January 1856, as a reward for 'Valour'. After the Crimean War, 111 awards were made.

An amendment of August 1858 stated that the Victoria Cross is to be awarded 'For acts of conspicuous courage and bravery under circumstances of extreme danger.' The medal is open to all ranks and is becoming increasingly difficult to win, so much so that it is now almost always awarded posthumously.

Badge	*A bronze straight-armed cross pattee. Front: a medallion, with a standing crowned lion on a Victorian crown. A draped scroll with the inscription FOR VALOUR. Reverse: the recipient's name, details, and date of the act of valour.*
Ribbon	*Crimson ribbon for all services.*

1 Commando

No 1 Commando was but one of the many British Army Commandos raised during the war. The shoulder flash depicts a salamander, a mythical lizard-like creature able to endure fire, the implication being that the troops who wore this flash had the same quality.

The first Commando was raised in June 1940 to operate as a unit of storm troops. One of the key reasons why the Commandos were successful was that they were small, tightly organised units with a great deal of operational flexibility and imagination.

Each Commando was composed of 10 troops of 50 men, but in early 1941 the number of troops was reduced to six, each fielding 65 men. The Commandos retained a high level of discipline and cohesion in battle. Such conduct earned a higher-than-average number of awards. At Kangaw in Burma in February 1945, for example, Lieutenant Knowland of No 1 Commando won a Victoria Cross for gallantry during a heavy Japanese attack.

1st Airborne Division

Bellerophon astride a Pegasus in pale blue on a dark maroon background. The word 'Airborne' appears in pale blue on a separate strip below. 6th Airborne Division wears the same.

The 1st Airborne Division initially saw action in North Africa in 1942 in support of the British First Army landings. The formation fought as an infantry division during the winter of 1942–43, helping bring about the collapse of the Axis forces in Tunisia. Thereafter it played a key role in the invasion of Sicily, and the invasion of the Italian mainland, and was afterwards withdrawn to the United Kingdom.

The Division next jumped into Holland in September 1944, winning undying fame at Arnhem. It spearheaded Operation Market Garden, and holding out against overwhelming odds for eight days, sustained 80 percent casualties. The formation withdrew to England to regroup, and in May 1945 landed in Norway as part of the British liberation forces.

Battle Honours

- *Vaagso, December 1941*
- *St Nazaire, March 1942*
- *Dieppe, August 1942*
- *Kangaw, February 1945*

Battle Honours

- *North Africa, 1942*
- *Sicily, July 1943*
- *Taranto and Castellaneta, 1943*
- *Arnhem, September 1944*

Second Army

A blue cross in the style of St George on a white shield, with a crusader's sword super-imposed on the upright of the cross.

The Second Army was raised in summer 1943 to spearhead the invasion of Northwest Europe, and went ashore on D-Day as part of 21st Army Group. It saw much hard fighting in establishing the beachhead, and later at Caen, and in the advance to Falaise. After the breakout, it crossed the Seine and the Somme before liberating Brussels.

The Second Army became embroiled in the sweep up to the banks of the Maas during the winter of 1944–45, and in the spring found itself engaged in clearing the remaining pockets of resistance between the Maas and the Rhine. In March 1945, its 12 and 30 Corps forced the northern crossing of the Rhine, thereafter driving across Northwest Germany to Munster, Osnabrook, Bremen and Hamburg.

6th Armoured Division

A clenched mailed gauntlet in white, on a square black background.

The 6th Armoured Division fought as part of the First Army in Tunisia in 1942–43, and was the first to link up with the Eighth Army advancing from the east. It served throughout the Italian campaign, and in the spring of 1945 as part of the Eighth Army. It also participated in the Fifteenth Army Group's operations in the Po Valley.

During the final weeks of the war the Division advanced at speed to Gorizia, accelerating the crumbling of German resistance in the Italian theatre.

The Division was subsequently renumbered, becoming the 1st Armoured Division.

Battle Honours
● *D-Day, 6 June 1944*
● *Normandy, June–August 1944*
● *Rhine crossing, March 1945*
● *Northwest Germany, March–May 1945*

Battle Honours
● *North Africa, 1942*
● *Tunisia, 1943*
● *Italy, 1943–45*
● *Po Valley, April–May 1945*

7th Armoured Division

A red desert rat, or jerboa, in a white circle on a red square, later changed to a brown rat, picked out in white, on a black background.

The 7th Armoured Division was the first to deploy in the Western Desert after Italy entered the war. The 'Desert Rats' nickname came from its 'scurrying and biting' activities, and its jerboa emblem. The Division formed part of the Army of the Nile and fought against the Italians. Later it won plaudits in the desert operations as part of Eighth Army, and with 21st Army Group in the invasion of Northwest Europe and the Rhine. With the British force, it entered Berlin.

7th Gurkha Rifles

The cap badge of this regiment shows two kukris pointed upwards, the handles crossed in saltire, the blades pointed upwards. First raised in 1902 at Thayetmyo as the 8th Gurkha Rifles, a year later the unit became the 2nd Battalion, 10th Gurkha Rifles.

The regiment fought in the Middle East during World War I, fighting at Megiddo, Sharon, and in Palestine. In World War II the Gurkhas fought in Italy, winning more laurels for their courage at Monte Cassino. After the abbey had been bombed the Germans moved troops into the ruins and turned them into an impregnable fortress. The Gurkhas charged up the slopes but were caught in a merciless crossfire that turned back the tough Nepalese fighters. The 7th Gurkha Rifles went on to fight in Burma against the Japanese Army.

Battle Honours
• *Sidi Barrani, December 1940*
• *Battle of El Alamein, October–November 1942*
• *Northwest Europe, 1944*
• *Germany, 1945*

Battle Honours
• *Burma, 1942*
• *Italy, 1944*
• *Imphal, March–June 1944*
• *Burma, 1945*

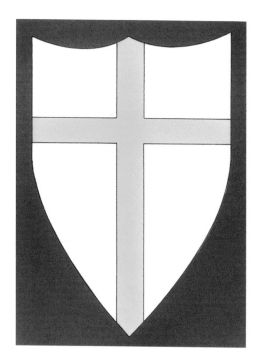

Eighth Army

A golden crusader's cross on a white shield set on a dark blue background. The badge owes its origin to the Army's first action, code-named 'Operation Crusader'.

The Eighth Army was formed from the original Army of the Nile in November 1941. Comprising 13 and 30 Corps, together with other formations, it fought hard in 1942, initially against the Italians and later against Rommel's Afrika Corps. Although forced to a defensive line at the gateway to Egypt, in October it won a great victory at El Alamein under General Montgomery. Thereafter it swept onward into Tunisia. Its next action was the invasion of Sicily, and then the bloody slog northwards through Italy. With Fifteenth Army Group, it forced the Sangro and Volturno crossings, and played a decisive role in the Po Valley.

Battle Honours

- *North Africa, 1941–42*
- *Battle of El Alamein, October–November 1942*
- *Sicily, July 1943*
- *Italy, 1943–45*

---

9 Squadron

No 9 Squadron, Royal Flying Corps, in existence today, was formed at St Omer, France, in December 1914. Under the command of Major Hugh Dowding, it crossed to France in December 1915. After flying in support of the artillery, it became involved in night raids, offensive patrolling and tactical bombing.

The Squadron was disbanded in 1919, but reformed as a bomber unit in 1924. It took part in the first raid against Germany, attacking Brunsbuttel on 4 September. In May 1941, it undertook a series of raids against the industrial heartland of the Ruhr. In August 1942 it transferred to No 5 Group, with whom it remained for the rest of the war. Arguably its most crucial and successful sortie was that against the German V-2 testing site at Peenemunde in August 1943.

Battle Honours

- *Germany, 1939*
- *Ruhr, 1941*
- *Peenemunde, August 1943*
- *Germany, 1943–45*

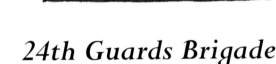

Fourteenth Army

A red shield with a narrow white inner border, the centre divided by a black horizontal band on which the Roman figures XIV were inscribed in white, set across a white sword, hilt uppermost. The badge was chosen from an anonymous entry in a competition open to all ranks, the winner being none other than the Army Commander, General Bill Slim.

The Fourteenth Army was formed in November 1943. Until its disbandment in1945 it held the longest battle line, from the Bay of Bengal to the borders of India and China, and was the war's largest single army. Its nearly one million personnel were grouped into the 4th, 15th and 33rd Indian Corps and a fourth corps, the 34th, formed for the invasion of Malaya. It won a series of vicious but crucial victories in the Arakan, at Imphal, Kohima, Kennedy Peak, Mandalay and Meiktila, leading to the defeat of the Japanese and liberation of Burma and Malaya.

Battle Honours
● *Imphal, March–June 1944*
● *Kohima, Summer 1944*
● *Northern Burma, December 1944*
● *Mandalay, March 1945*

24th Guards Brigade

An heraldic pinion (wing) in the form of a crest in red, set on a dark blue background.

The 24th Guards Brigade was one of the most highly trained units in the British Army during World War II. It was deployed to North Africa in March 1943 to join the British First Army, and was in action almost immediately upon arrival, preventing a German breakthrough near Beja. During the final offensive in North Africa between April and May 1943, the Brigade played a decisive role in the assault on the Bou feature.

Following the German surrender in North Africa, the Brigade took part in the campaign in Italy, being deployed to Anzio in January 1944. The fighting was hard, and the Brigade suffered heavy casualties (the Grenadier Guards suffered 60 per cent casualties) forcing the German defences of the Gothic Line as part of the Eighth Army. The winter of 1944 was particularly hard, made worse by the fact that the Brigade had to endure it in the Apennines.

Battle Honours
● *Beja, March 1942*
● *Tunisia, April 1943*
● *Anzio, January 1944*
● *Gothic Line, September 1944*

50th Northumbrian Division

Two capital 'Ts', for the Rivers Tyne and Tees, in red on a black square. When looked at sideways, the two 'Ts' formed an 'H', representing the Humber, the divisional area's third river.

Composed of Territorials from Northumberland, Durham and Yorkshire, the Division saw action in France and Belgium in 1940, with hard fighting during the withdrawal to Dunkirk. It embarked for the Middle East in 1941, taking part in the offensive operations in Libya. It acquitted itself well in the Battles of Knightsbridge and the Omars, and as part of 30 Corps at El Alamein. Thereafter it participated in the successful advance through Cyrenaica and Tripolitania.

Prominent in the invasion of Sicily, and heavily engaged in the fighting at Catania, it was withdrawn from Italy in 1944, joining the 21st Army Group in England prior to the Normandy landings. It was withdrawn from operations in autumn 1944 and returned to England after four years of continuous fighting.

51st Division

The letters 'HD' in red joined together within a red circle on a blue background. Formed from various Highland Regiments' Territorial Army battalions, the 51st Division joined the B.E.F. in France in January 1940, moving up to the Belgian border in March and from here through the Maginot Line to the Saar front.

The Division was ordered north when the Germans attacked, and it saw much hard action, sustaining heavy casualties from the German advance through Normandy. The 152nd and 153rd brigade were cut off at St. Valery-en-Caux and surrendered.

The Division was reformed around the surviving brigade, and in 1942 fought at El Alamein with the Eighth Army, pushing the enemy into Cyreanaica and Tunisia. After invading Sicily in July 1943, and landing in Italy in August, it returned to Britain from where, as part of 21st Army Group, it played a crucial part in the Normandy landings. Having participated in the liberation of Belgium, and advanced across the Rhine, it had reached the Elbe by the time Germany surrendered.

Battle Honours

- *France, 1940*
- *North Africa, 1941–43*
- *Sicily and Italy, 1943–44*
- *Northwest Europe, 1944*

Battle Honours

- *France, 1940*
- *North Africa, 1942–43*
- *Sicily and Italy, 1943*
- *Northwest Europe, 1944–45*

55th West Lancashire Division

The red rose of Lancashire is represented in this Division's badge. The rose has five petals inside, and five outside, and the leaves are arranged five on each side of the stem, thereby repeating the Divisional number '55'.

The Divisional vehicle marking did not include this stem and these leaves.

When worn as an arm badge, the rose was red with a green stem and leaves, set on a khaki circular background. The badge was originally adopted by the West Lancashire Division in 1916.

A Territorial Army Division was composed of Territorials from Liverpool and West Lancashire. The Division did not serve in action abroad, but rather formed part of the Home Forces, latterly in a training role.

56th London Division

A black cat set on a red background. The badge, reputedly 'Dick Whittington's cat', was chosen by Major General Sir Claude Liardet, the first Territorial Army officer to command a division.

The 56th (London) Division formed part of the Home Forces until 1942, when it was posted to the Middle East as part of the garrison in Palestine, Syria and Iraq. It joined the Central Mediterranean Force in 1943, taking part in the Salerno and Anzio landings. It was constantly in the front line during the unrelenting advance through Italy, earning plaudits for its role in the Garigliano crossing.

As part of the Eighth Army the Division took part in the Po Valley campaign, forcing the Agenta Gap, winning the Reno bridgehead, and sweeping northeast towards Venice (the Italian campaign was one of the war's most vicious and unrelenting).

Battle Honours

- *Home Defence only*

Battle Honours

- *Salerno, September 1943*
- *Anzio, January 1944*
- *Monte Cassino, January–May 1944*
- *Po Vally, 1945*

71 Squadron

No 71 Squadron, the first Eagle Squadron, was formed in September 1940 from American volunteers. It was joined in May 1941 by the second Eagle Squadron, No 121 Squadron, initially equipped with Hurricanes, but which in October 1941 converted to Spitfires. In February of that year, it took part in the unsuccessful channel dash operation against the battle-cruisers *Scharnhorst* and *Gneisenau.*

No 133 Squadron, the third Eagle Squadron, was formed in July 1941 and commanded by Squadron-Leader George Brown, a veteran of the Battle of Britain. It, too, was initially equipped with Hurricanes, but in the spring of 1942 converted to Spitfires. It was heavily engaged in the Dieppe raid.

Battle Honours

- *Battle of Britain, 1940*
- *North Sea, 1941*
- *Northern France, 1941*
- *Dieppe, August 1942*

---

100 Group

No 100 Group was formally established in November 1943 under the command of Air-Vice Marshal Addison. The Group specialised in electronic counter-measures to confuse the Luftwaffe night-fighters and radar, and as such constantly found itself engaged in a deadly game of cat-and-mouse with the ever-improving German air-defence measures.

The Group became fully operational in the early summer of 1944 by which time its jamming forces comprised four squadrons of heavy bombers, subsequently supplemented by No 92 Squadron, flying Halifaxes, Wellingtons and Mosquitoes fitted with special receiving equipment. The Group was disbanded in December 1945.

Battle Honours

- *The Low Countries, 1944*
- *Northwest Germany, 1944*
- *Germany, 1945*

120 Squadron

No 120 Squadron was formed in Kent in January 1918. Designated a day-bombing squadron, as the war progressed it was assigned the more mundane task of transporting mail between England and France. The Squadron was disbanded in 1919 and reformed in June 1941 in Belfast. Tasked with countering the U-boat threat in the North Atlantic, it was one of the first Coastal Command squadrons to be equipped with Liberators.

The Squadron remained in the anti-submarine role throughout the war. When it was disbanded in June 1945 it had 16 confirmed U-boat kills, the highest score in Coastal Command.

148 Squadron

No 148 Squadron was formed in February 1918, and saw action in France that year in night operations against German railheads and airfields. It was disbanded twice before April 1940, then reactivated in Malta in December. It played an important role in support of the Eighth Army in North Africa until December 1942, when it was again temporarily disbanded.

Reformed in March 1943 and equipped with Liberators and Halifaxes for supply drops into the Balkans, it was redesignated No 148 (Special Duties) Squadron. From January 1944 it operated from forward bases in Italy supplying Partisan missions in Poland, Greece and the Balkans.

Battle Honours

- *Belfast, 1941*
- *North Atlantic, 1941*
- *North Atlantic, 1942–44*
- *North Atlantic, 1945*

Battle Honours

- *Malta, 1940*
- *North Africa, 1940–42*
- *Reformed, 1943*
- *Italy, 1944–45*

231st Independent Infantry Brigade

161 Squadron

The Special Operations Executive (SOE) was formed by Churchill with the express aim of 'setting Europe ablaze'. Shortly thereafter No 419 Flight, equipped with Lysanders and Whitleys, was formed to enable the new resistance groups to receive both agent drops and essential supplies. No 419 Flight was expanded, and in August 1941 became No 138 Squadron.

In February 1942 No 161 Squadron was formed as a second Special Duties Squadron under the command of Wing-Commander 'Mouse' Fielden. From then on 'A' Flight flew Lysanders for pick-up missions, while 'B' Flight flew Whitleys, and later Halifaxes and Sterlings, for parachute drops. In all, No 161 Squadron made over 400 drops and 600 extractions.

A white Maltese cross on a scarlet shield.

The Brigade had several titles: the Malta Infantry Brigade; the Southern Infantry Brigade; 1st (Malta) Infantry Brigade; 231st Infantry Brigade; and finally the 231 (Malta) Independent Brigade Group. It comprised the three regular battalions which formed the Malta garrison.

The Brigade was ready to oppose any attempt at Italian invasion, and for months withstood the combined ordeals of constant air attack and near famine of the siege. In April 1943, the Brigade was withdrawn from Malta to Egypt, where it undertook the special training for required for an Independent Brigade Group. After taking part in the invasion of Sicily, and the landings on the toe of Italy, it returned to the United Kingdom in 1943. The Brigade made its third assault landing on D-day. At the end of 1944, after the breakout and advance into Northwest Europe, by now exhausted, it was relieved.

Battle Honours

- *Northern France, February 1942*
- *France, 1943*
- *D-Day, 6 June 1944*
- *France and the Low Countries, 1944*

Battle Honours

- *Sicily, July 1943*
- *Italy, 1943*
- *D-Day, 6 June 1944*
- *Northwest Europe, 1944*

249 Squadron

Originally formed as Royal Naval Air Squadron, Killingholme, in 1917, the Squadron was redesignated No 249 Squadron, RAF, a year later. It reformed on 18 May 1940 as a gift squadron from the Gold Coast at Church Fenton.

Re-equipped with Hurricanes, it redeployed and during the Battle of Britain, Flight Lieutenant Nicolson won the only Victoria Cross to be awarded to Fighter Command. On 21 May 1941, the Squadron was transferred by aircraft carrier to Malta where it played a decisive role in the defence of the island.

In October 1942, the Squadron converted to Spitfires and later transferred to Italy. After serving in Yugoslavia, it returned to Italy where it was disbanded in August 1945, having destroyed 244 enemy aircraft.

Battle Honours

- *Battle of Britain, 1940*
- *Malta, 1941*
- *Italy, 1944*
- *Yugoslavia, 1945*

609 Squadron

No 609 Squadron was originally formed as a bomber unit in 1936, but on the outbreak of war was equipped with Spitfires. Initially tasked with convoy protection, following the Dunkirk evacuation it moved to Southampton. It was heavily involved in the Battle of Britain, claiming over 100 enemy aircraft by 20 October.

In early 1941 the Squadron moved to Biggin Hill, taking part in bomber escort duties over Northern France. In March 1942, the Squadron converted to Typhoons and again found itself in action over northern France. It transferred to France after the D-Day landings, joining the 2nd Tactical Air Force in action against enemy ground targets.

Battle Honours

- *English Channel, 1940*
- *Battle of Britain, 1940*
- *France, June 1944*
- *Germany, 1945*

67

616 Squadron

No 616 Squadron was formed in November 1938 and initially equipped with Hawker Hinds. In October 1939, it was redesignated a fighter squadron and re-equipped with Spitfires. The Squadron moved south, and in 1940 distinguished itself during the Battle of Britain, downing 30 enemy aircraft.

In 1942 the Squadron was equipped with Spitfire Mk VI and undertook a high-altitude defensive role against enemy reconnaissance aircraft. In September 1943 it received Mk VIIs, and in 1944 switched to escort duties in support of bombers attacking targets in Northern France. In July 1944 the Squadron moved to Manston, and in January 1945 received a consignment of Meteors, Britain's first jet fighter.

617 Squadron

No 617 Squadron was formed, contrary to RAF tradition, as an élite of élites. It was intensively trained as a prelude to possibly the most famous sortie of the war, the 'dambusters' raid on the Mohne and Eder dams.

Both dams were breached, causing immense damage to the industrial areas in the 'flood-plains' below. The Ruhr was back to full production within a few backs; the psychological impact, however, both on British and German morale, was immense. Wing Commander Guy Gibson, in command of the raid, was awarded the Victoria Cross, and 33 other members of the Squadron were decorated. The Squadron took part in a number of highly successful subsequent high-level raids.

Battle Honours
● *Battle of Britain, 1940*
● *North Sea, 1941–44*
● *Northern France, 1944*
● *Germany, 1945*

Battle Honours
● *The Dam raids, May 1943*
● *Dortmund-Ems Canal, 1943*
● *Norway, 1944*
● *Germany, 1945*

3rd Indian Division (Chindits)

A golden Burmese Dragon (a Chinthern-Pagoda Guardian) on a blue circular background.

As part of the Fourteenth Army the 3rd Indian Division, Wingate's Chindits, spearheaded the British fight back against Japan in Burma. They entered Japanese-held Burma from the west, crossing the Chindwin River in February 1943 and the Irrawaddy a month later. By then the enemy were fully aware of them. Wingate was forced to withdraw circuitously to India, having lost a third of his troops and most of his equipment. Despite his limited success he was given leave to prepare a more ambitious raid by six brigades with its own air unit. The expedition was air-dropped into Burma in February 1944 and immediately ran into difficulties. Wingate was killed in a jungle air crash on 24 March 1944; thereafter the Chindits came under United States command, with disastrous results.

Battle Honours

- *Chindwin, February 1943*
- *Irrawaddy, March 1943*
- *Burma, 1944*

Coldstream Guards

The insignia is the Star of the Order of the Garter. The Garter and motto are on a blue enamel ground, the cross in red enamel. The badge is silver for officers, warrant officers and certain other appointments, anodized gold for other ranks.

The Regiment was formed in 1650 as a unit of the Commonwealth Army. The Star of the Order of the Garter was granted by King William III in 1696, and the Regiment was expanded to six battalions during World War II. The 1st and 2nd Battalions fought in France in 1940, and retired in good order to Dunkirk following the German breakthrough. The 3rd Battalion fought in the North African desert, and was later joined by the 2nd Battalion in Italy. The 1st and 5th Battalions took part in the liberation of France and the Low Countries after D-Day, and were later joined by the 4th Battalion in the final advance into Germany in early 1945.

Battle Honours

- *France, 1940*
- *Tobruk, 1941*
- *Italy, 1943–44*
- *Northwest Europe, 1944–45*

Combined Operations

In February 1941, Nos 7, 8 and 11 Commandos were sent to the Middle East to join forces with Nos 50, 51, 52 and 53, who amalgamated to form the Combined (Middle East) Commando. Later this force became D Battalion of 'Layforce', a brigade of the Eighth Army's 6th Division.

After fighting in North Africa, Syria and Crete, Layforce was disbanded and Laycock returned to Britain to lead the Special Service Brigade. The cloth shoulder flash illustrated above carries one of the favourite weapons of the Commandos, the Thompson submachine gun. This weapon, plus the famous Commando dagger, was ideally suited to the type of hit-and-run raids mounted by the Commandos. It was customary for each soldier to wear a should flash which carried the number of his Commando unit. These flashes could be red or white lettering on a navy blue background. Other flashes were dark green with yellow lettering.

Commandos

The Commandos had a proud history dating back to October 1664. King Charles II was very much in favour of creating a standing force of men trained to fight on land and sea, and foresaw the creation of the Regiment of professional servicemen trained to crew his warships. The sea soldiers took the title 'Marines' in 1672, and became a strong backbone to the crews of the ships of the line. They saw considerable action against the Dutch, and were formed into a Corps in 1755. It won its first VC at the Battle of Inkerman in 1854.

During World War I the 4th Battalion took part in the amphibious raid at Zeebrugge in April 1918, winning its eighth and ninth VCs, both of which were awarded by ballot.

During World War II, the government formed a number of Commando units, the name and concept taken from the Afrikaner raiding parties which had carried out swift strikes across the Transvaal in the Boer War. These British Commando units were intended to be relatively small, highly mobile and capable of carrying out surgical attacks against tactical or strategic targets. Commando units were raised from Army and Royal Navy personnel, as well as from the Royal Marines, but at the end of the war, with the exception of a small Royal Navy contingent, the title and training standards were retained by the Royal Marines alone.

Battle Honours
● *North Africa, 1941*
● *Syria, 1941*
● *Italy, 1944*
● *Far East, 1945*

Battle Honours
● *North Africa, 1941*
● *Middle Easta, 1941*
● *Italy and France, 1944*
● *Far East, 1945*

Essex Regiment

The insignia depicts the Castle of Gibraltar with a key in the lower centre of the base and turned to the left. Above the castle is Sphinx sitting on a tablet carrying the inscription 'Egypt'. The castle is enclosed in an oak wreath, upon the lower portion of which is inscribed the Regiment's name.

Formed in 1881 from the 44th Foot and the 56th Foot, the castle and key insignia were granted for service at the siege of Gibraltar in 1779-83, while the Sphinx was granted for service in the Egyptian campaign of 1801. The Regiment captured the eagle of the French 62nd Regiment at Salamanca in the Napoleonic Wars, which resulted in officers wearing an eagle on their collar badges.

The Essex Regiment fought with the British Expeditionary Force in France in 1940, being evacuated from Dunkirk. It went on to fight in North Africa, specifically at the Battle of El Alamein under Montgomery. It also fought in Burma.

Gloucester Regiment

The badge depicts a Sphinx resting on a tablet inscribed 'Egypt' above two sprays of laurel, in gold embroidery.

In 1881, the 28th (North Gloucestershire) Regiment was amalgamated with the 61st (South Gloucestershire) Regiment to form the Gloucestershire Regiment. It enjoyed the unique privilege of wearing a second badge in the rear of caps in commemoration of fighting back-to-back at the Battle of Alexandria in 1801. This tradition endures today, though the unit is titled The Royal Gloucestershire, Berkshire and Wiltshire Regiment).

The Regiment first saw action in World War II in France, where a member of the 5th Battalion became the first Territorial Army soldier to be awarded the Military Medal, before the unit's evacuation from Dunkirk. In the Korean War, the Regiment received a United States Presidential Citation in 1951 in recognition of its heroic stand on the River Imjin against overwhelming Chinese odds.

Battle Honours

- *France, 1940*
- *North Africa, 1941–42*
- *Burma, 1944*
- *Northwest Europe, 1945*

Battle Honours

- *France, 1940*
- *Normandy, June 1944*
- *Falaise, August 1944*
- *France, September 1944*

Gordon Highlanders

The headdress badge showed the crest of the Marquess of Huntly, a stag's head issuing from a ducal coronet within a wreath of ivy. On the bottom of the wreath was a scroll with the words 'Bydand' (Stand Fast) inscribed in silver plate or white metal.

The Gordon Highlanders were formed in 1881 from the amalgamation of the 75th Stirlingshire Regiment and the 92nd Gordon Highlanders. During World War II they fought in France in 1940, throughout the North African campaign, through Sicily and north into Italy. As part of 51st (Highland) Division they were returned to England in time for D-Day, advancing through Normandy and onwards into the Low Countries. They spent more time in action than almost any other regiment in the British Army. Among their most notable actions are St Valery-en-Caux, Odon, Caen, Northwest Europe 1940, 1944-45, Sidi Barrani, El Alamein, Adrano, Sicily 1943, North Africa 1940-43, and the Gothic Line.

Battle Honours
● *France, 1940*
● *North Africa, 1941–43*
● *Sicily, 1943*
● *Italy, 1944*

Grenadier Guards

A grenade in gold embroidery. On the ball in silver the Royal Cypher is interlaced and reversed with the crown above.

The regiment was raised by Charles II. In September 1939 all three battalions were posted to Europe, engaged in a quiet 'Phoney War'. In 1940–41, 4th, 5th and 6th Battalions were raised. Whereas the 1st, 2nd, and 4th Battalions were converted to armoured units, the 3rd, 5th, and 6th saw active service in 1942. The 6th Battalion were the first Grenadiers to land in Italy, but the 5th Battalion suffered such heavy losses at Anzio that its survivors withdrew to reinforce the 6th and returned to England as a cadre. They then fought on northwards to make a breakthrough at Battaglia.

The armoured units battled through Normandy, and as part of 30 Corps secured the bridge at Nijmegen, thereafter clearing the enemy out of the area between the Maas and the Rhine, before forcing the Rhine itself onwards into Germany. The Grenadiers reached the Elbe before the final German collapse.

Battle Honours
● *Dunkirk, 1940*
● *North Africa, 1942–43*
● *Gothic Line, 1944*
● *Italy, 1943–45*

Guards Armoured Division

A white eye (denoting vigilance) on a blue shield with a red border. The badge was selected from designs of the late Rex Whistler.

The Guards Armoured Division was formed in September 1941. As part of 8 Corps, 21st Armoured Group, it landed in Normandy in June 1944, fighting through the bocage to Caen and Falaise. It participated in the breakout and dash to the Somme, and was the first formation to enter Brussels on its liberation in September 1944. Thereafter it assisted in clearing the area from the Meuse to the Rhine, crossing the Rhine under command of 12 Corps.

The Division fought its way across Germany to Bremen and Cuxhaven, accepting the latter port's surrender shortly before V.E. Day. It moved to the Rhineland, parading in armour on 10 June 1945 for the last time. Thereafter it was renamed the Guards Division, forming part of the British Army of the Rhine.

Honourable Artillery Company

The badge sports an old-fashioned cannon with a scroll above inscribed 'H.A.C.' and a scroll below which a Latin inscription which translates as 'arms are the fulcrum of peace'. The whole badge is surmounted by St Edward's crown.

Henry VIII issued letters of patent on 25 August 1537 to the Overseers of the Fraternity or Guild of Saint George authorising them to establish a corporation for the better increase of the defence of the realm (at this time artillery included any type of projectile-launching weapon, such as the crossbow and longbow, as well as firearms).

The officers of the London Trained Bands were trained by the Artillery Company from its corporation until 1780. The prefix Honourable was first used in 1685 and confirmed by Queen Victoria in 1860. Contingents from the Regiment served in the both Boer Wars, and it raised three infantry battalions and seven batteries of artillery in World War I. In World War II the 12th (HAC) Regiment saw action.

Battle Honours
● *Normandy, June 1944*
● *Northern France, 1944*
● *Operation Market Garden, September 1944*
● *Germany, 1945*

Battle Honours
● *North Africa, 1941–43*
● *Sicily, 1943*
● *Italy, 1944*
● *France, 1944*

Inniskilling Fusiliers

The insignia depicts a grenade, on the ball of which is the Castle of Inniskilling with St George's flag flying.

Raised in 1689 by William III from the defenders of Enniskillen when it was besieged by the forces of James II, the Regiment saw service throughout the eighteenth and nineteenth centuries as Britain established her empire. In World War I, the Regiment saw action at Mons in August 1914, at Gallipoli in 1915 and in Palestine in 1917-18.

In World War II, the Regiment was heavily engaged in France in 1940 as part of the British Expeditionary Force. Like many British regiments, it went on to fight in North Africa and the grim campaign of attrition on the Italian mainland.

Irish Guards

The badge depicts the Star of the Order of St Patrick, with a motto in Latin which translates as 'Who Shall Separate Us?'

The Regiment was formed in 1900 by Order of Queen Victoria 'to commemorate the bravery shown by the Irish Regiments in the operations in South Africa in the years 1899 and 1900.'

During World War II many men from the Irish Republic joined Irish units serving in the British Army, which went some way to offset the duplicitous attitude of the government in Dublin towards the war and the Third Reich in general.

During World War II, the Irish Guards saw action in Norway and in the defence of Boulogne in 1940. Ejected from France by the victorious German Army, the Regiment went on to fight in North Africa and then Italy. One of its notable actions was at Anzio at the beginning of 1944, while its men also served in France and the Low Countries after D-Day.

Battle Honours
● *France, 1940*
● *North Africa, 1942*
● *Burma, 1943*
● *Italy, 1944*

Battle Honours
● *France, 1940*
● *North Africa, 1943*
● *Italy, 1944*
● *France and the Low Countries, 1944*

London Irish Rifles

The insignia for the London Irish Rifles is the Tara Harp surmounted by St Edward's crown in silver.

The London Irish Rifles were raised in 1859 as the 28th Middlesex (London Irish) Rifle Volunteers, and in 1908 were renamed the 18th (County of London) Battalion, The London Regiment. As part of 56th (London Division), they saw service during World War II in Italy in arguably the most forgotten of campaigns, fighting their way north against not only a determined enemy, but the terrain, the weather and perpetual shortages, suffering high losses and illnesses as a result.

They were later affiliated to The Royal Irish Rifles, and today, as a Territorial Army unit, form 'D' Company, The London Regiment.

London Scottish

Within a wreath a lion rampant superimposed on a Cross of St Andrews. The Regimental name and the Regimental motto, *Strike Sure*, were inscribed on the cross.

In 1936 the Regiment was a single Territorial Battalion of the Gordon Highlanders, but by 1939 was three. Accordingly the 97th HAA Regiment RA, TA (The London Scottish) was formed. Its battalions were in reserve from 1939–41, but the 3rd Battalion acted as an AA unit in the Battle of Britain.

The 1st Battalion went to the Middle East in 1942 and later to the invasion of Sicily. With the 56th Division after the invasion of Italy, under both American and British command, it fought in all the major battles, from the River Volturno to the Garigliano crossing, at Anzio, the Gothic Line break, and the subsequent battle at the River Po. The 3rd Battalion was converted from a static to mobile anti-aircraft unit and transferred to Egypt in December 1942. It subsequently fought through Sicily and Italy. The Regiment was de facto disbanded in 1947.

Battle Honours
● *Salerno, September 1943*
● *Central Italy, 1944*
● *Gothic Line, 1944*
● *Northern Italy, 1945*

Battle Honours
● *Sicily, July 1943*
● *Anzio, January 1944*
● *Gothic Line, August–September 1944*
● *Northern Italy, 1945*

Merchant Navy

Not all members of the Merchant Navy wore the same uniform, several companies having liveries of their own. Officers wore special insignia, and had titles according to their speciality. Captains wore four stripes, the two at the centre joined to form a diamond. Other officers, namely 1st, 2nd and 3rd officers, wore three, two and one stripes respectively. Surgeons wore red cloth backings to their insignia, engineers purple, and pursers white. The wireless officers wore waved stripes, while stewards were identified by one straight stripe below six-pointed gold stars.

Merchant seamen throughout the war suffered severe losses, particularly those who served on North Atlantic and Russian convoys yet, inexplicably, theirs was regarded as a reserved occupation and they were not granted military status. This appears rather unjust, given that they kept Britain fed.

Battle Honours
• *North Atlantic, 1940*
• *The Arctic, 1941*
• *English Channel, 1943*
• *North Atlantic, 1942–45*

Military Police

The Royal Cypher with crown above within a wreath of laurel; below the wreath a scroll inscribed 'Royal Military Police'.

Provision was first made for a Provost Company by Henry VIII in 1513. A small mounted detachment of 12 N.C.Os. formed in 1855, formed the Military Mounted Police 20 years later. The Military Foot Police was founded in 1885, the two wings merging in 1926 in the Corps of Military Police.

Throughout the war, the Military Police undertook close security duties, and acted as beach marshals during landings, as well as their normal duties. They fought in every theatre and were attached to the vast majority of independent units.

Although a large number of individual decorations were awarded to Military Policemen, the Regiment never fought as an entity, and as such was not liable for battle honours. In 1946, in recognition of its crucial role in the war, it was granted the title 'Royal'.

Battle Honours
• *Not applicable*

Parachute Regiment

Upon a spread of wings, an open parachute; above, the Royal Crest.

This Regiment was formed in September 1941, raising three battalions in the 1st Parachute Brigade. With a 4th Battalion, the selected and trained volunteer force grew to two airborne divisions. In February 1942, the 2nd Battalion's elements conducted a successful airborne sabotage raid against a German radar site in France. In 1942 the Airborne Forces Depot was formed, and a 2nd Parachute Brigade raised. That year the 1st Parachute Brigade fought a number of actions in Tunisia, and later in the invasion of Sicily. The Division took part in the invasion of Italy prior to returning home; the 2nd Brigade stayed on as an independent unit. The Regiment trained intensely for D-Day; the 6th Airborne Division spearheaded the invasion, but the 1st Division was not deployed.

As part of Operation Market Garden, the 1st Airborne Division jumped into Arnhem to capture and hold the bridge pending the arrival of 30 Corps. But the area was German-held. Elements of the Division held out against the enemy for eight days, although over 1200 troops were dead and 3000 taken prisoner. In March 1945 the British 6th and American 17th Airborne Divisions undertook Operation Varsity, the war's final and largest single airborne operation.

Popski's Private Army

Founded and led by Major Vladimir ('Popski') Peniakoff, a Belgian engineer who had worked in Egypt, Popski's Private Army was spurned by the North African campaign. Peniakoff had wanted to join the Long Range Desert Group; considered too eccentric, he was allowed to form his own independent raiding unit, the smallest in the British Army.

Initially comprising five officers and 18 other ranks, it dashed into the Libyan desert in jeeps and trucks, wrecking Axis military installations, aircraft and petrol dumps behind the lines. At its maximum of 120 men, it was part of the Eighth Army order of battle, although never fully appreciated by the British High Command.

Battle Honours
• *Bruneval, February 1942*
• *D-Day, 6 June 1944*
• *Arnhem, September 1944*
• *The Rhine, March 1945*

Battle Honours
• *Cyrenaica, 1941*
• *Mareth Line, 1943*
• *Tunisia, 1943*
• *Italy, 1944*

Royal Horse Artillery

The headdress badge of the Royal Horse Artillery depicts the Royal Cypher within the Garter, ensigned with the crown. Below is a scroll inscribed 'Royal Horse Artillery'.

Two troops of the Royal Horse Artillery were raised in 1793 for the support of cavalry forces. In 1899, the Royal Artillery was reorganised into two broad groups: The Royal Horse Artillery and Royal Field Artillery in one, and the Royal Garrison Artillery in the other. In 1924, the groups were merged into a single regiment, the Royal Regiment of Artillery, though the Royal Horse Artillery retained its title and distinctive badge. In 1945, King George VI ordered that a mounted troop of the Royal Horse Artillery be raised for ceremonial duties, and this was formed in 1946.

Rifle Brigade

The badge depicts a Maltese Cross inscribed with the regimental battle honours and surrounded by a laurel wreath, in the centre of which is a bugle horn.

The Rifle Brigade was formed in 1797 for service in America. Its worth was quickly realised, and an 'experimental corps of riflemen' was raised from 14 line regiments a year later.

In 1937, the 9th London Regiment became the Queen Victoria's Rifles, the King's Royal Rifle Corps (KRRC). The 1st Battalion was equipped with motor-cycles and was lost at Calais in 1940; the survivors were redesignated the 7th Battalion, KRRC, in 1941, and two years later were placed in suspended animation. The 9th and 11th Battalions went on to see much hard fighting, particularly in North Africa and Italy. The 11th Battalion had formerly been the Queen's Westminsters.

Battle Honours
● *Ceremonial duties*

Battle Honours
● *France, 1940*
● *Crete, 1941*
● *North Africa, 1940–43*
● *Italy, 1944*

Royal Artillery

An old-fashioned muzzle-loading gun; above, a scroll inscribed with the motto *Ubique* (Everywhere) ensigned by a crown; below the gun the motto *Quo Fas et Gloria Ducunt* (Whither Right and Glory Lead), in gilt or gilding metal.

The Royal Artillery was formed by the Board of Ordnance in 1716. It was granted its two mottoes on 10 July 1832, and in the following year the badge was adopted. One of the largest Regiments in the Army, the Royal Artillery served in every theatre during World War II, in roles as diverse as close support, anti-aircraft, and coastal defence. Volunteers even manned the guns on troop ships and armed merchantmen, setting a fine record during the Battle of the Atlantic.

The Royal Artillery's battle honours are incorporated into the names of its batteries. Its guns constitute its colours.

Battle Honours

- *France and the Low Countries, 1940*
- *North Africa, 1940–43*
- *Italy and Northwest Europe, 1943–45*
- *Southeast Asia, 1941–45*

Royal Engineers

The badge of the Corps is the Royal Cypher of the reigning monarch within the Garter, surrounded by a laurel wreath, the crown above and the title below. The motto, 'Wherever right and glory lead' indicates the worldwide nature of the Corps.

The electric telegraph was first used in the Crimean War in 1854, and a Telegraph Troop RE was formed in 1870. However, it was not until 1920, after World War I, that a separate Corps of Signals was formed. Engineers fought n all theatres in World War II, performing a host of different duties, ranging from building field defences, demolishing enemy defences, building and strengthening roads and bridges, and also destroying the same as the army withdraws. In addition, engineers were involved in the making safe of unexploded bombs and the camouflage and concealment of forces.

Battle Honours

- *All theatres*

Royal Fusiliers

The badge of the Royal Fusiliers is a flaming grenade, with a rose over within the Garter, which sports a motto that translates as 'Evil to him who evil thinks'.

The Regiment was first raised at the Tower of London by James II in 1685, and in May 1881 was redesignated The City of London Regiment (Royal Fusiliers). The primary role of the fusiliers was to escort the Train of Artillery, which at the time was housed in the Tower of London.

In 1968 the Royal Regiment of Fusiliers was created by amalgamating the Royal Northumberland Fusiliers, The Royal Warwickshire Fusiliers, The Royal Fusiliers and The Lancashire Fusiliers. The new badge was a flaming grenade in brass with the Queen's crown thereon, superimposed on the body of the grenade is St George and the Dragon.

Battle Honours

- *France, 1940*
- *North Africa, 1941*
- *Italy, 1943*
- *France, 1944*

Royal Green Jackets

The badge comprises a Maltese Cross inscribed with the selected battle honours thereon a bugle-horn stringed and encircled with the title of the Regiment, all within a wreath of laurel ensigned with the crown resting upon a plinth inscribe 'Peninsula. Across the tie is a naval crown inscribed with 'Copenhagen 1801' to commemorate the Regiment's first honour, and the death in action of the first officer of the Experimental Corps of Riflemen.

The Green Jackets first fought in World War II in northern France, earning the honour 'Calais' for their dogged resistance against the Germans. The 2nd Battalion was in the Air-Landing Brigade of the 6th Airborne Division and earned the battle honour 'Pegasus Bridge', an honour unique to line infantry at the time.

Battle Honours

- *France, 1940*
- *North Africa, 1941–43*
- *D-Day, 6 June 1944*
- *France, 1944*

Royal Marines

This insignia depicts the Royal Crest, which was initially displayed on the officers' shoulder plates in 1797; a laurel wreath, awarded after the Battle of Belle-Ile in 1761; and the globe, granted by King George IV in 1827.

The Royal Marines, which became a permanent corps in 1775, can trace its origins to the Duke of York and Albany's Maritime Regiment of Foot which was formed in 1664. Traditionally they formed landing parties, provided infantry support and maintained discipline aboard ship. During World War II, their duties expanded to include the defence of naval bases abroad, the provision of crews for landing craft, beach control parties and armoured units for close support on the beaches. They also formed specially trained Commando units, which launched hit-and-run raids on German-occupied Europe, as well as missions against the Japanese.

Royal Navy Commandos

Formation signs were adopted during World War II and were worn on the upper sleeves of the battledress. Royal Navy titles were curved, embroidered in white thread on a dark blue background. There were three independent badges in total: one with the straightforward designation 'COMMANDO'; a second issued to Royal Marines Beach Commandos with the designation 'R.N. COMMANDO'; and a third, issued to Royal Navy personnel attached to the Royal Marines, inscribed 'ROYAL NAVY COMMANDO.'

Royal Navy Commandos were particularly responsible for the control of beach-heads and naval gunfire support. The badge shown above is the shoulder flash for a Royal Navy Beach Commando. During World War II beach assaults and naval gunfire support were critical to the success of Allied amphibious operations, especially on D-Day. In addition, once units were ashore they had to be marshalled and directed off the beaches, where they were vulnerable to enemy fire. All this required specialist personnel, who had to work under fire.

Battle Honours

- *Italy, 1943–44*
- *D-Day, 6 June 1944*
- *Northwest Europe, 1944–45*
- *Far East, 1941–45*

Battle Honours

- *North Africa, 1942*
- *Sicily, 1943*
- *Italy, 1943*
- *D-Day, 6 June 1944*

Special Air Service

A winged dagger striking downwards with the motto 'Who Dares Wins'.

The SAS was the brainchild of a young subaltern, David Stirling, of No 8 Commando in the Western Desert. His plan was to disrupt German maneouvres by making hit-and-run raids on targets well behind the German lines. The Commander-in-Chief authorised the formation of 'L Detachment', 66 men who would be trained like the Long Range Desert Group.

Some spectacular successes followed; L-Detachment destroyed over 100 aircraft. In October 1942, it became 1st Special Air Service Regiment, with 390 men and officers. In January 1944, an SAS brigade was formed in Scotland, of four regiments (British and French), and a Belgian parachute squadron. Before D-Day, the SAS jumped into Occupied Europe to assist the Resistance.

Battle Honours
● *North Africa, 1941–43*
● *Sicily and Italy, 1943–45*
● *Adriatic, 1943–44*
● *Northwest Europe, 1944–45*

Welsh Guards

Officers: A leek of 70mm (2.75in) high, in gold embroidery on a black cloth ground. Soldiers: A leek in gilding metal.

The Welsh Guards was formed from serving officers and Guardsmen on St David's Day, 1915.

On 20 May 1940 the Welsh Guards fought a valiant rear-guard action withdrawing from Arras, and later assisted the First Guards Brigade in taking up a covering position in the retreat to Dunkirk. The remnants of the 1st Battalion were among the last troops off the beach-head.

They later fought in North Africa, Italy and Northeast Europe, assisting in the liberation of Brussels, and were at the vanguard of the advance into North Germany immediately prior to the enemy surrender.

Battle Honours
● *Defence of Arras, 1940*
● *Boulogne 1940*
● *France and the Low Countries, 1944*
● *Germany, 1945*

HMS Amazon

The ship's badge depicted the helmeted, stern features of a martial female; her motto *Audacater*, meant 'Boldly'. The ninth ship to carry the name was built by Yarrow and Thornycroft in 1926. Displacing 1189 tonnes (1170 tons), with a length of 95m (312ft), she was large for the day. This, together with her excellent top speed of 37 knots and main armament of four 12cm (4.7in) guns and six 53.3cm (21in) torpedo tubes, gave her a potency which made her the blue-print for destroyer construction.

Amazon enjoyed a long and distinguished war, serving off the Norwegian coast in May 1940. She later assumed an escort destroyer role with increased anti-submarine capability. Although she served mainly in the North Atlantic until 1943, she undertook a number of Arctic and Malta convoys in 1942, and was present during the November North Africa landings.

In 1943, too old for front-line duties, *Amazon* was converted into an anti-submarine training vessel.

HMS Ark Royal

The motto of HMS *Ark Royal*, *Desire n'a pas repos* (Desire Has No Rest), was that of Lord Howard of Effingham, the Lord High Admiral, commander of the first *Ark Royal* against the Spanish Armada in the 1580s.

The second *Ark Royal* was built as a seaplane carrier, and served throughout World War I, renamed *Pegasus* in 1935. The third, an aircraft carrier, was launched in 1937; she displaced 22,353 tonnes (22,000 tons) and had a complement of 1575. She served in the Mediterranean, in the attack on the French fleet at Oran, in a number of Malta convoys, and was later detached to take part in the hunt for the battleship *Bismark* when *Ark Royal*'s aircraft scored a hit on the enemy's steering mechanism, so that British ships could overhaul and sink her. German propaganda so often 'sank' the Ark Royal, that when she really *was* sunk by torpedoes the authorities could hide the fact.

Battle Honours
• *Norway, 1940*
• *North Atlantic, 1940–43*
• *Malta convoys, 1942*
• *North Africa, 1942*

Battle Honours
• *Oran, July 1940*
• *Sinking of the* Bismarck, *May 1941*
• *Malta convoys, 1942*
• *Gibraltar, November 1941*

HMS Danae

In classical history, Danae was the daughter of Acrisius, King of Argos, and mother of Perseus. For a ship, hers was not an auspicious name; the first two *Danae* were both 5th raters taken as prizes, and the third mutinied in 1800.

The fifth HMS *Danae* was built in 1918, the name-ship of a new enlarged class of light cruiser. She was 4725 tonnes (4650 tons), 144m (471ft) long, and had a beam of 14m (46ft). Her armament was six single 15.2cm (6in) guns, two 7.6cm (3in) AA guns, and torpedoes of 12 53cm (21in) tubes. With a crew of 400, she was capable of a speed of 29 knots. A hybrid, she had neither the size nor endurance to patrol distant waters' sea lanes, yet was too slow to undertake a heavy destroyer's duties. She served on the China Station from 1939 to 1941 and when the Japanese annihilated the Allied fleet during the Java invasion, escaped destruction and transferred to the East Indies Fleet. In home waters in 1944, she then took part in the bombardment during the Normandy landings.

Battle Honours

- China Station, 1939–41
- Given to Free Polish Navy, 1944
- Home waters, 1944
- D-Day, 6 June 1944

HMS Devonshire

The badge is derived from the arms of Devonshire, as is the motto, *Auxilio Divino* ('By the Help of God'). The seventh ship to bear the name was launched in October 1927. She was a heavy cruiser of the 'County' class, displacing 10,000 tonnes (9850 tons), with a crew of 650 and armament comprising eight 20.3cm (8 in) and eight 10.1cm (4in) guns.

When war broke out *Devonshire* was serving as flagship to Rear-Admiral Cunningham at Malta. She returned home in late 1939 to join the Home Fleet, where she remained until 1942, when she was sent to join the Eastern Fleet in the Indian Ocean. She returned to the Home Fleet a year later, and was part of the escort force when *Queen Mary* carried Winston Churchill across the North Atlantic to meet President Roosevelt.

Devonshire remained with the Home Fleet for the rest of the war, and in 1947 was converted into a training ship. She was scrapped in 1955.

Battle Honours

- Home Fleet, 1939–42
- Eastern Fleet, 1942
- Home Fleet, 1943–45

HMS Glorious

HMS Glowworm

HMS *Glorious* was only the second ship in the history of the Royal Navy to carry that name.

Glorious, together with *Courageous* and *Furious*, was designed for World War I service as a 'large-light cruiser' whose shallow draught would enable her to operate in the Baltic. Originally armed with four 38cm (15 in) and 18 10.1cm (4in) guns, a maximum speed of 31 knots, and a complement of 835, all three ships entered service in 1917 and were converted into aircraft carriers between 1924 and 1930. *Glorious* gained a flight deck, an island bridge and anti-aircraft weapons in the rebuild and lost her main armament. She had the capacity to carry 49 aircraft.

Glorious was serving in the Mediterranean at the outbreak of war, but was soon reassigned to the Home Fleet. As part of the 1940 Norwegian campaign, on the return to Scapa Flow her Captain sought permission to sail directly home. With only two destroyers, she met two German battle-cruisers en route, and was quickly sunk. Only 38 men out of 1200 survived.

Launched in 1935, a destroyer of the 'Gallant' class, *Glowworm* displaced 1382 tonnes (1360 tons) and carried four 12cm (4.7in) guns and twin quintuple 53cm (21in) torpedo tubes. She was built for night torpedo attacks against capital shipping lines; her crew were specialists in night fighting and manoeuvre.

In 1939 *Glowworm* was with the 1st Destroyer Flotilla, whose survivors from Harwich were transferred to Norway. From there, *Glowworm* was to be part of a force which would help seal Narvik in 1940. But a German naval force was on a collision course. *Glowworm,* given leave to search for a man lost overboard, was steaming to rejoin the force when on 8 April, she was met by two enemy destroyers, which, with help from *Admiral Hipper*, scored lethal wounds on her. Although *Glowworm* rammed her adversary, she went down; all but 38 of her men drowned. The commander, Lt Cdr Roope was awarded the posthumous Victoria Cross, the Royal Navy's first of the war.

Battle Honours

- *Mediterranean, 1939*
- *Home Fleet, 1940*
- *Norway, 1940*
- *Sunk in April 1940*

Battle Honours

- *Sunk by* Admiral Hipper, *April 1940*

HMS Grenville

The name derives from Sir Richard Grenville, *Revenge*'s commander who gallantly lost his life in 1591 against 53 Spanish ships. *Revenge*'s motto *Deo Patriae Amicis* (For God, Country and Friends) was transferred to *Grenville* in 1922; the crest is that of the Grenville family.

The third ship was launched in 1935. She led the 1st Destroyer Flotilla in the North Sea at the outbreak of war but in January 1940 struck a mine.

The fourth *Grenville* joined the fleet in May 1943. She displaced 1819 tonnes (1790 tons), had a top speed of 35 knots, and mounted four 12cm (4.7in) guns, an array of air defence weapons, and eight 53.3cm (21in) torpedo tubes. With four other destroyers in October 1943, she put two German destroyers out of action for six months.

The flotilla moved to the Mediterranean where it fought numerous actions in the Adriatic, at Anzio in 1943–44, and in 1945 in the invasion of Okinawa.

HMS Hermes

HMS *Hermes*, the first ship to be built as an aircraft carrier, was completed in 1923. Of only 10,669 tonnes (10,500 tons) she could carry only 15 aircraft, had a complement of 664, and could make 25 knots. A 'graceful little experiment', by 1939 she was relegated to the East Indies where her aircraft were employed in the search for enemy shipping.

After the sinking of the *Courageous* and the *Glorious* in mid-1940, her aircraft were promoted to more active duties against the French *Richelieu* at Dakar. She returned to the East Indies to continue her former tasks but was ordered to join the newly formed fleet at Ceylon when Japan entered the war. En route to Australia she put in at the naval base of Trincomalee to pick up stores; when Japanese aircraft attacked the installation she was ordered to put out to sea for 'safety'. Without aircraft, and with only the destroyer *Vampire* for protection, she was sighted by the enemy, and sunk by 80 Japanese dive-bombers in 15 minutes.

Battle Honours

- *North Sea, 1940*
- *Adriatic, 1943–44*
- *Anzio, January 1944*
- *Okinawa, April 1945*

Battle Honours

- *Mediterranean, 1940*
- *East Indies, 1940*
- *Ceylon, 1941*
- *Sunk by Japanese aircraft, April 1941*

HMS Hood

The battlecruiser HMS *Hood* was launched in 1920 as a class of four, and was to be fast enough to catch a cruiser, yet powerful enough to sink a battleship. Technically the largest ship in the Royal Navy, even so, her lack of deck armour made her vulnerable.

Even later modifications to her side armour did not take into account steady improvements in gunnery. *Hood* served with the Home Fleet until 1935, rejoining it at Scapa Flow when war was declared. In July 1940, after the destruction of the Vichy French fleet, she returned to Scapa Flow, patrolling the Greenland-Iceland Gap through the winter of 1940–41. In May 1941 she was sunk by a salvo from the German battleship *Bismarck*. All but three of her crew of 1415 officers and men perished.

HMS King George V

The first vessel to bear the name was launched in October 1911. A seagoing gunnery training ship in 1923, she was scrapped in 1926.

The second *King George V*, a 35,560 tonne (35,000 ton) battleship with 10 35.5cm (14in) and 16 13.3cm (5.25in) guns, was launched by George VI in 1939 as the first British battleship designed to carry aircraft and with most of her guns in quadruple mounts.

King George V played a pivotal role in locating and sinking the German battleship *Bismarck*, closing with her to inactivate her guns. Her vigorous actions in 1942 against German raiders in the North Atlantic caused the enemy to retain its capital ships in the safety of home or captured bases. As part of a fleet, *King George V* was dispatched to the Far East in 1945 and saw considerable action, particularly off Okinawa, and in the final bombardment of the Japanese home islands.

Battle Honours
● *Mers-el-Kebir, July 1940*
● *Scapa Flow, 1940–41*
● *Sunk by the* Bismarck, *May 1941*

Battle Honours
● *Sinking the* Bismarck, *May 1941*
● *North Atlantic, 1942*
● *Far East, 1945*
● *Okinawa, April 1945*

HMS Nelson

The badge of HMS *Nelson* was adapted from a supporter of the arms of Lord Nelson. The motto reads *Palmam Qui Meruit Ferat* ('Let Him Bear the Palm Who Has Deserved It').

Although built to the constraints of the 1922 Washington Treaty, the *Nelson* of 1927 remained the largest, most heavily armed battleship in the fleet for over 12 years. Her displacement of 34,495 tonnes (33,950 tons) and comparatively small engines gave *Nelson* only 21 knots, yet her armament of nine 41cm (16in) guns, all triple mounted forward, tremendous potency. Prior to 1939 she was a flagship to a series of Commanders-in-Chief, but saw action during World War II with Force H through the Malta convoys, and supporting the landings in North Africa, Sicily, Salerno, and Normandy. After Normandy, she sailed for the Pacific, and as flagship of the East Indies Fleet saw the surrender of the Japanese forces in Malaya.

Battle Honours
● *Home Fleet, 1940*
● *Force H, 1942*
● *D-Day, 6 June 1944*
● *Far East, 1945*

HMS Prince of Wales

A 35,561-tonne (35,000-ton) battleship of the 'King George V' class, *Prince of Wales* was armed with 10 36cm (14in) and 16 13.3cm (5.25in) guns. She saw her first action against the *Bismarck,* when she was so new that her crew had not yet had the opportunity to work up. HMS *Hood* was sunk in the engagement and *Prince of Wales* damaged, being forced to make smoke and disengage.

She served with vigour and distinction in 1941, helping to fight through the Malta convoys, although she was lost later that year when, as part of Force Z, she was dispatched to the Far East. In company with the battlecruiser *Repulse,* with no air cover, and with a protective umbrella of only four destroyers, she was sighted off the coast of Malaya by a strike-force of Japanese land-based aircraft, attacked and sunk.

Battle Honours
● *Home Fleet, 1941*
● *Malta convoys, 1941*
● *Force Z, 1941*
● *Sunk by Japanese aircraft, December 1941*

HMS Renown

The ninth ship to bear this name, and the illustrious motto *Antiquae Famae Custos* ('Guardian of Ancient Renown'), was a battle-cruiser completed in 1916. Sacrificing armour protection in favour of speed, *Renown* and her sister ship *Repulse* were regarded as liabilities by the Grand Fleet. However, due to their speed of 32 knots they were retained.

By 1939 *Renown* was extensively refitted. Her armament of eight 38cm (15in) and 20 11.4cm (4.5in) guns, four eight-barrelled pom-poms, and 64 20mm (0.7in) Oerlikons slowed her down, but she remained the Royal Navy's fastest capital ship. She first saw action during the 1940 Norwegian campaign, and then with Force H at Gibraltar. In November 1940, at the Battle of Spartivento, she engaged the Italian battleship *Vittoria Veneto*, and in 1941 supported the *Ark Royal* in the hunt for the *Bismarck*.

Battle Honours

- *Norway, 1940*
- *Battle of Spartivento, November 1940*
- *Hunt for Bismarck, May 1941*
- *East Indies Fleet, 1944–45*

HMS Rodney

The motto *Non Generant Aquilae Columbas* ('Eagles Do Not Breed Doves') was one of the strangest to grace one of His Majesty's capital ships. Built as a sister ship to the *Nelson*, she displaced 34,495 tonnes (33,950 tons) and was thus marginally lighter than her sister. Her heavy displacement and comparatively small engines made her both slow and prone to breakdown. Yet her armament of nine 41cm (16in) guns, all triple mounted forward, gave her tremendous potency, particularly as they were able to elevate to 40 degrees and fire in the anti-aircraft role.

En route to the United States for a major refit, *Rodney* was ordered to rendezvous with *King George V*, and with her took part in the hunt for the *Bismarck*, crippling the enemy at maximum range.

Battle Honours

- *Hunt for the Bismarck, May 1941*

HMS Sea Lion

HMS *Sea Lion* was one of the original 'S'-class submarines built 1932–37. She displaced 681 tonnes (670 tons) surfaced, 975 tonnes (960 tons) submerged, carried a crew of 38 all ranks and was armed with one 7.6cm (3in) gun and six bow-mounted 53.3cm (21in) torpedo tubes.

The 'S' class boats were ideally suited to patrolling; when war broke out, a massive building programme started. *Sea Lion* operated against German convoys in the North Sea in 1940; whilst patrolling in the Skagerrak, she sighted and chased the German minelayer *Ulm,* and a few days later penetrated the Kattegat, sinking the transport *August Leonhardt.* During the winter of 1941 *Sea Lion* was transferred to Murmansk to assist the Russian naval forces, and in January 1942 she was on watch for the *Scharnhorst* and *Gneisenau* in the French coastal training area. By 1943 *Sea Lion* was no longer fit for front-line duties, but continued to play an active training role.

Battle Honours
- *North Sea, 1940*
- *Murmansk, 1941*
- *French coast, 1942*
- *Training duties, 1943–45*

HMS Sikh

HMS *Sikh* was a member of the large 'Tribal' class of destroyers built prior to World War II. Completed in 1938, she was stationed in the Red Sea when war broke out, remaining there to escort local convoys until December when she returned home to join the 4th Flotilla at Scapa Flow.

She served off Norway in 1940 during the British evacuation, and attacked a German convoy there that year in October. In May 1941, under the command of Admiral Vian, she took part in 4th Flotilla's harrying attack on the *Bismarck* the night before her destruction.

The 4th Flotilla was transferred to Gibraltar as part of Force H in 1941. In December, *Sikh* was sent to reinforce the main fleet at Alexandria. En route, with *Maori, Legion* and the Dutch *Isaac Sweers,* she surprised and sank two Italian cruisers off Cape Bon. In September 1942, attacking German-held positions at Tobruk, *Sikh* and her sister ship *Zulu* were hit and sunk.

Battle Honours
- *Norway, 1940*
- *Force H, 1941*
- *Battle of Sirte, March 1942*
- *Sunk off Tobruk, September 1942*

HMS Southampton

HMS *Southampton* was built in 1936 as the first of an enlarged class of light cruisers displacing 10,160 tonnes (10,000 tons) with a maximum speed of 32 knots, each mounting 12 15.2cm (6in) guns in four triple turrets together with eight 10.1cm (4in) anti-aircraft guns. She was the fifth ship to bear the name *Southampton*, the fourth having fought with distinction at the Battle of Jutland.

Southampton served in the Mediterranean before the war, transferring to the Home Fleet in 1939. In June 1940 she took part in the battle for Norway, transferring to Gibraltar later that year from where she transported R.A.F. personnel to Malta.

She took a regular part in convoy duties, participating in the Battle of Spartivento as part of Force H on 27 November 1940. On 11 January 1941, she was attacked and sunk by a force of ten Stuka dive-bombers to the east of Malta.

HMS Sussex

The badge, which features a golden martlet on a blue field, derived from the arms of the Sussex county. The motto is *Fortiter In Re*. HMS *Sussex*, the fourth, was built as a heavy cruiser in 1929 to Washington Treaty specifications; displacing 9988 tonnes (9830 tons), she was 193.3m (633ft) long, and had a crew of 650 all ranks. Her armament comprised eight 20.3cm (8in) guns, eight 10.1cm (4in) guns, and eight 53.3cm (21in) torpedo tubes.

The 'County' class cruisers' endurance made them ideally suited for distant stations, and large enough to perform the duties of flagship in smaller stations. From the 1st Cruiser Squadron in the Mediterranean in 1935, to the South Atlantic Station where she took part in the hunt for the German pocket battleship *Graf Spee*, thereafter *Sussex* moved to the East Indies, returning home to participate in the Norwegian campaign in May 1940. In 1943 she sailed for the East Indies, remaining with the Eastern Fleet until 1945.

Battle Honours

- *Norway, 1940*
- *Battle of Spartivento, November 1940*
- *Malta, 1940*
- *Sunk near Malta, January 1941*

Battle Honours

- *Hunt for* Graf Spee, *December 1939*
- *Norway, 1940*
- *Home Fleet, 1940–43*
- *Eastern Fleet, 1943–45*

HMS Upholder

In January 1941, HMS *Upholder* joined the 10th Submarine Flotilla based in Malta and was tasked with severing the vital Axis supply line from Italy to North Africa. Her first four patrols were unsuccessful. The fifth raid, however, resulted in the sinking of the *Antonietta Laura*, after which *Upholder's* luck changed and a series of kills followed. On 20 May 1941, in a particularly daring attack, she sunk the troopship *Conte Rosso*. Her Captain, Malcolm Wanklyn, was awarded the Victoria Cross.

In September, *Upholder* conducted what was arguably the most skilful exercise of her career, sinking two North-Africa bound troopships, the *Neptunia* and *Oceania*, within five hours. *Upholder* was the world's most successful submarine; she sunk in total 131,824 tonnes (133,940 tons) of enemy shipping.

Battle Honours

- *Malta, January 1941*
- *Conte Rosso, May 1941*
- *Neptunia and Oceania, September 1941*

HMS Victorious

The first *Victorious* was launched in 1785. The fourth ship of that name was a fleet aircraft carrier completed in 1941.

That year her aircraft, flying at night at extreme range, took part in the hunt for the *Bismarck*, scoring a crucial hit on the battleship, which forced her to slow and head for French waters. En route she was met and sunk by British capital ships.

In 1942, in conjunction with the carrier *Furious*, *Victorious*'s aircraft sank an entire German convoy off the Norwegian coast from where, that same year, she took part in an attack on *Tirpitz*. The presence of her Albacores caused the Germans to return to port, thus preventing a potentially disastrous encounter with the Russian-bound convoy PQ13. *Victorious* was dispatched to the Far East in 1945 and was at the assault on Okinawa. Her aircraft were active to the war's end.

Battle Honours

- *Attack on the* Bismarck, *May 1941*
- *Attack on the* Tirpitz, *March 1942*
- *Far East, 1945*
- *Okinawa, April 1945*

HMS **Warspite**

Credited with the greatest number of battle honours of any ship in the Royal Navy, *Warspite* has as her motto, *Belli dura despicio*: 'I despise the hardships of war'.

The seventh *Warspite*, a battleship of the Queen Elizabeth class, joined the Grand Fleet in 1915, and was extensively rebuilt in the 1930s . During the German occupation of Norway in 1940 she led a force of British destroyers into Ofotfiord, and without loss, sunk eight German destroyers and a U-boat. Soon thereafter she was the flagship of Admiral Sir Andrew Cunningham at Alexandria. In 1940 and 1941 she saw action against Italian battleships, cruisers and destroyers. Extensively damaged during the evacuation of Crete, she became flagship of the East Indies fleet in 1942. She was present at the Italian fleet's surrender in 1943, and at the Normandy beaches in June 1944.

HMS **Wild Swan**

This Modified 'W' class destroyer, the second *Wild Swan*, was laid down in 1918. Displacing 1130 tonnes (1112 tons), with a complement of 134 all ranks, a top speed of 34 knots, and armament of four 11.9cm (4.7in) guns, two 2-pdr pom-poms, and two sets of 53.3cm (21in) torpedo tubes, she was among the finest escort vessels afloat. Thus, she was retained in service with the coming of peace.

Wild Swan returned to active service from the reserve in 1939. She was refitted and joined the 18th Flotilla in the Western Approaches, remaining on convoy duty until 1942, but for a short yet vicious spell providing supporting gunfire at Dunkirk.

On 23 May 1940 *Wild Swan* helped the 20th Guards Brigade to land in Boulogne, destroying the the enemy armour's lead tank. *Wild Swan* returned to previous escort duties but in June 1942 was sunk near Gibraltar by a squadron of 12 Ju 88 bombers.

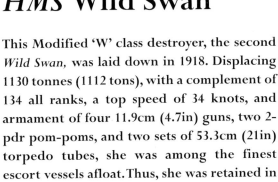

Battle Honours
• *Norway, 1940*
• *Mediterranean, 1940–41*
• *East Indies Fleet, 1942*
• *D-Day, 6 June 1944*

Battle Honours
• *Dinkirk, May 1940*
• *Convoy duties, 1939–42*
• *Western Approaches, 1942*
• *Sunk by German aircraft, Gibraltar, June 1942*

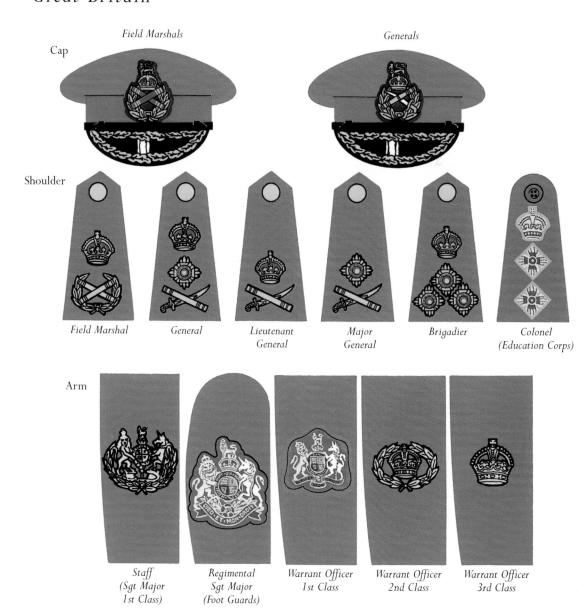

Cap

Field Marshals

Generals

Shoulder

Field Marshal — General — Lieutenant General — Major General — Brigadier — Colonel (Education Corps)

Arm

Staff (Sgt Major 1st Class) — Regimental Sgt Major (Foot Guards) — Warrant Officer 1st Class — Warrant Officer 2nd Class — Warrant Officer 3rd Class

British Army

Rank was identified primarily by badges worn on the shoulder of officers, on the sleeve of warrant officers, and on the upper arm of sergeants and below. Warrant officers and non-commissioned officers wore their insignia either on the right arm or on both, depending upon their regimental tradition.

Head-dress varied for General officers, regimental officers and other ranks. The field marshals' cap badge displayed crossed batons (and other officers of general rank a crossed baton and sword) on a wreath of laurel, surmounted by the Royal Crest, while that of brigadiers displayed the Royal Crest.

Field-marshals and generals wore scarlet gorget patches with gold leaves and acorns embroidered along the centre on the lapels of their service dresses, or a gold gimp on the patches in battledress. Brigadiers and substantive Colonels were identified by red gimps on their patches.

Officers' rank badges were worn on the shoulder strap. As a generalisation subalterns wore stars (commonly known as 'pips'), field officers crowns plus a star for each superior rank, and general officers crossed batons and swords. Field marshals were denoted by crossed batons on a laurel wreath with a crown above. Crowns and stars were made from

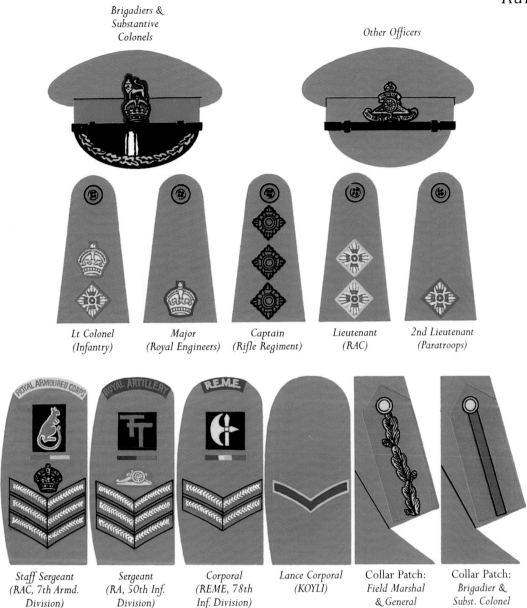

Brigadiers &
Substantive
Colonels

Other Officers

Lt Colonel
(Infantry)

Major
(Royal Engineers)

Captain
(Rifle Regiment)

Lieutenant
(RAC)

2nd Lieutenant
(Paratroops)

Staff Sergeant
(RAC, 7th Armd.
Division)

Sergeant
(RA, 50th Inf.
Division)

Corporal
(REME, 78th
Inf. Division)

Lance Corporal
(KOYLI)

Collar Patch:
Field Marshal
& General

Collar Patch:
Brigadier &
Subst. Colonel

diverse materials such as embroidery, blackened brass, gilt, enamel, and bronze; worsted was normally employed on battledress.

Dependent upon rank, appointment, and regimental tradition, warrant officers wore a diversity of emblems on their sleeves. Most warrant officers class 1 (WO1s) wore a badge depicting the Royal Arms surrounded by a coloured border dependent upon their arm-of-service. Regimental sergeant-majors and superintending clerks in the Foot Guards, however, wore a badge depicting the Royal Arms in full colour embroidered on khaki material. Warrant officers class 2 (WO2s), including company sergeant majors, wore

a plain crown approximately 5.8cm (2in) wide on the sleeve. Squadron corporal-majors of the Life Guards wore a smaller crown, some 3.8cm (1.5in) wide. Squadron quartermaster-corporals and staff corporals of the Household Cavalry wore four chevrons pointing upward, below a crown. Sergeants, and in the case of the Foot Guards' lance-sergeants, wore three stripes on the arm, corporals (lance-corporals in the Foot Guards) wore two stripes, and lance-corporals one. Formations and arms-of-service were depicted by the style of head-dress and by a series of regimental cap badges and insignia which are described in greater detail elsewhere in this book.

95

'Air' Ranks

Group Captain

Cuff

Marshal
of the RAF

Air Chief
Marshal

Air Marshal

Air Vice
Marshal

Air Commodore

Cuff

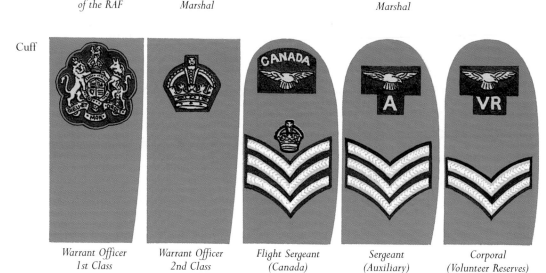

Warrant Officer
1st Class

Warrant Officer
2nd Class

Flight Sergeant
(Canada)

Sergeant
(Auxiliary)

Corporal
(Volunteer Reserves)

Royal Air Force

All ranks wore a grey-blue uniform based on that of the Army, and were issued with a tunic worn open with collar and tie.

Officers wore service dress consisting of a peaked or field service cap with a cloth covered peak, a black mohaired band and a gold-embroidered badge. Their tunic was worn open with a blue shirt, black tie, and long matching trousers. In addition, for protection colder weather, they were issued with a double-breasted greatcoat with matching cloth belt, a mackintosh and a raincoat.

When on service in the Mediterranean officers wore a tropical dress similar to that issued to the Army. Both long and short trousers were worn, the latter with khaki shirts.

For service in Europe, other ranks were issued with a service dress identical to that worn by officers but made of serge. In the Mediterranean or North Africa, however, they wore a formal khaki drill tunic with brass (later black plastic) buttons, a khaki shirt, long or short trousers, and khaki socks. Gradually the blue-grey field service cap, worn with the RAF badge

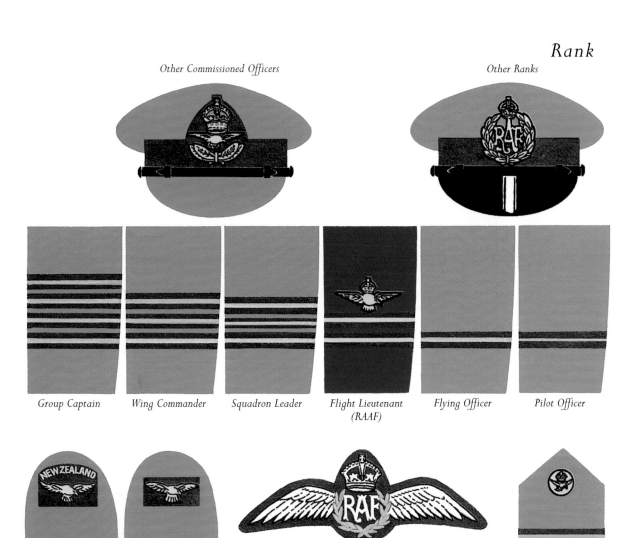

Other Commissioned Officers

Other Ranks

Group Captain

Wing Commander

Squadron Leader

Flight Lieutenant
(RAAF)

Flying Officer

Pilot Officer

Leading Aircraftman
(RNZAF)

Aircraftman

Navigator's Wings

Observer's Wings

Greatcoat
Shoulder Strap:
Marshal of the RAF

on the left side, was replaced by a grey-blue beret, particularly in the RAF Regiment. The RAF regiment served in both the Middle East and Italy where it received khaki battledress. On the khaki-drill uniform the propeller badge of leading aircraftmen was in red.

Badges or rank, and indeed rank titles, were unique to the RAF. Officers wore rank distinction lace on the cuffs of their tunics, on the shoulder straps of their greatcoats, and when in shirt-sleeve order. Officers of air rank were distinguishable by two rows of gold embroidery on their cap peaks, group captains

by one. Warrant officers 1st class wore the Royal Coat of Arms on their sleeves, whereas warrant officers 2nd class wore a crown. NCOs wore chevrons on both sleeves of their tunics and greatcoats. All ranks below warrant officer 1st class wore an eagle on both upper arms.

Unusually the RAF had no special rank badges for wear on flight clothing. There were no arm-of-service badges as such, but air crew wore highly distinctive, and much prized, insignia above their left breast pockets.

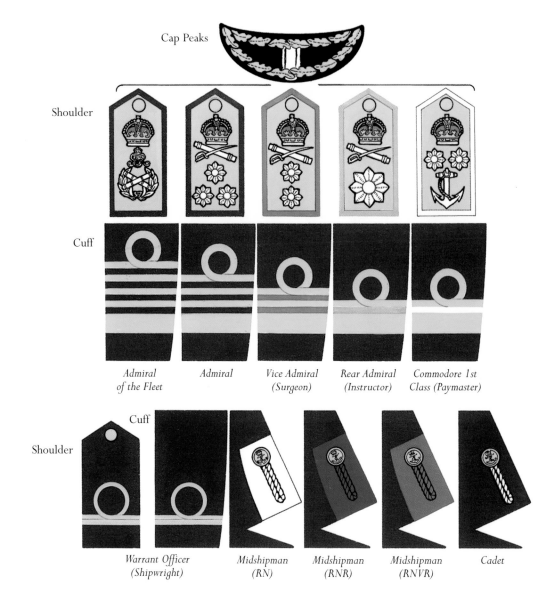

Cap Peaks

Shoulder

Cuff

Admiral of the Fleet   *Admiral*   *Vice Admiral (Surgeon)*   *Rear Admiral (Instructor)*   *Commodore 1st Class (Paymaster)*

Cuff

Shoulder

Warrant Officer (Shipwright)   *Midshipman (RN)*   *Midshipman (RNR)*   *Midshipman (RNVR)*   *Cadet*

British Navy

By the outbreak of war Royal Navy uniform and insignia had been evolving over many years, and was the model for the vast majority of European navies.

The basic uniform for officers consisted of a peaked cap worn with a white cover, a double-breasted reefer jacket, with white shirt and black tie, matching long trousers, and black shoes. The greatcoat was double-breasted and worn with brown leather gloves.

Chief petty officers wore a similar uniform, although they would usually change into a single-breasted working rig when operational. Ratings wore the traditional 'square-rig' supplemented by a single-

breasted greatcoat, and were issued with thick white woollen pullovers and duffle coats for inclement weather. When serving in the Mediterranean or in tropical climates all ranks were issued with a white uniform for everyday wear. Officers, chief petty officers, and petty officers wore a cap with a white cover (or, very rarely, a sun helmet), white open-necked shirts, white shorts and socks and canvas shoes. Ratings either wore a similar uniform with black socks and shoes, or a white shirt with blue dungaree binding around the collar.

Flag officers and senior officers could be identified by the gold embroidery on their cap peaks, while all

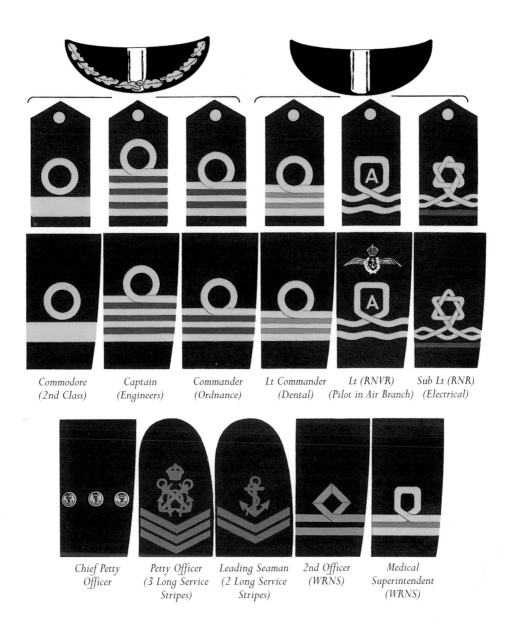

Commodore
(2nd Class)

Captain
(Engineers)

Commander
(Ordnance)

Lt Commander
(Dental)

Lt (RNVR)
(Pilot in Air Branch)

Sub Lt (RNR)
(Electrical)

Chief Petty
Officer

Petty Officer
(3 Long Service
Stripes)

Leading Seaman
(2 Long Service
Stripes)

2nd Officer
(WRNS)

Medical
Superintendent
(WRNS)

officers wore rank distinction lace on the cuffs of their reefer jackets and on their greatcoat shoulder straps. When in shirt sleeve or greatcoat order, officers of the rank of captain or below wore insignia similar to that worn on the sleeve. However, when so dressed commodores and above wore individual rank badges similar in broad design to those worn by senior Army officers.

Officers of the Royal Navy Volunteer Reserve wore 'wavy' rank distinction lace; whereas officers of the Royal Naval Reserve differed in that they wore rank distinction lace in which the 'curl' formed a six-pointed star.

Chief petty officers were distinguished by three buttons on each cuff; petty officers and ratings by rank badges on the upper left sleeve, crossed fouled anchors for a petty officer and a single fouled anchor for a leading seaman. On the outbreak of war the name of his ship on the cap tally of a rating's head-dresses was replaced with either the letters HM Submarine or, in the case of the surface fleet, HMS (His Majesty's Ship). Certain officers, such as doctors and engineers, wore arm-of-service 'lights' between their rank distinction lace. Chief petty officers wore specialist distinguishing badges on the collar, petty officers and ratings on the right arm.

Generals   Brigadier & Colonel   Lt Colonel & Major

Cap

Shoulder

Collar Patch: Generals   General   Lieutenant General   Major General   Collar Patch: Brigadier & Colonel   Brigadier

Cuff

Collar Patch

Warrant Officer (intro. 1943)   Sergeant Major   Q.M. Sergeant (P.T. Instructor)   Colour Sergeant (non-sub badge on right cuff)   Bandmaster 1st Class (equiv. to Col.Sgt.)   Sergeant (Gunnery Instructor)

Royal Marines

The Royal Marines were active in the Far East as commandos, as well as their role as part of the complement of the Royal Navy vessels. Their special qualities as élite soldiers were used to good effect in Burma in the No 3 Commando Brigade. A typical Marine commando detachment would be 100-men strong with a small HQ and three troops of 30 officers and men. Despite their strong traditions with the Royal Navy, the Royal Marines wore uniform

and insignia more identifiable with that of the Army. Most distinctive was their headdress; a dark blue peaked cap with a red band, often worn with a white top. In tropical dress a distinctive feature of the Royal Marine uniform was a fabric belt in the corps' colours.

Officers of general rank wore scarlet gorget patches with gold leaves, and cap badges of cross batons on a wreath of laurel surmounted by the Royal Crest; brigadiers and colonels wore gorget patches of scarlet

Other Officers &
W.O. & RSM

Q.M. Sergeant

Other NCOs

Colonel

Lieutenant Colonel

Major

Captain

Lieutenant

2nd Lieutenant &
Comm.W.O.

Bandmaster 2nd Class
(equivalent to Sgt.)

Corporal
(Military Training
Instructor)

Lance Corporal

Marine
(Signals, G.C. Badge)

Provost Sergeant
or Cook Sergeant

cloth with a red gimp, and cap badges depicting the Royal Crest.

Officers' rank badges were worn on the shoulder strap. As a generalisation subalterns wore stars (commonly known as 'pips'), field officers crowns with a star added for each superior rank, and general officers crossed batons with swords. Thus a second-lieutenant wore one star, to which a second was added on promotion to lieutenant and a third on promotion to captain. A major wore a crown, a lieutenant colonel a crown above a star, a colonel a crown above two stars, and a brigadier a crown above three stars set in triangular formation. Lieutenant colonels and below wore their rank insignia above the letters RM. Other ranks wore badges of rank based on those of the Army with arm-of-service insignia above.

It should be remembered that many Royal Marines saw action in commando engagements in which rank was often not worn and uniform was personalised for comfort.

Bomb Aimer's Badge

Introduced in 1942, it comprised a half-wing badge with a 12-feathered wing, was either flat or padded, and was embroidered on dark blue or black backing cloth. Bomb aimers in Pathfinder squadrons, who were employed in finding and marking targets for the main bomber force, wore an additional distinctive badge depicting an eagle on their left breast pockets.

In the RAF pre-war badges were made of brass, while wartime versions were produced in cloth purely for reasons of economy (there were thousands of wearers). The vast majority of badges were worn by NCOs and airmen, and these badges had a dark blue or black background. For their part, officers wore badges embroidered on a grey-blue background.

Bombing was an art which came to the RAF slowly, and during the early war years the tactic of area bombing was used by bomber crews to try to hit a target. The Germans were way ahead in the use of bombing and training of bomb aimers.

Navigator's Badge

The observer's badge, which was adopted in September 1915, depicted a wing with 14 feathers protruding from an 'O'. This was replaced in 1942 by the Navigators' badge, with 12 feathers protruding from the letter 'N.'

Navigation was a crucial and complex art, even with the increased introduction of advanced direction-finding equipment as the war progressed. As such, it was not at all unusual for the navigator to be the senior officer in a bomber crew.

Most trade and other badges were worn on the sleeve. The RAF eagle was worn on both upper sleeves, below the shoulder seam, and only nationality titles could be worn above the eagle. This badge was adopted in 1918 and was originally red for the khaki uniform of that period. However, its colour was changed to light blue when the grey-blue uniform was introduced. Red eagles as well as other badges were worn on the khaki tropical uniform worn in the Pacific and North African theatres.

Badge	Cloth badge in embroidered and printed pattern, in light blue with a dark blue background for grey-blue uniforms and red on khaki for khaki tropical uniforms.

Badge	Cloth badge in embroidered and printed pattern, in light blue with a dark blue background for grey-blue uniforms and red on khaki for khaki tropical uniforms.

Italy

Many units in the Italian armed forces had a proud history and wore distinctive insignia. The Alpini and Bersaglieri, for example, had coloured cuffs and wore embroidered flames on a black velvet collar. The Bersaglieri, who fought in North Africa, wore a wide-brimmed black hat with a cluster of cockerel feathers.

Medal for Aeronautical Valour

There are two designs; each awarded in gold, silver and bronze. Established in 1927 and awarded for bravery and exceptional deeds of distinction associated with flying.

Badge	*Front: the head of the King with the legend VITTORIO EMANUELE III RE D'ITALIA. Reverse: a flying eagle and crown upon a wreath containing the recipient's details. The circumscription reads MEDAGLIA MILITARE AERONAUTICA.*
Ribbon	*Blue watered silk.*

Badge	*Front: the arms of Savoy held in the talons of a flying eagle with a crown above; the words AL VALORE AERONAUTICA appear below. Reverse: the engraved details of the recipient with fasces appearing on either side.*
Ribbon	*Blue with thick and thin red side stripes.*

Medal for Maritime Valour

Established in 1836 in three grades: gold, silver and bronze. Awarded for bravery in saving life at sea.

The Italian Royal Navy was derived from the Sardinian Navy, which in turn traced its origins back to a single oared galley belonging to the Country of Savoy in the late thirteenth century. Much later the rule of Victor Emmanuel II (1849–78) witnessed a rapid expansion in the size of Italy's navy, as the country became politically unified and a seafaring nation due to its geographical position in the centre of the Mediterranean Sea.

Badge	*In gold, silver or bronze according to the grade. Front: the arms of Savoy surmounted by the crown and centred between a branch of oak and a sheaf of rushes. The circumscription reads AL VALORE DI MARINA. Reverse: engraved details of the recipient within two branches of foliage.*
Ribbon	*Blue with thick and thin white stripes to each edge.*

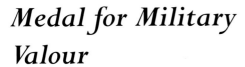

Medal for Military Valour

Established in 1833, awarded to officers and men of the armed forces for gallantry in action against the enemy. The gold medal, highly regarded as the supreme reward, is presented only in exceptional circumstances.

During the years 1943–45, the medal's design changed by order of the new government. Obverse the arms of Savoy became a Roman sword, inscribed ITALIA, and in 1945, a star in a cogwheel surrounded by a wreath above the words REPUBLICA ITALIANA.

Badge	*In gold, silver or bronze according to the grade. Front: the arms of Savoy surmounted by the crown, and centred between two branches of foliage, surrounded by the wording AL VALORE MILITARE (For Military Valour). Reverse: engraved details of the recipient within two branches of laurel.*
Ribbon	*Bright blue watered silk. When the ribbon only is worn the gold and silver medals are denoted by gold or silver five-pointed stars.*

Military Order of Italy

Instituted in 1815 as the Military Order of Savoy, renewed in 1855, and established in its present form in 1947. In five classes (Grand Cross, Grand Officer, Commander, Officer and Knight), it is awarded to the armed forces for exceptional abilities of command and for bravery.

Badge	*A white enamelled Key cross in gold with a garland of green oak and laurel between the arms of a cross. Front: a red medallion with crossed swords and the dates 1855 and 1947 in gold. Reverse: medallion has the monogram RI in gold on white with the words AL MERITO MILITARE (For Military Merit).*
Ribbon	*Dark blue with a crimson centre stripe.*

Italy

War Cross

Established in January 1918 and amended in 1943, the War Cross is awarded for meritorious service over a prolonged period in a combat area where individual acts of bravery have not warranted the award of a higher decoration. Many of these medals were awarded during World War II in recognition of the bravery shown by Italian troops in battle against a superior enemy.

Badge	*A Greek cross in bronze. Front: on the traverse arms the words MERITO DI GUERRA, the lower arm of the cross has an upright Roman sword entwined in a spray of oak, on the upper arm the crowned Royal monogram. The monogram was replaced in 1943 with the letters RI. Reverse: a central five-pointed star set upon diverging rays.*
Ribbon	*Light blue with two white stripes. Subsequent acts of meritorious service are denoted by a small bronze crown worn upon the ribbon.*

7th Bersaglieri

The *Bersaglieri* were traditionally regarded as an élite, and as such were granted permission to wear gold cap badges, a privilege only extended to the rest of the Italian Army in 1933. Officers, warrant officers and non-commissioned officers wore gold wire, hand-embroidered cap badges; corporals and below brass or machine-embroidered badges in black rayon.

The first companies of *Bersaglieri* were raised as light infantry detachments in 1836. A total of 21 regiments were raised during World War I. They wore standard tropical dress in the desert like other units, but were much better equipped. A distinctive feature of their uniform was the plume of cockerel feathers worn in the helmet.

Battle Honours
● *Sidi Barrani, December 1940*
● *Tripolitania, 1941*
● *Sicily, 1943*
● *Italy, 1943*

106

10th Assault Regiment

Crossed Roman swords behind a wreath, with the Roman numeral 'X' within a shaded black velvet centre, the whole beneath a flame. Embroidered in gold and edged in black.

An independent parachute unit, its members were specially trained to undertake specialist behind-the-lines commando-style raids. Traditionally, in the Italian Army the infantry, cavalry and service corps connected with them wore silver badges. With the introduction of the 1933 army regulations, gold was granted to all the army with the exception of generals, who retained their silver badges. There were two sizes of embroidered badges: a large size worn by officers on the peaked cap, embroidered on grey-green, black or brick red felt. A cap badge on grey-green was also worn on the summer cap.

Alpine Infantry

The first 15 companies of *Alpini* were formed in 1872, and by 1909 had expanded to 26 battalions. The 8th *Alpini*, part of the 3rd *Julia* Alpine Division, was deployed on all fronts save for North Africa. It suffered heavy casualties against the Red Army fighting in southern Russia.

Regiments of mountain gunners and companies of pioneers, miners and signalmen were also raised in support of the infantry. The alpine battalions were never numbered, but instead named after the town, mountain, village or valley in the battalion's recruiting area. A small enamel badge, a different one for each battalion, was also worn on the hat near the feather holder.

In total there were six alpine divisions, each made up of two *Alpini* regiments and an artillery regiment. The titles of the divisions were *Taurinense*, *Tridentina*, *Julia*, *Cuneense*, *Pusteria* and *Apli Graie*. Though these units did not serve in North Africa, they were decimated in the fighting in the Balkans and on the Eastern Front.

Battle Honours
• *Tripolitania, 1940*
• *Cyrenaica, 1941*
• *Sicily, 1943*
• *Italy, 1943*

Battle Honours
• *Greece, 1940*
• *Albania, 1940*
• *Russia, 1941–42*
• *Italy, 1943*

Alpine Division

The first 15 companies of Alpini were raised in 1872, and by 1909 had expanded to 26 battalions. They were joined by specialist regiments of Alpine Artillery, and companies of pioneers, miners, and signallers to form independent divisions.

Unusually, the battalions were not numbered, but instead were named after the towns and valleys in which they were formed. They were identified by small enamel badges worn on the hat near the feather holder, and black rayon or worsted cap badges. Divisional arm shields were adopted by the Italian Army in the mid-1930s. Mostly they were of identical design, but had different background colours and divisional titles.

Alpine divisions wore green badges with Roman or Arabic numerals, and the Frontier Guard also wore green with the sector number in the centre.

Colonial Rifles

Crossed rifles beneath crossed horns, the whole within a circle with a cross and beneath a crown. Embroidered in gold with a black, green or red centre.

The Colonial Rifles were originally named the *Cacciatori d'Africa*, and were raised in July 1887 in Eritrea. They adhered to the *Bersaglieri* tradition and suffered heavily in action against the British in North Africa in the 1940 campaign.

The cap badge shown above was worn by officers and NCOs from 1933 until 1943. Cap badges of corps that were divided into regiments had a black velvet centre where the regimental number was applied, or, as here, in the case of unassigned officers, a cross.

Battle Honours
● *France, 1940*
● *Russia, 1943*
● *Sicily, 1943*
● *Italy, 1943*

Battle Honours
● *Somaliland, August 1940*
● *Egypt, September 1940*
● *Sidi Barrani, December 1940*
● *Bardia, January 1941*

Folgore *Brigade*

Italy was among the pioneers of military parachuting, having established a fully trained parachute company as early as 1938. By 1939, this had been expanded into two battalions each of 250 men, both of which were deployed to Libya. A third battalion of 300 officers and men was raised at Castel Benito in 1940, and in 1942 all three battalions, together with their logistic support, were reformed into the **Folgore Airborne Division.**

After Italy's surrender, many members of the Division elected to fight on the side of the allies. The *Folgore* was composed of two parachute regiments, each of four battalions. An artillery regiment of two batteries was divided among the parachute regiments. Each battalion comprised a headquarters unit and three parachute companies and had a strength of 326 men, all armed with automatic weapons.

Infantry Division 61

The 61st *Sirte* Infantry Division wore a red embroidered divisional badge and was one of the nine infantry divisions called *Autotrasportabile tipo Africa Settentrionale*. Divisional arm shields were on a blue background if in enamel, black if on a painted background. Other shields were woven and some embroidered.

Most infantry divisions in the Italian Army were named after their infantry brigade. By 1943 infantry divisions were for the most part the only units left, as th armoured and motorised divisions were all destroyed in North Africa. The 61st Division comprised the 69th and 70th Infantry Regiments and the 43rd Artillery Regiment. Like most Italian units, when pitted against good opponents it suffered heavily, especially in Greece and North Africa, where there was chronic shortages of supplies.

Battle Honours

- *North Africa, 1940*
- *Cyrenaica, 1942*
- *Tunisia, 1943*
- *Italy, 1943*

Battle Honours

- *Greece, October 1940*
- *Albania, February 1941*
- *El Agheila, December 1941*
- *Egypt, October 1942*

Naval Commandos

The Underwater Division of the 10th MAS Flotilla, the *Gamma* Group, was raised at La Spezia with a view to taking the battle to the formidable British by unconventional means. In retaliation for the sinking of several of their capital ships by the Fleet Air Arm, the Italians swore revenge and began a number of daring and highly successful raids against British shipping and coastal installations.

The first, in March 1941, by an Explosive Motor Boat, sank the cruiser *York* off northern Crete. The first human torpedo raid, which followed shortly thereafter, sank three cargo ships in Gibraltar harbour. After a series of abortive raids on Malta, members of the Flotilla attacked the harbour of Alexandria in December 1941, sinking a tanker, and severely damaging the battleships *Valiant* and *Queen Elizabeth*.

The 10th MAS Flotilla was unique when first introduced, and became the blue-print for the highly successful British human torpedo raids which followed.

San Marco *Battalion* Cap Tally

At one stage of the war, units bearing the title *San Marco* Marines fought on both sides. Following World War I, the name, which was chosen in honour of Saint Mark, the patron saint of Venice, was originally given to a naval infantry unit which adopted the city's symbolic Lion of St Mark as its insignia. Although larger than a conventional battalion, the unit bore the title *Battaglione San Marco*, which was worn on the cap tallies on their traditional caps and sun helmets.

During World War II, the *San Marcos* fought against the Allies in North Africa but, following the Armistice, joined the Allies in fighting the Germans. When Mussolini formed the Italian Social Republic in the north, a rival *San Marco* Division was raised to fight against the Allies. Marines were issued with grey-green uniforms of army pattern during World War I. Following their defection to the Allies, the Marines wore British battledress.

Battle Honours
• *Crete, March 1941*
• *Gibraltar, April 1941*
• *Malta, summer 1941*
• *Alexandria, December 1941*

Battle Honours
• *Tripolitania, 1940*
• *Cyrenaica, 1941*
• *Sicily, 1943*
• *Italy, 1943*

Battleship Badge

On 27 May 1944, a set of badges was introduced to reward long and distinguished service in war time. Bronze badges were awarded for 18 months of embarkation, or 1000 hours at sea including taking part in at least one military engagement. Silver badges required 30 months of embarkation, or 3000 hours of navigation and three war engagements. Gold badges were awarded for 48 months of embarkation, or 5000 hours at sea and six war engagements.

By mid-1944 the Italian Navy was a shadow of its former self, having suffered at the hands of the Allies for three years. In addition, personnel had been drained from ships to fight on land, further weakening the force. The British attack against the port of Taranto in November 1940 had delivered a massive blow to the pride of the Italian Navy.

Pilot Underwater Assault Craft

Northern Italy became a fascist republic following the Italian defection to the Allies in 1943. The insignia of the new regime thus did not sport crowns and royal emblems. In the case of the navy, the crown was cut off from badges, should straps and tabs. The Republican Eagle replaced the crown on cap badges and the anchor alone embroidered in the centre of shoulder straps and tabs.

Naval personnel as a whole continued to wear their old uniforms with the new badges, which were in reality the same as before but minus royal emblems. A number of badges were introduced for wearing on the breast or upper sleeve. The underwater assault units were among the most effective formations in the Italian Navy.

Badge	War Navigation (2nd Degree). Silver badge bearing a foul anchor bisected by waves. This badge was also awarded to personnel who served on cruisers. Also awarded in gold and bronze. For wear on grey-green uniforms.

Badge	War Navigation (2nd Degree). Silver badge bearing an arm brandishing a harpoon. Also awarded in gold and bronze. Issued by the government of the Italian Fascist Social Republic in northern Italy.

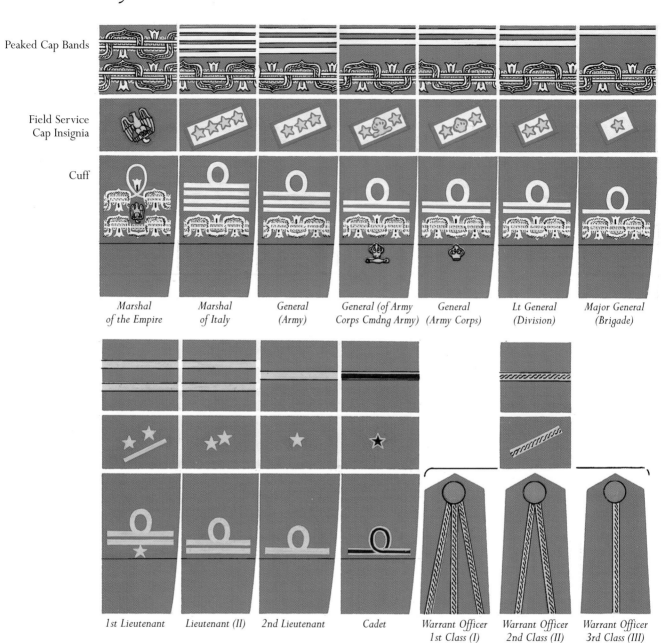

Peaked Cap Bands

Field Service Cap Insignia

Cuff

Marshal of the Empire	Marshal of Italy	General (Army)	General (of Army Corps Cmdng Army)	General (Army Corps)	Lt General (Division)	Major General (Brigade)

1st Lieutenant	Lieutenant (II)	2nd Lieutenant	Cadet	Warrant Officer 1st Class (I)	Warrant Officer 2nd Class (II)	Warrant Officer 3rd Class (III)

Italian Army

In most cases, Italian uniforms were as inadequate as they were diverse. While officers uniforms were made of a light shade of twill, other ranks' were of coarse dark green cloth. Although the issue greatcoat was single-breasted, many officers purchased a superior double-breasted garment.

Head-dress included the side cap (*bustina*), which was intended to replace the peaked cap on active service, the steel helmet, the grey-green felt hat with

feather for the *Alpini*, and the dark crimson fez with light blue tassel for the *Bersaglieri*. In 1942 issue of the highly successful Africa Corps *bustina* was extended to all troops.

Officers wore two basic uniforms: a khaki service dress with a khaki or white peaked bustina; and grey-green field dress.

Rank badges were worn on a combination of the head-dress, shoulder straps, sleeves, cuffs, and on the front of various types of protective clothing. Officers

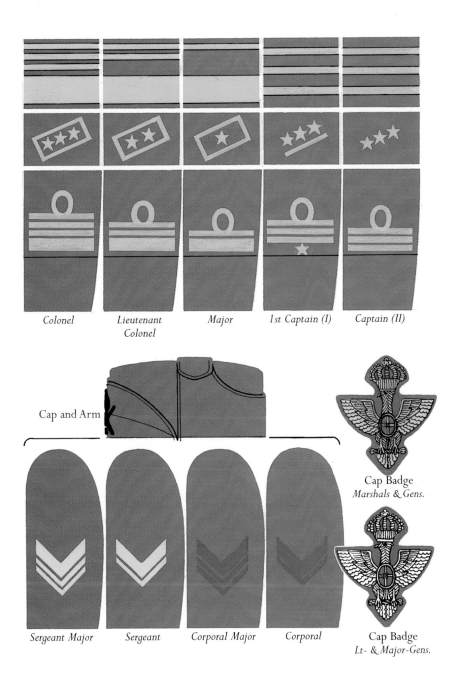

Colonel Lieutenant Major 1st Captain (I) Captain (II)
Colonel

Cap and Arm

Cap Badge
Marshals & Gens.

Sergeant Major Sergeant Corporal Major Corporal Cap Badge
Lt- & Major-Gens.

and warrant officers wore rank distinction on their peaked cap bands, on the left side of their *bustinas*, and in the form of chevrons on the left side of their Alpini hats. General officers' cap badges depicted the crowned eagle of Savoy, embroidered in gold for marshals and generals, and silver for subordinates.

On their temperate weather greatcoats and tunics, officers' rank was worn in the form of gold or silver stripes and stars on the cuffs, whereas they wore their rank on detachable shoulder straps on their tropical jackets and shirts. The ranks of 1st captain and 1st lieutenant were awarded after 12 years in rank or 20 years in commissioned service, and were denoted by a star below the lower band.

Warrant officers were distinguished by one, two or three gold cords worn on the shoulder, and by a single gold cord on the cap band.

Sergeant majors and sergeants wore gold chevrons (replaced by yellow weave as the war progressed) and corporals red chevrons, inverted, on both upper sleeves.

Italy

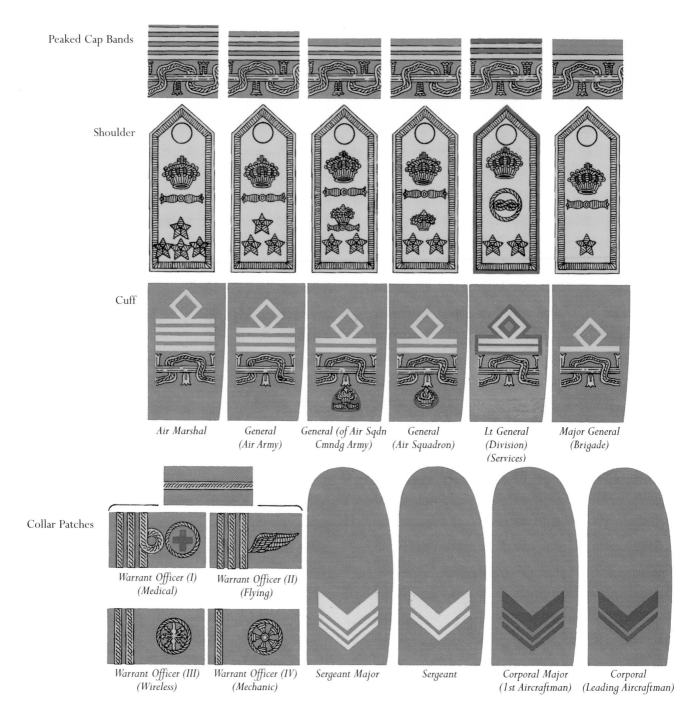

Peaked Cap Bands

Shoulder

Cuff

| *Air Marshal* | *General (Air Army)* | *General (of Air Sqdn Cmndg Army)* | *General (Air Squadron)* | *Lt General (Division) (Services)* | *Major General (Brigade)* |

Collar Patches

Warrant Officer (I) (Medical) — *Warrant Officer (II) (Flying)*

Warrant Officer (III) (Wireless) — *Warrant Officer (IV) (Mechanic)*

Sergeant Major — *Sergeant* — *Corporal Major (1st Aircraftman)* — *Corporal (Leading Aircraftman)*

Italian Air Force

Grey-green in colour, the uniform was basically that of the Army. Officers tended to wear long trousers; however, other ranks were provided with narrower pantaloons and puttees, and jackets had three-pointed pocket flaps instead of straight ones. Officers tended to wear black shoes more often than their Army colleagues. The side cap, with a pleat in the crown, was more ornate than the Army's, but in conjunction with many refinements tended to be abandoned as the war progressed.

Officers wore distinctive rank bands, with an elaborately embroidered gold badge at the centre, on their peaked hats. Rank insignia was also worn on the cuffs,

Colonel | Lt. Colonel (Commissariat) | Major | Captain (Fitter) | Lieutenant | 2nd Lieutenant (Engineers)

Cap Badges:
Gen. of Air Sqdn. to Marshal (left) Other Officers (right)

Generals

Senior Officers

Junior Officers

Pilot's Wings

Observer's Wings

Flying Branch Passants

similar in style to the Army's except that the loop on the upper ring was replaced by a diamond. On tropical jackets and shirts, rank badges were worn on grey-cloth shoulder straps.

Arm-of-service was denoted by a small circular badge worn at the bottom of the cap badge. A similar small circular badge was worn by other ranks on their

shoulder straps, and, embroidered in gold wire on the grey cloth, passants tended to be worn by officers on both shoulders.

Pilots and observers displayed gilt metal wings on the left breast above their medal ribbons, whereas other aircrew displayed a variety of specialist badges on the left breast pocket.

115

Italy

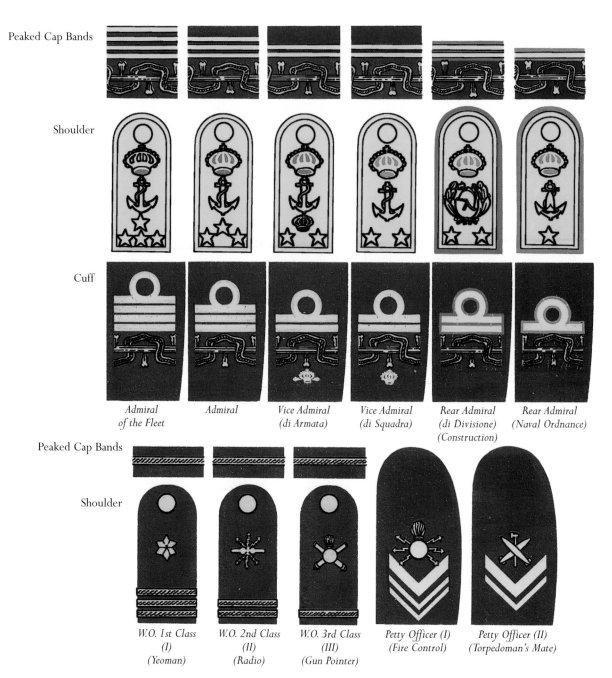

Peaked Cap Bands

Shoulder

Cuff

| Admiral of the Fleet | Admiral | Vice Admiral (di Armata) | Vice Admiral (di Squadra) | Rear Admiral (di Divisione) (Construction) | Rear Admiral (Naval Ordnance) |

Peaked Cap Bands

Shoulder

| W.O. 1st Class (I) (Yeoman) | W.O. 2nd Class (II) (Radio) | W.O. 3rd Class (III) (Gun Pointer) | Petty Officer (I) (Fire Control) | Petty Officer (II) (Torpedoman's Mate) |

Italian Navy

Officers' service dress was of conventional European design with peaked cap, reefer jacket, matching long trousers and black shoes. In summer months, or in tropical waters, officers wore a white cap cover and single-breasted white tunic trimmed with white lace. Warrant officers were similarly attired, save that in summer the white tunic was simpler with open patch pockets and no lace.

Ratings wore a conventional 'square', and were issued with three-quarter length pea-coats in inclement weather, and white cap covers and shirts with blue denim collars and cuffs for summer.

Uniforms became more relaxed and personalised when at sea, particularly aboard small ships, although officers tended to continue to wear their regulation peaked caps, or peaked field caps with a reduced rank badge on the left.

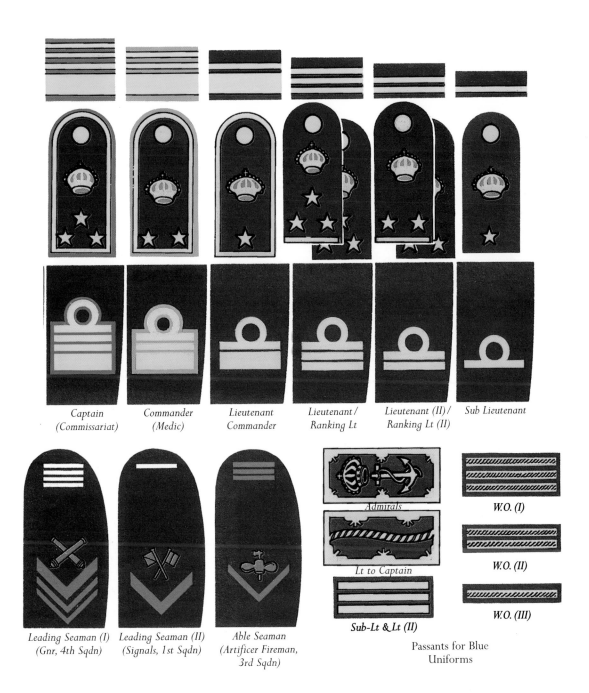

Captain
(Commissariat)

Commander
(Medic)

Lieutenant
Commander

Lieutenant/
Ranking Lt

Lieutenant (II)/
Ranking Lt (II)

Sub Lieutenant

Leading Seaman (I)
(Gnr, 4th Sqdn)

Leading Seaman (II)
(Signals, 1st Sqdn)

Able Seaman
(Artificer Fireman,
3rd Sqdn)

Admirals

Lt to Captain

Sub-Lt & Lt (II)

W.O. (I)

W.O. (II)

W.O. (III)

Passants for Blue
Uniforms

Officers wore rank distinction lace on their peaked caps, as well as bars on the cuffs of their service dress, and on the shoulder straps of their greatcoats, white tunics, and tropical jackets. Only line officers wore a curl at the top of their rank distinction lace on the cuffs.

Others identified their specialisation by a colour in the centre of their cap badge, as 'lights' between the rank distinction bars on their cuffs and shoulder boards, and as piping on their passants and shoulder straps. Commissioned warrant officers wore officers' uniforms with a small metal branch badge above the rank distinction bars on their cuffs.

Petty officers and ratings wore Army-style badges of rank below their branch badges on their arms. Marine officers wore naval rank distinctions on the cap and cuffs, other ranks the distinctive Lion of St Mark on their cuffs.

117

Japan

Japan mobilised over 9,000,000 men to fight in World War II. The typical Japanese serviceman was hardy, devoted to his Emperor and did not lack for courage. Indeed, the Japanese Army alone suffered a staggering 1,526,000 casualties; killed and wounded, testimony to the often suicidal battle tactics used in the Pacific theatre.

Order of the Golden Kite

Established in 1890 as the most important gallantry decoration of Japan, it was awarded to officers of the Army, Navy, and Air Force for acts of bravery in the face of the enemy. Due to its association with aggression the Order was abolished in 1947.

Badge	*Gold and silver overlaid in red enamel, forming an eight-pointed star with lesser points between the angles. Two crossed traditional Japanese war shields in blue with golden swords and flags form a cross Saltire, through the centre of which an upright ribboned lance forms a perch for the golden kite, wings outstretched. The medal is suspended from a large ring. The Breast Star of the Order is identical in design to the badge, but without the suspender ring.*
Ribbon	*Light green with a white stripe towards each edge.*

Order of the Rising Sun

Established in 1875 in eight classes, the first class being in two degrees. This medal is awarded to naval and military officers for gallantry in time of war, and is also awarded to citizens for notable and distinguished service in peacetime.

Field-Marshal Earl Haig, Commander-in-Chief of the British Expeditionary Force in France and Flanders, was awarded the Order of the Rising Sun, Paulownia Flowers, Grand Cordon, for service to the Allies in 1918.

Badge	*An unfaceted red garnet centre with 32 divergent rays, hanging from a suspender crest of green paulownia flowers and leaves. The badge for the senior class (Order of the Rising Sun, Paulownia Flowers, Grand Cordon) has a background of additional rays making four points with blue paulownia flowers appearing between the angles.*
Ribbon	*White with edge stripes of crimson.*

Order of the Sacred Treasure

Established in 1888 in eight classes. Awarded to naval and military officers for gallantry in time of war; it may also be awarded to citizens for notable and distinguished service in peacetime. During World War I it was occasionally awarded to Allied officers for gallantry. The eight classes of the Order have recently been retitled, the most senior being the Order of the Sacred Treasure, Grand Cordon.

Badge	*Twenty white enamelled rays representing sword blades, edged in gold or silver according to class, with a central frame of eight large and eight small rubies surrounding a blue medallion holding an eight-pointed silver star. The Breast Star of the Order comprises 40 white enamelled rays divided into groups of five by a small blue ray; 16 rubies encircle the blue medallion which holds a silver eight-pointed mirror star.*
Ribbon	*Pale blue with a wide gold stripe towards each edge.*

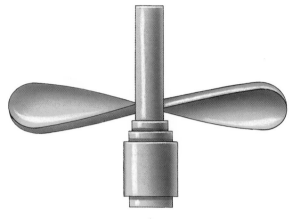

Anti-Aircraft Regiment

Japanese anti-aircraft units were armed with a broad spectrum of weapons, from 7.62mm machine guns to 105mm heavy guns. As the war progressed and equipment became more difficult to acquire, naval guns were occasionally pressed into service.

The 13.2mm Hotchkiss dual-purpose heavy machine gun acquired a good reputation in China, as did the 20mm quick-firing Oerlikon-type gun, but in both instances against limited opposition.

Some anti-aircraft battalions deployed primarily in the defence of the home islands were equipped with 105mm guns. Despite their age (they were of 1925 vintage), their heavy shell and and vertical range of 10,972m (36,000ft) made them highly effective. However, once the Americans were able to use B-29 Superfortress heavy bombers against the Japanese home islands, the anti-aircraft batteries were found wanting. The bombers flew at high altitudes, and were able to stay out of range of the guns while they rained down a hail of destruction on the cities below.

Badge	*Brass badge, worn on the collar patches of the M90 uniform and later, after the rank patch, on the collar of the M98 uniform. Badges were worn on both sides of the collar.*

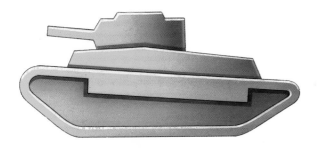

Armour

Japanese interest in armoured fighting can be traced back to the 1920s, when her army purchased its first Vickers armoured car. Most of her early vehicles were adaptations of European models. Although they were used with success against the Chinese in the 1930s, against an enemy that had almost no motorised or armoured forces, they were obsolete by the time World War II broke out. Nevertheless, the Japanese were lulled into an unusual degree of complacency.

In 1939, the Japanese introduced a new tank of its own, the medium Type 97 of Chi-Ha, which went into full production in 1942. By European standards its armour was thin, although its armament was comparable with equivalent British and American tanks. The Japanese had little opportunity to deploy their armour in the jungles of Burma and Southeast Asia, but where they were used they were generally found to be effective in the infantry support role.

Aviation

The Japanese possessed a powerful and efficient navy on the outbreak of war. Her aviators scored a considerable success at Pearl Harbor; crucially, however, the US fleet of carriers escaped to fight another day. In February 1942, raids by US carrier groups on Japanese-held positions caused the Japanese to realise that they would have to neutralise the US carrier fleet. The Battle of the Coral Sea was the first strategic defeat sustained by the Japanese in the war. Although the US lost a carrier, the Japanese lost the light carrier *Shoho* and the carrier *Shokak* was damaged.

In the subsequent Battle of Midway, Japanese naval air power was all but destroyed, leaving the US as the absolute masters of the Pacific. There can be no doubt that the Japanese naval aviators were extraordinarily brave and, at times, resourceful. They were simply worn down by better aircraft and by the sheer strength of the United States carrier force.

Badge	Brass badge, worn on the collar patches of the M90 uniform and later, after the rank patch, on the collar of the M98 uniform. Badges were worn on both sides of the collar.

Badge	A round, cloth badge displaying a red crossed aircraft device on a dark blue background. This badge was for wear on the blue uniform. Blue device on white were worn on the white uniform.

Naval Bomber Crews

The Japanese Navy was one of the most powerful and efficient of the war. During early actions its aviation wing scored a number of striking successes, notably against the Royal Navy when it attacked and sunk the battleship *Prince of Wales* and battlecruiser *Repulse*. However, as the war progressed Japan began to suffer heavily at the hands of the overwhelming might of the United States Navy. Japan never recovered from the loss of four vital carriers, *Akagi*, *Kaga*, *Soryu* and *Hiryu* during the Battle of Midway in June 1942, and was forced onto the defensive thereafter.

The design of several badges was modified during the course of the war. Red or blue Good Conduct chevrons, according to uniform, were worn above the badge; chevrons with a small cherry blossom at the apex identified Excellent Conduct. In the Japanese Imperial Navy all rate and corps badges were round and cloth.

Gunnery

Japanese artillery support was provided by field artillery regiments in infantry divisions or by artillery battalions attached to independent infantry brigades. Most guns were old, light and relatively slow. However, they were extremely robust, as were their crews, and often surprised the Allies by their appearance far forward in extremely hostile terrain. The principle medium guns in service were the Type 14, issued in 1925, and Type 92, which entered service in 1932. Both were 105mm-calibre weapons towed by tractors.

On uniforms which sported colloured collar patched that indicated the wearer's arm of service, personnel wore only regimental numbers. The badges could be worn on both sides of the collar, or the badge on one side and an Arabic number on the other. Roman numerals were worn usually by personnel of independent units.

Badge	An anchor with wings outstretched, the whole in red on a dark blue or white circular background. Petty Officers were identified by a wreath on their badges. Worn on the dark blue or white uniform.

Badge	Brass badge, worn on the collar patches of the M90 uniform and later, after the rank patch, on the collar of the M98 uniform. Badges were worn on both sides of the collar.

Horse Artillery

The Japanese maintained a number of independent cavalry brigades right up to the end of the war, although they played only a minimal role in the war, rarely operating outside of Manchuria. Each brigade comprised two regiments and supporting arms. The regiments themselves consisted of four sabre companies of 186 men and a machine-gun company of 167, all ranks divided into four medium machine-gun and one anti-tank platoons.

Each independent cavalry brigade was supported by a horse artillery regiment equipped with eight 75mm mountain or field guns, a light tank unit of 12 light tanks, an anti-tank company, and four anti-aircraft machine guns. Horse artillery personnel wore yellow badges of rank and an arm-of-service badge depicting crossed cannon barrels superimposed over a quartered, square background.

Mountain Artillery

Japanese divisional mountain regiments were organised into three battalions each equipped with 12 75mm guns, developments of an early Krupp design with a range of 10,972m (36,000ft).

Independent mountain artillery regiments differed from their divisional counterparts in having two battalions instead of three. They were approximately 1500 officers and men strong, although one regiment operating in the Southwest Pacific was half-strength, and were equipped with 24 guns. Each battalion had three companies and battalion transport.

Chevrons were also worn to denoted arm of service, and went on to replace badges and numerals. Yellow chevrons denoted artillery, though because they were made from locally available cloth the varying colours caused a considerable amount of confusion. They were usually worn above the right breast pocket of the service uniform.

Badge	Brass badge, worn on the collar patches of the M90 uniform and later, after the rank patch, on the collar of the M98 uniform. Badges were worn on both sides of the collar.

Badge	Brass badge, worn on the collar patches of the M90 uniform and later, after the rank patch, on the collar of the M98 uniform. Badges were worn on both sides of the collar.

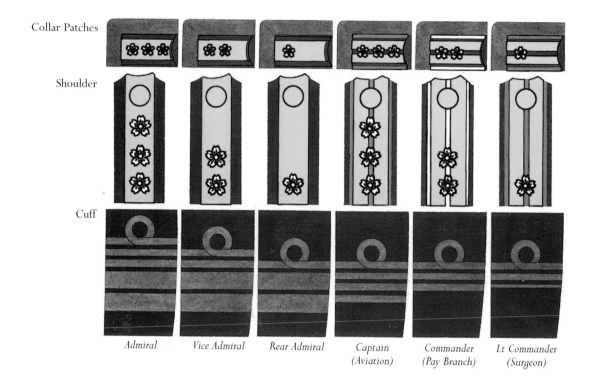

Collar Patches

Shoulder

Cuff

| Admiral | Vice Admiral | Rear Admiral | Captain (Aviation) | Commander (Pay Branch) | Lt Commander (Surgeon) |

Arm

| C.P.O. (Line) | P.O. 1st Class (I) (Aviation) | P.O. 2nd Class (II) (Medical) | Leading Seaman (I) (Justice) | Leading Seaman (II) (Construction) | Able Seaman (Pay) |

Japanese Navy

Officers wore a peaked cap with an embroidered cap badge and undress tunic, with a stand collar trimmed with black lace.

Chief petty officers were issued with a peaked cap with a special badge, a single-breasted tunic in navy blue or white with a single row of five gold buttons, matching long trousers, and black shoes. In winter their double-breasted watch-coat had twin rows of six gold buttons and a fur collar. In summer they were

issued with a white cap cover and white lightweight uniform. Ratings wore the traditional 'square-rig', matching trousers, shoes or sandals, and as headdress, the conventional round hat with a silk tally bearing Japanese characters. An identical white uniform was worn in summer.

An Army-style field cap, worn with a yellow or light-blue anchor badge at the front was issued to all ranks. Personnel serving ashore wore an olive-drab

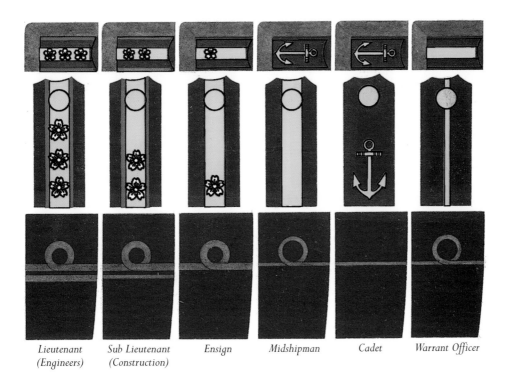

Lieutenant (Engineers) Sub Lieutenant (Construction) Ensign Midshipman Cadet Warrant Officer

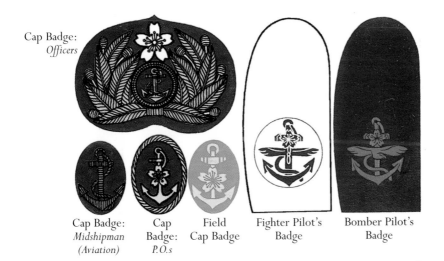

Cap Badge: *Officers*

Cap Badge: *Midshipman (Aviation)* Cap Badge: *P.O.s* Field Cap Badge Fighter Pilot's Badge Bomber Pilot's Badge

cotton drill, officers with brown leather equipment and short leather boots.

Officers' badges of rank were worn on the collar and occasionally on the tunic lapels, and on the shoulder straps of the white tunic and greatcoat. Ratings wore rank badges on their sleeves, initially in red on their blue, and light blue on their white uniforms, but later in yellow on blue backing on all uniforms. Initially, officers wore two and ratings one stripe on their

hats. However, as the war progressed ratings had the stripe removed, lieutenants wore one stripe and captains two. From January 1944 officers began to wear from one to three narrow lace rings above one, two, or three cherry blossoms on the cuffs of their tunics.

Specialisations were denoted by red emblems which were worn on a circular blue badge on the right sleeve. After 1944, the colour of the cherry blossoms on the cuff indicated the branch of service.

Marksman Badge

Fortunately for Allied troops the average Japanese infantryman was not a good shot, nor was his Arisaka rifle a good weapon for sustained or accurate shooting. Nonetheless, it was adequate and the Japanese infantry developed an effective method of firing from a squatting position, which most British and American soldiers found uncomfortable.

Most accounts of actions in Southeast Asia and the Pacific refer to the effectiveness of Japanese snipers in trees. Although the Japanese tended to use trees more for observation purposes than for sniping, they were extremely dangerous and difficult to locate when they did. Not only were their snipers experts at camouflage, but many tied themselves into position to enable them to carry on firing even when wounded.

Snipers were issued with the Meiji 38 6.5mm Sniper Rifle, fitted with a telescopic sight and folding monopod. It had few exceptional properties and was of little practical use at ranges in excess of 600m (1969ft).

Badge	As well as the badge shown above, a metal marksman badge was issued. This was made of enamel and displayed two crossed rifles over a cherry blossom. It was worn on the breast as an award.

Naval Aviation Badge

As has been mentioned, Japanese possessed a powerful and efficient navy on the outbreak of war. One of the reasons for the high rate of success of Japanese naval aviators at the beginning of the war was their high standard of training. Training was so intense that fewer than 100 naval aviators graduated from flying school each year. This was fine when Japan was not at war, but as soon as hostilities began pilot attrition rate increased faster than replacements could be trained.

In the great naval battles of Midway, Leyte Gulf and the Philippine Sea Japan's naval aviation force was all but destroyed. There can be no doubt that the Japanese naval aviators were extraordinarily brave and resourceful, but they worn down by better aircraft and by the sheer strength of the United States' economic power. The loss of her carriers and naval air arm dealt a fatal blow to the expansionist aims of the Japanese Empire, and paved the way for the eventual American victory in the Pacific.

Badge	The Army aviation badge was worn on both sides of the collar. The naval pilot's wings shown above was worn above the right-breast pocket. It depicted a single wing and the cherry blossom.

126

USSR

No other Allied nation made a larger or more sustained contribution to the defeat of the Axis alliance than the Soviet Union. Millions of men and women were mobilised to fight on the Eastern Front in what the Russians called the Great Patriotic War. Russian awards were hard won, especially the Order of Glory, awarded for extreme bravery.

Gold Star 'Hero of the Soviet Union'

Established in August 1939 in the form of the Gold Star Medal as the supreme mark of distinction within the Soviet Union. It was awarded for heroic deeds both military and civilian, and for outstanding achievement in scientific or technical development. The recipient was automatically awarded the Order of Lenin and bestowed with the title 'Hero of the Soviet Union', itself first instituted in 1934.

Second and subsequent awards were recognised with an additional Gold Star medal and a further Order of Lenin. A second award also carried the honour of having a bust of the recipient placed in his home town. During the Great Patriotic War (1941–1945) the second award was bestowed 109 times.

Badge	*A solid pure gold five-pointed star with a small top ring attached for the suspender. Reverse: the raised inscription HERO OF THE USSR is engraved below the recipient's award registration number.*
Ribbon	*Red.*

Order of Glory

Established in November 1943 in three classes. Awarded to junior officers and men and women of the Red Army and Air Force for extreme bravery, it was considered by the armed forces as the most coveted of all awards.

Initially only the 3rd Class Order was awarded. Recipients who performed further acts of bravery were promoted to the 2nd Class and thereafter to the 1st Class, the subsequent award being worn next to the original, until all three Orders were worn together. A total of 980,000 awards of the Order of Glory 3rd Class were made, over 46,000 awards of the Order 2nd Class, and 2582 Order of Glory 1st Class.

Badge	*A five-pointed star, with a central medallion depicting above the Kremlin Spassky Tower a red star, around it laurel sprays, and below it, GLORY on a red banner. Reverse: the letters CCCP and the recipient's award registration number engraved on the top arm of the star.*
Ribbon	*Orange with three equal black stripes, thinly edged in orange.*

Order of Lenin

Established in April 1930 as the highest decoration of the Soviet Union. Military and civilian personnel, including foreigners, were eligible, as were cities and public or commercial organisations rendering conspicuous service.

The City of Leningrad received the Order in 1945 in recognition of its citizens' heroism during the 900-day siege. A total of 36,000 Orders of Lenin were awarded to military personnel and partisans during the Great Patriotic War (1941–1945), and a further 5000 to civilians. Three British and Commonwealth officers and one N.C.O., all of whom flew Hurricanes as part of 151 Wing, received the Order.

Badge	*A circular badge bearing the portrait of Lenin in platinum surrounded by a gold wreath of rye, overlaid in red enamel a banner with the name LENIN inscribed in gold. The hammer and sickle with Soviet star appear in red. Reverse: the recipient's award registration number and a detailed mint mark.*
Ribbon	*Red with two thin gold stripes towards each edge.*

Order of the Patriotic War

Established in May 1942 in two classes. Awarded to members of the armed forces, partisans or security forces showing great courage during battle, either by destroying enemy equipment, or completing several successful attacks on enemy positions. Members of the Red Air Force who destroyed two enemy aircraft in combat were automatically eligible for the award. Non-combatants were eligible for the award of the Order of the Patriotic War, Second Class.

Badge	*A gold hammer and sickle on a red medallion encircled by PATRIOTIC WAR on a white border; all set on a red star with crossed rifle and sword in silver. The background rays are gold for 1st Class and silver for 2nd Class. Reverse, the recipient's registration number. The 1st Class is of a three-piece and 2nd Class of a one-piece construction.*
Ribbon	*First Class: claret with central stripe of light red. Second Class: claret with edge stripes in light red.*

Order of the Red Banner

Originated in September 1918 and redesigned in August 1924. Awarded to military units, members of the armed forces, and civilians of the Soviet Union in recognition of conspicuous bravery contributing to the success of Soviet arms in time of war, or to outstanding achievement in time of peace.

Leningrad was awarded the Order in 1919 for the defence of the city during the Civil War. During the Great Patriotic War 580,000 awards were made.

Badge	*A silver oval design of golden oak leaves, with a white enamelled background with a silver ploughshare, a bayonet and hammer overlaid by a red star with hammer and sickle. A red banner with WORKERS OF ALL NATIONS UNITE, its staff crossing a torch staff. A riband with the letters CCCP forms the base. Reverse: the recipient's award number.*
Ribbon	*Equal stripes of red, white, and red with thin white edges.*

Order of Suvorov

The Order takes its name from Count Alexander Suvorov, promoted Field Marshal by Catherine II for military success against the Turks.

Established in three classes in July 1942, and awarded to senior commanders for outstanding success in leadership and logistics resulting in the defeat of numerically superior enemy forces. From 1941 to 1945, 390 First Class, 2800 Second and 4000 Third were awarded.

Badge	*First Class: a platinum rayed star, a superimposed red star at the top. The central medallion, overlaid with the gold bust, encircled with the legend above a wreath. Second Class: a gold star, smaller than the 1st Class, with a medallion of silver, and red enamel legend. Third Class: a Star and central medallion in silver, the legend in red enamel.*
Ribbon	*First Class: green with wide central stripes of orange. Second Class: green with orange stripe to each edge. Third Class: green with three orange stripes, one to each edge and one central.*

Order of Ushakov

The Order takes its name from Feodor Ushakov, the Black Sea fleet commander who enjoyed considerable success against the Turks.

Established in March 1944 for senior naval officers for victory against superior forces. First Class awarded to senior ranks; Second Class awarded to lower. In all, 47 First and 200 Second Class Orders were awarded.

Badge	*First Class: a platinum star and superimposed silver anchor encircle the blue medallion showing the gold bust and legend of ADMIRAL USHAKOV. Below, gold laurel and oak sprays around the hammer and sickle. Reverse, the recipient's registration number. Second Class: a gold star on a silver anchor. The medallion has a silver bust and legend over blue. Below, hammer and sickle. Reverse: plain but for the recipient's registration number.*
Ribbon	*First Class: white with three light blue stripes, one to each edge and one wide central stripe. Second Class: white with two wide light blue stripes inset from the edge.*

3rd Tank Brigade

During the early stages of the war on the Eastern Front, the Red Army's vehicles were almost totally devoid of markings. However, soon vehicles began to have geometric shapes painted on their turrets, with numbers carried within the markings. By 1943, most of the squares, rectangles and circles had disappeared, leaving only the diamond shape. This was an obvious choice, as the diamond was the Red Army map symbol for a tank.

As shown above, the marking was usually applied to the turret in 400mm (1575in) white or yellow paint. The original pattern had the brigade number on the bottom and the battalion number on top. In other examples, though, the brigade number was not coded and would be at the top rather than the bottom. When the lettering system was used, the battalion number usually appeared at the top of the diamond. The different systems used to mark tanks was probably designed to confuse the Germans.

Battle Honours

- *White Russia, 1942*
- *Battle of Kursk, July 1943*
- *Ukraine, 1944*
- *Poland, 1944*

36th Guards Tank Brigade

85th Heavy Tank Regiment

One of the more unusual marking systems used in the Red Army was that used by the 4th Guards Mechanised Corps, of which the 36th Guards Tank Brigade was a part. This system consisted of animal symbols for each of its brigades: a bear, donkey, rhino and running dog. These markings were usually painted in white, though yellow was also used on occasion.

Up to 1941 the mechanised corps of the Red Army do not appear to have used any divisional insignia. Some independent armoured fighting vehicle regiments were also given animal insignia, especially heavy tank and self-propelled gun regiments. Birds were another favourite animal that featured on the vehicles of such units. At the other end of the scale, some units used very rudimentary symbols, such as the three white bars of the 11th Guards Tank Corps.

The 85th Heavy Tank Regiment was one of the heavy tank regiments to receive the fearsome IS-2 tank in early 1944. Each regiment had four companies of five tanks each, two recovery tanks, three armoured personnel carriers, one BA-64 armoured car and 48 assorted trucks. The IS-2 soon proved itself an excellent fighting machine, able to take on the German Panthers and Tigers, and so the High Command increased production to allow the allotment of one heavy regiment to each tank corps.

The device shown above was painted in white on the green hulls of the tanks. However, by the end of the war the marking had changed to incorporate a solid red star behind a solid white animal. The 85th Heavy Tank Regiment was part of the 4th Guards Tank Army which fought in Berlin in 1945.

Battle Honours

- *Eastern Russia, 1941*
- *Central Russia, 1943*
- *Poland, 1944*
- *Germany, 1945*

Battle Honours

- *White Russia, 1944*
- *Poland, 1944*
- *East Prussia, 1945*
- *Berlin, April 1945*

109th Tank Brigade

This device was painted on the sides of T-34 Model 1943s of the 16th Tank Corps. Soviet tanks during the war were finished only in olive green. Tanks were sent into combat during the 1939-40 Russo-Finnish War in green, even though the terrain was covered in snow. The result of seeing its tanks knocked out because they stood out so much against the background led the Red Army to issue Type B paint, a water-soluble whitewash.

There was little interest in pattern-painted camouflage. One type of marking which did become popular was air identity symbols. The square was used as a tactical symbol towards the end of the war. This contained the same arrangement of numbered information as the diamond, but was usually divided into three or four segments with up to four sets of numbers. The system was most common among self-propelled units, though it was also used on tanks, armoured cars and other military vehicles.

Naval Infantry

The Soviet Naval Infantry could trace its roots back to Peter the Great. During the Great Patriotic war it reached a peak of 350,000 personnel, but was hampered by the inactivity of the fleet and was rarely used for its true purpose. However, Soviet naval special forces played a crucial part in the war. In three years of fighting, they spearheaded many of the 110 tactical and four operational beach landings undertaken by the conventional Naval Infantry. More fundamentally, they were the **first naval forces to pioneer agent penetration and deep reconnaissance behind the enemy lines.**

In particular, the 181st Special Reconnaissance Detachment, formed from volunteers drawn from within the Murmansk area, operated often hundreds of kilometres from their home base in Poliarnyi, undertaking aggressive search and destroy missions, target acquisition, coast watching, prisoner snatching and field interrogation.

Battle Honours

- *White Russia, 1941*
- *Moscow, 1941*
- *Batle of Kursk, July 1943*
- *Poland, 1944*

Battle Honours

- *White Sea, 1941*
- *The Baltic, 1941–43*
- *Black Sea, 1942*
- *Pacific Ocean, 1945*

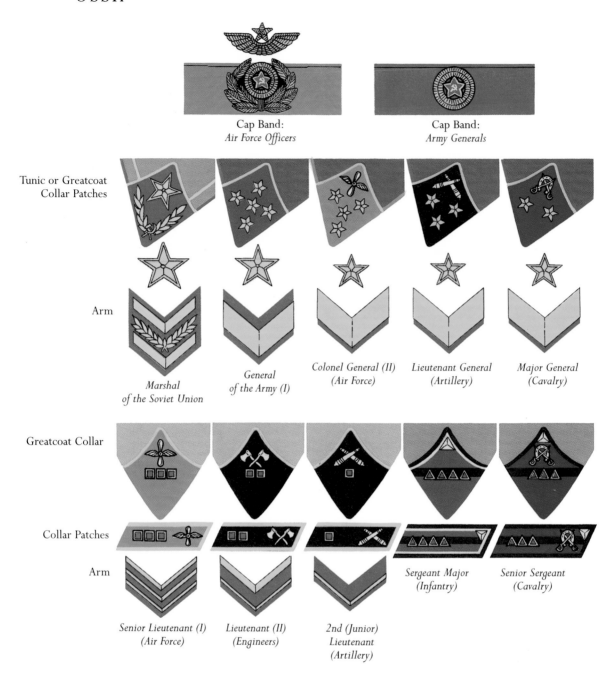

Cap Band:
Air Force Officers

Cap Band:
Army Generals

Tunic or Greatcoat
Collar Patches

Arm

*Marshal
of the Soviet Union*

*General
of the Army (I)*

*Colonel General (II)
(Air Force)*

*Lieutenant General
(Artillery)*

*Major General
(Cavalry)*

Greatcoat Collar

Collar Patches

Arm

*Sergeant Major
(Infantry)*

*Senior Sergeant
(Cavalry)*

*Senior Lieutenant (I)
(Air Force)*

*Lieutenant (II)
(Engineers)*

*2nd (Junior)
Lieutenant
(Artillery)*

Russian Army & Air Force 1941–1943

The theories of Marxism were allowed to interfere with military doctrine in the early stages of the war. Although by 1941 the inevitability of rank had been accepted, outward signs of privilege in the form of superior uniform and rank insignia were still unpopular.

The ranks of lieutenant, captain, major and colonel were reintroduced in 1935, as was a new officers' service dress uniform. The basic uniform for other ranks comprised a peaked cap (*fourashka*) or side cap (*pilotka*), a khaki shirt (*rubaha*) worn outside the matching breeches or trousers, boots, and in winter a double-breasted greatcoat. The trousers had no pockets, nor were the soldiers issued with socks. Officers wore a single-breasted tunic, a shirt with piping and good quality cloth greatcoat with piping and brass buttons.

Cap Band:
Army Officers (Artillery)

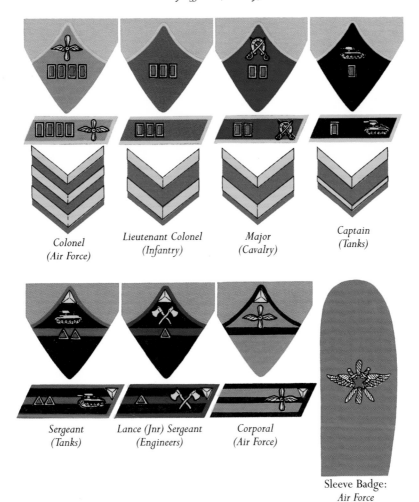

Colonel
(Air Force)

Lieutenant Colonel
(Infantry)

Major
(Cavalry)

Captain
(Tanks)

Sergeant
(Tanks)

Lance (Jnr) Sergeant
(Engineers)

Corporal
(Air Force)

Sleeve Badge:
Air Force

Tank crew were issued with a steel-grey dress and undress uniform, but continued to wear khaki in the field. Air Force personnel, as members of the Red Army, wore a dark blue dress and undress uniform, but retained the standard khaki in the field.

A brass and red enamel cap badge depicting a red star was worn by all ranks until 1940, when the rank of general was reintroduced and a new badge instigated for those general officers fortunate enough to have survived the earlier purges. Despite their obvious practicality, badges of rank on shoulder boards were regarded as élitist. A new system of rank designation was therefore developed, worn on the arm and tunic or greatcoat collar. These were comprised of a series of red enamel geometrical shaped triangles for non-commissioned officers, squares for company, oblongs for field and lozenges for general officers.

Chevrons worn on the cuff were introduced for officers in 1935, five-pointed guilt metal stars for generals in 1940. Arm-of-service was denoted by colour on the cap badge and collar, and by symbols worn as an integral part of the collar rank badge.

135

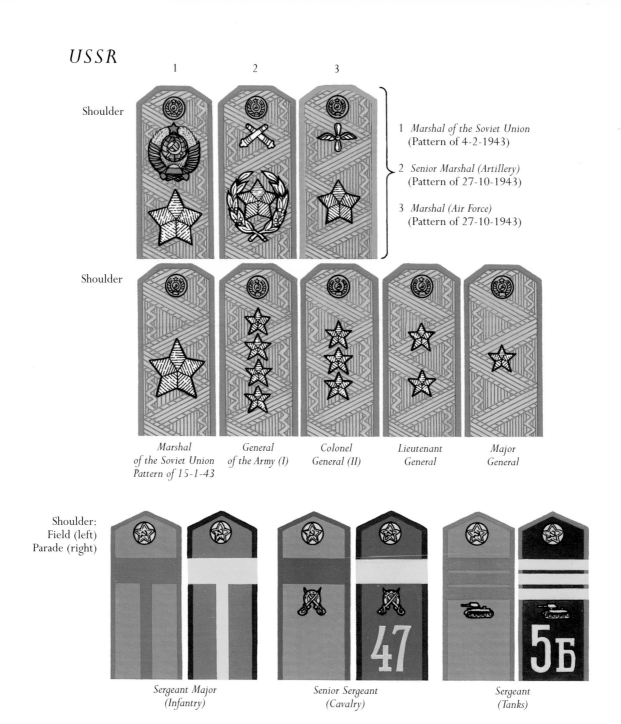

Shoulder

1 *Marshal of the Soviet Union*
   (Pattern of 4-2-1943)

2 *Senior Marshal (Artillery)*
   (Pattern of 27-10-1943)

3 *Marshal (Air Force)*
   (Pattern of 27-10-1943)

Shoulder

Marshal
of the Soviet Union
Pattern of 15-1-43

General
of the Army (I)

Colonel
General (II)

Lieutenant
General

Major
General

Shoulder:
Field (left)
Parade (right)

Sergeant Major
(Infantry)

Senior Sergeant
(Cavalry)

Sergeant
(Tanks)

Russian Army & Air Force 1943–45

On 6 January 1943, after fierce lobbying from his senior officers, Stalin re-introduced the old Tsarist shoulder boards. Both rank titles and rank badges were fully restored although not identical to those worn in the Tsarist army since Stalin reintroduced the rank of major, abolished in 1881. Marshals of the Soviet Union and generals retained, with some minor alterations, the uniforms adopted in 1940. Other officers wore a khaki parade uniform consisting of a peaked cap and single-breasted tunic with five brass buttons.

Red stars continued to appear on the head-dress of all below general officer rank; worn plain on the peaked cap and fur hat, and on a star-shaped arm-of-service coloured cloth backing on the field cap. Mar-

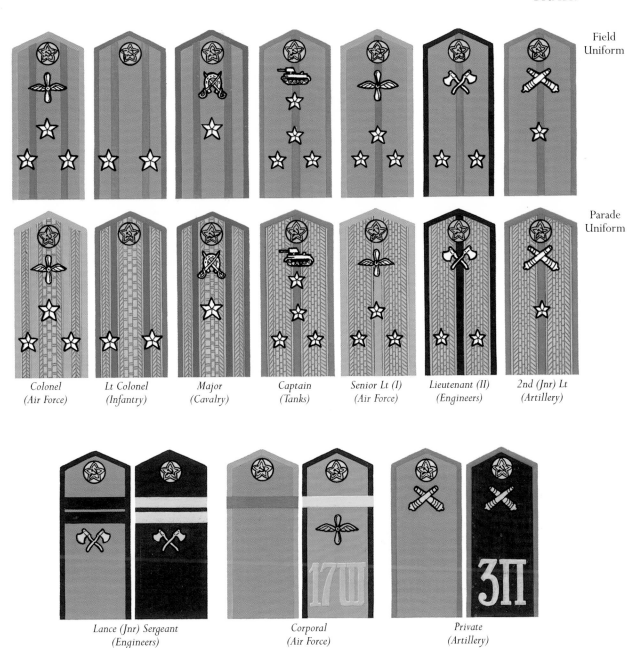

Colonel
(Air Force)

Lt Colonel
(Infantry)

Major
(Cavalry)

Captain
(Tanks)

Senior Lt (I)
(Air Force)

Lieutenant (II)
(Engineers)

2nd (Jnr) Lt
(Artillery)

Field
Uniform

Parade
Uniform

Lance (Jnr) Sergeant
(Engineers)

Corporal
(Air Force)

Private
(Artillery)

shals wore red cap bands and arm-of-service piping, and had gold oak leaves embroidered on their cap badges, collars and cuffs.

Officers' shoulder boards were of gold background, plain in the field and woven in the parade uniform, and comprised a single- and twin vertical bars in the case of subalterns and field officers respectively, superimposed by one, two, or three five-point-ed stars. General officers wore from one to four silver five-pointed stars; marshals a single, enlarged star. Non-commissioned officers wore a series of stripes on their shoulder boards.

Arms of service were depicted by small metal emblems worn in conjunction with the rank badges, and divisional subordinations by colour patches worn on the lapels and other ranks' shoulder boards.

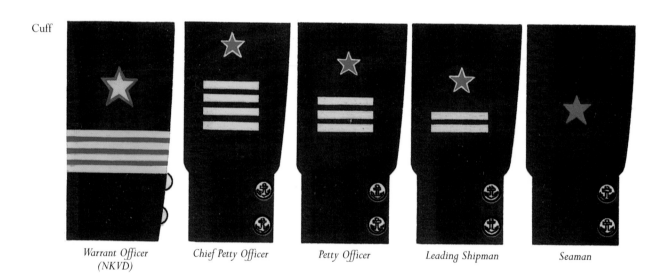

Cuff

Admiral of the Fleet	Admiral	Vice Admiral	Rear Admiral	Captain (I) (Legal Branch)

Cuff

Warrant Officer (NKVD)	Chief Petty Officer	Petty Officer	Leading Shipman	Seaman

Russian Navy 1941–43

Ratings' uniforms were largely conventional, although unusually the 'square-rig' was also worn by petty officers, but with a peaked cap for those with more than five years' service. A dark blue jumper was provided to be worn over bell-bottomed trousers. The cap had a long ribbon or 'tally' on which appeared the name of the ship or fleet in gilt cyrillic letters.

Warrant officers (*mishman*) and chief petty officers (*starshina*) wore officers' uniform with a special cap badge; the officers a peaked cap, black reefer jacket, matching trousers, white shirt, black tie, and black shoes. Their black greatcoat was double-breasted with twin rows of six guilt metal buttons.

During the summer, or in hot climates, all ranks wore a white uniform, including a white top on the head-dress.

Captain (II)
(Coastal Defence)

Captain (III)
(Administration)

Lt-Commander
(Naval Aviation)

Lieutenant
(Political Officer)

Lieutenant (II)
(Technical)

Arm

Cadet
(Parade Uniform)

Cadet
(2 yrs experience)

Cadet
(3 yrs experience)

Boatswain

Telegraphist
(plus 1 Service Stripe)

Badges of rank, which were reintroduced in 1925, was worn on the cuffs by all ranks. Officers wore gold lace rings on their standard black uniforms in the form of light blue rings on white, while all other ranks wore yellow or red on all items of dress.

Arm-of-service was defined by the colour of the rank lace and by the backing 'lights'.

Ratings' red specialist badges were worn on the upper left sleeve, and commissioned naval aviators were identified by sky blue 'lights'. They wore the same embroidered badges on the sleeve as their comrades in the army.

Political officers were identified by a large red star with gold surround above the rank lace.

The Naval Frontier Forces, which formed part of the NKVD, wore naval uniform with green lights and a green backing to the star which was worn on the cuffs.

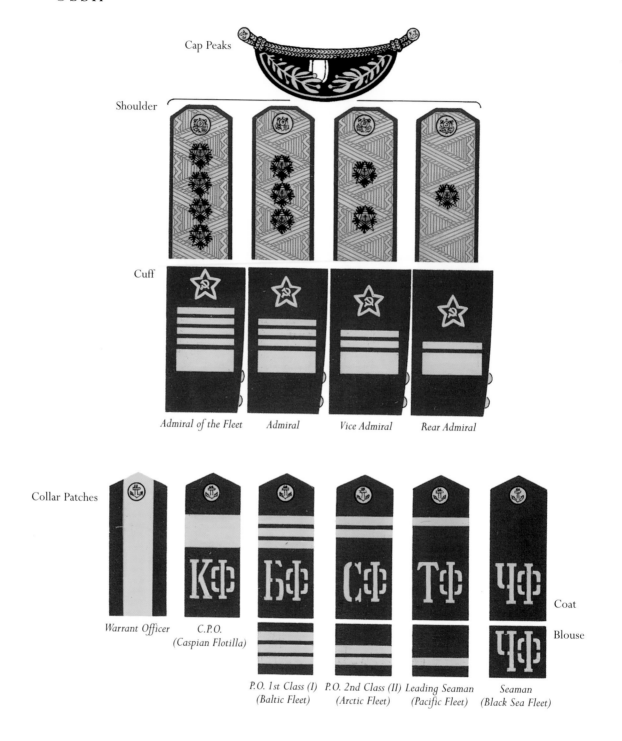

Cap Peaks

Shoulder

Cuff

Admiral of the Fleet *Admiral* *Vice Admiral* *Rear Admiral*

Collar Patches

Warrant Officer *C.P.O.*
(Caspian Flotilla)

Coat

Blouse

P.O. 1st Class (I) *P.O. 2nd Class (II)* *Leading Seaman* *Seaman*
(Baltic Fleet) (Arctic Fleet) (Pacific Fleet) (Black Sea Fleet)

Russian Navy 1943–45

Soviet naval uniform and insignia changed radically in 1943. It was in this year that shoulder boards were reintroduced, and only executive officers continued to wear badges of rank on the cuffs. Officers were issued with double-breasted jackets with twin rows of four buttons, matching trousers and black shoes; flag officers and captains could be identified by the gold embroidery on their peaked caps.

It was from 1943 on that only line or executive officers and line engineering officers retained their

140

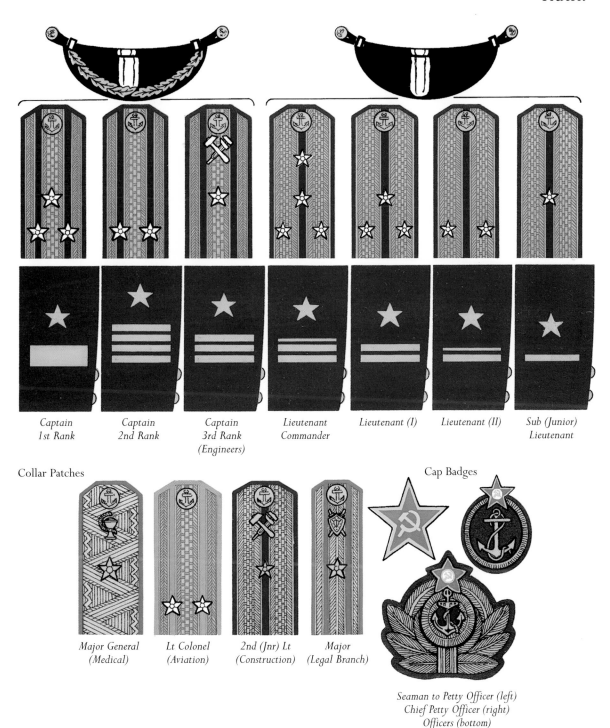

Captain 1st Rank	Captain 2nd Rank	Captain 3rd Rank (Engineers)	Lieutenant Commander	Lieutenant (I)	Lieutenant (II)	Sub (Junior) Lieutenant

Collar Patches

Major General (Medical)	Lt Colonel (Aviation)	2nd (Jnr) Lt (Construction)	Major (Legal Branch)

Cap Badges

Seaman to Petty Officer (left)
Chief Petty Officer (right)
Officers (bottom)

rank distinction lace on the cuffs. The traditional ratings' black hat was retained, with the addition of a black and orange guard tally awarded to ships for distinguished service and worn by the entire crew. Blue jumpers were worn over a blue-and-white striped vest, and carried the rank badges on shoulder patches.

Army-style rank badges were worn on the shoulder, although the ranks themselves remained traditionally naval, as did the officers' rank bars worn on the cuffs. A single five-pointed gold star was worn above the rank bars by all officers, solid for captains and below, and hollow with a central 'hammer and sickle' logo for admirals.

From warrant officer and below, other ranks advertised their home fleet or flotilla in cyrillic below their rank on their shoulder boards.

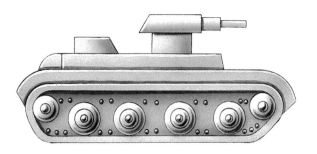

Armoured Troops

In the Red Army, metal collar patches were worn by all ranks on the collar patches. One of their uses was to identify the branch of service of the wearer, as often the colours of the collar patch and piping were inadequate for this purpose (this particularly applied to officers, who all wore gold piping on their collar patches).

In 1922 around 40 collar badges were introduced, though some were discontinued and others brought into use in the years after. All ranks wore brass badges on the collar, the exception being vets, whose badges were made of white metal. The armoured troops went through a major reorganisation in the 1930s, with the final 'armoured' badge being instituted in 1936. Armoured artillery and other service branches wore their own badges on the black collar patches of the armoured troops. The armoured formations of the Red Army were its cutting edge in battle, despite the artillery being termed the 'God of War'.

Commissariat

The red star with hammer and sickle was introduced into the Red Army in 1922. As well as appearing on collar badges, the red star was worn on its own on the peaked cap and fur hat, while on the field cap it was worn on a star-shaped coloured cloth backing.

It is a curious fact that though the red star was the traditional insignia of the Soviet Union, it was rarely used on vehicles. It was sometimes applied unofficially by tank crews, which increased dramatically in the last year of the war. Far more common were patriotic slogans, which appeared on thousands of tanks during the course of the war. At first these were inspired by political officers and were rather bland, but as the war went on they were more spontaneous and sentimental, directed towards the fascist invaders.

The commissariat played a crucial part in the war against Nazi Germany, providing food and other essentials for the fighting troops — a major logistical exercise.

Badge	The tank badge was instituted in 1936 for the tank units of the armoured troops. Those of the officers were of silver when worn on gold shoulder boards, or gold when worn on silver boards.

Badge	A brass badge depicting the hammer and sickle symbol of the Soviet Union, with a red star above. Worn on the collar. Adopted in 1942 by a special regulation dated 30 March of that year.

France

The defeat of France in the summer of 1940 was a severe blow to French martial pride. Nevertheless, elements of her armed forces continued the fight from foreign shores. The French Foreign Legion in particular made a heroic contribution to the Allied cause, fighting in North Africa, Italy and northwest Europe.

Croix De Guerre

Established in September 1939, but for the date stamp it was identical to the World War I medal of 1915. Awarded to all ranks of the armed forces and to French citizens individually mentioned in despatches. In exceptional circumstances it was conferred on units and towns.

Vichy France introduced a Croix de Guerre in 1941, and General Henri Giraud, High Commissioner of French North West Africa, introduced an unofficial medal of 1943. By order of the French National Committee of Liberation in January 1944, only the Croix de Guerre, 1939 was recognised.

Badge	*A bronze straight-armed cross pattee with crossed swords in the arms of the cross. Front: the medallion carries the female head of the Republic. Reverse: medallion is date-stamped 1939.*
Ribbon	*Green with five equally spaced red stripes and edges of red. Emblems were worn on the ribbon in the form of metallic palm or stars, the metal used dependent on the recipient's rank.*

Escaped Prisoner

Instituted in 1926 to reward prisoners who had escaped during World War I and made retoactive to incorporate the Franco-Prussian War. Extended in 1944 to encompass escapes during World War II.

Badge	*A bronze medal, its the motif and outline artificially patinated. Front: the bust of a right-facing female, standing proud from the medal's flat field, an oak branch wreath tucked into a bun at the back of her head. The words REPUBLIQUE FRANCAIS border the head from front to rear. Reverse: a flat field edged by a wreath of oak leaves, comprising 14 bunches, made up of three leaves to a bunch. In the centre the words MEDAILLE DES EVADES, one word on each line.*
Ribbon	*A green band with a central orange stripe, with an orange side stripe.*

Free French Forces

French Resistance

Introduced on 4 April 1946, and awarded to those who volunteered for service in the Free French Forces prior to 1 August 1943, or who had served in the territories administered by the French National Committee before 3 June 1943.

Established by General de Gaulle on 9 February 1943 as a reward for members of the active Resistance against German occupation of France.

Badge	A silver-coloured Cross of Lorraine with a 1mm (0.04in) recessed line running around the edge. Front: the word FRANCE on the upper arm of the cross, the word LIBRE on the lower arm. Reverse: the dates 18 JUIN 1940–8 MAI 1945. The entire inscription is patinated to give an impression of aging.
Ribbon	A 38mm (1.5in) royal blue band, with red diagonal stripes measuring 2mm (0.08) in width, spaced 7mm (0.28) apart, running from top right to bottom left. When the ribbon was worn on the undress tunic, a miniature emblem of the cross was worn on it.

Badge	A bronze medal artificially patinated to a dark brown colour, 37mm (1.46in) in diameter with a raised edge approximately 2mm (0.08in) in width. Front: the Cross Of Lorraine raised to the height of the outer edge, with the Roman figures XVIII.VI.MCMXL (the date of the German occupation) printed below the lower cross. Reverse: the inscription PATRIA NON IMMEMOR (The Fatherland is Not Forgetful) in large sloping capitals on a threefold scroll.
Ribbon	Black with 4mm (0.18in) red edges and four 1mm (0.04in) red stripes, two inset from the edge and two central. A rosette was occasionally attached to the ribbon.

Liberated France

Instituted in 1947 as a reward to French or Allied persons who had contributed a considerable effort towards the liberation of France, yet were not awarded the Legion of Honour, Medal of Gratitude, Order of Liberation, Medaille Militaire or Medal of the French Resistance. The receipt of any of these medals for other military actions did not preclude its award.

Badge	*A bronze medal. Front: a map of France with a raised 1944. Edged by a chain broken by an eight-pointed star with a central pellet in the relative position of Great Britain; a second seven-pointed star in the position of North Africa. The stars emanate particles like a shell burst. Reverse, a Phrygian Cap of Liberty on a fasces. The initials R.F. on either side, with the words LA FRANCE – A SES LIBERATEURS above and below in a curve.*
Ribbon	*A double rainbow merging.*

1st Algerian Spahis

The 1st Algerian Spahis were among the finest of France's colonial troops. Jealous of their fine uniforms and traditions, the Regiment re-introduced 'oriental' full dress, almost identical to that worn in 1914, for its other ranks in 1927. Its officers wore a black tunic without epaulettes, and with rank distinctions in elongated Austrian knots. Officers wore conventional kepis, other ranks light khaki chichi covers.

Although poorly armed the Spahis gave a good account of themselves in action during the early stages of the war. There were two branches of the French Army: the Colonial branch and the Metropolitan branch. Colonial officers wore the khaki uniform of their Metropolitan counterparts, and a summer version of the same which was made of light khaki material. Note the integration of the crescent motif into the Spahis' insignia – a common feature of French North African units.

Battle Honours

- *North Africa, 1939*
- *France, 1940*

1st Regiment Etranger de Cavalrie

The 1er REC was formed in 1921 in Tunisia and recruited from three sources: the 2nd French Foreign Legion Regiment of Infantry, French Army cavalry regiments, and from Russian emigrés fleeing from the Soviets. Posted to Syria to control a Druze insurrection, in 1925 it fought a series of vicious engagements first at Messi, en route to Damascus, and later at Rachaya, west of the Djebel Mountains.

Until 1938, 1er REC took part in the pacification of Morocco and Algeria, fighting bands of rebels and conducting security patrols along the Saharan highways. Between 1939 and the French Armistice of 1940, with the 2nd French Foreign Legion Regiment, it fought on French soil as part of the 97th Divisional Reconnaissance Group. In 1943, its survivors fought in Tunisia, helped liberate southern France in 1944, and led French armoured units into Germany in 1945.

Battle Honours
● *France, 1940*
● *Tunisia, 1943*
● *France, 1944*
● *Germany, 1945*

1st Zouaves

The French colonies provided a powerful addition to the infantry, with no less than 14 regiments of Zouaves on active service on 10 May 1940. Recruited from Frenchman resident in North Africa or metropolitan France, the Zouaves were well equipped, albeit with often aged hardware. Officers were distinguished by their dark blue kepi bands and garance kepi tops, gold braid and plain buttons. Soldiers were issued with a light khaki cotton jacket in North Africa and the Levant, with detachable collar.

The *chechia* was officially worn without a badge, although it was not unusual for Zouaves to wear a small crescent inscribed with their regimental number. When in walking-out dress, members of the 1st Algerian Zouaves could be distinguished by their yellow and green *fourragere* (lanyard) attached to the second chest button.

Battle Honours
● *France, 1940*
● *North Africa, 1941–43*
● *Southeast Asia, 1945*

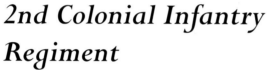

2nd Colonial Infantry Regiment

The insignia of the 2nd Colonial Infantry, in the form of a metal or enamelled badge worn by all ranks pinned on or above a breast pocket of the tunic, depicted a sailing ship on a plaque supported by an anchor above the figure '2' in gold. Officers wore red anchors, regimental numbers and piping, native soldiers yellow anchors and numbers, but without any piping.

Colonial troops were based almost exclusively in Africa, with the basic task of maintaining loyalty in the French protectorates, particularly after the Armistice and installation of the Vichy Government. In general they proved loyal Vichy troops.

Battle Honours
● *North Africa, 1940–43* ● *Southeast Asia, 1945*

12th Cuirassier Regiment

The French cavalry was reorganised during the inter-war years and largely mechanised or re-rolled. Although many Cuirassier regiments adopted helmets and cuirasses within their motifs, the 12th Cuirassiers were unusual in introducing a seahorse emblem.

The Regiment did, in fact, utilise three versions of its badge: that depicted at the outbreak of war; an entirely different badge in 1941; and a third, larger, badge basically similar to the original but with a thicker outer border. Like many French regiments, the 12th Cuirassiers had a proud history, but in France in 1940 were swept up in the collapse of the French war machine in the face of the German Army.

Battle Honours
● *France, 1940*

13th DBLE

The 13th Foreign Legion (Mountain) Half-Brigade (the 13th DBLE) was fighting in Norway in June 1940 when France was forced to surrender to Nazi Germany. The force was eventually repatriated to Britain, where its members were given the opportunity of joining General de Gaulle. Most chose to join the Free French forces and were sent to Syria, where it was understood that the Vichy forces were about to change sides. When this rumour proved false, the 13th DBLE found itself in action against the Vichy 6th Foreign Infantry Regiment, which it overcame in July 1941.

The 13th DBLE was posted to Egypt in December 1941, and six months later fought its most heroic action at Bir Hakeim, where for 14 days it held a fortified position against Rommel's troops before receiving orders to break out on the night of 10–11 June.

15th Infantry Regiment

Both officers and men of the infantry units wore a metal regimental badge, often enamelled, on or above the breast pocket. Badges, which were of personal design and often indicated the area of origin of the unit, were introduced in 1916 and became widespread in the 1920s. Their use proliferated shortly before the outbreak of World War II, due to the expansion of the Army on mobilisation.

The badge of the 15th Infantry Regiment depicted a brown bear on a mountain background with the number 15 in the foreground. The badge was made of enamelled metal and was worn pinned above the left breast pocket. The origin of this, and other, French unit badges goes back to 1916, when members of the 3rd Air Force started to wear a stork, their squadron emblem, on their uniforms. Soon other squadrons adopted insignia and the trend grew.

Battle Honours
- *Norway, 1940*
- *Syria, July 1941*
- *Bir Hakeim, May–June 1942*
- *France, 1944*

Battle Honours
- *France, 1940*
- *Northern France, 1944*
- *Low Countries, 1944*
- *Germany, 1945*

75th Alpine Fortress Regiment

Regiments d'Infanterie de Fortresse were usually comprised of two or three machine-gun battalions, each with two or three machine-gun companies and a mixed infantry/heavy weapons company. All ranks wore berets, which, in the case of Alpine units, were blue with a grade representing a flaming grenade. Officer's badges were embroidered in gold and worn horizontally on the beret, while other ranks wore a special round badge made of metal.

The Alpine battalions fought well when attacked by the Germans in the south, and were particularly spiritedly when combating the Italians. Mussolini declared war on Britain and France on 10 June 1940, in the hope of an easy victory. However, French troops fought Italian units to a standstill, and then threw them back to their start positions. There followed a France-Italian armistice on 24 June.

Chasseurs Alpin

The *Chasseurs Alpin* were among the élite of the French infantry. Six battalions under the command of General Bethouart formed the corps of the High Mountain Brigade which was dispatched to Norway in 1940. Although well equipped, the Brigade deployed so quickly that many of its members left their skis behind, completely neutralising their specialist potential. Elements of the Brigade returned to France in time to frustrate Italian expansionist ambitions when Mussolini declared war on France shortly before her surrender.

Chasseurs Alpin were easily distinguished by their dark blue alpine berets. Other clothing included gaiters and skis, which were standard issue for French mountain troops. Sheepskin jackets were also issued for protection against the cold and wet conditions encountered in mountain regions, which was usually rolled on top of the rucksack when not in use. The horn insignia was made of brass and was worn to the right on the beret. In combat the traditional French helmet, which had a stamped badge on the front. Standard *Chasseurs Alpin* armament was the bolt-action 7.5mm MAS 36 carbine.

Battle Honours
● *Grenoble, 20 June 1940*
● *Provence, 22 June 1940*
● *Monaco, 24 June 1940*

Battle Honours
● *Trondheim, April 1940*
● *Narvik, June 1940*
● *Provence, June 1940*
● *Toulon, June 1940*

Colonial Troops

In 1939, France had a massive empire extending throughout Africa, South America, the Middle East and Southeast Asia. On the outbreak of war most regular troops were recalled to France, leaving the defence of the area in the hands of colonial troops, supported by elements of the Foreign Legion. The 59 regiments of colonial troops, about one-third recruited from Frenchmen, the others from Senegalese, Malagasies and Indo-Chinese, were organised along traditional French metropolitan lines and were thus well equipped.

After 1940, most remained loyal to the Vichy Government, and resisted the Allies when steps were taken to reclaim territories for the exiled Government, but afterwards many sided with the Free French.

Fortress Units

Pre-war France laid great store by her fortress defences, specifically the Maginot Line, and as such regarded those who manned them as élite troops. Maginot Line units were distinguished by three aspects of uniform: a small dark khaki beret bearing the motto *On ne passe pas* (made famous at the Battle of Verdun in 1916), a dark khaki wool sash, and a shoulder title, worn on the left arm only, bearing the name of the unit's fortress zone.

The potential of the Fortress Units to defend the Maginot Line was never tested. The Germans simply outflanked the line to the north and forced its surrender as part of the general armistice. At the beginning of the war in the West in May 1940 there were 13 garrison divisions in the Maginot Line defences. When hostilities began these units were effectively neutralised, as they had to sit and wait for an attack that never came. Meanwhile, German units streamed past them into the Low Countries and northern France.

Battle Honours
- *Lebanon, June 1941*
- *Syria, July 1941*
- *North Africa, 1943*
- *Indo-Chine, 1945*

Battle Honours
- *Maginot Line, 1940*

France

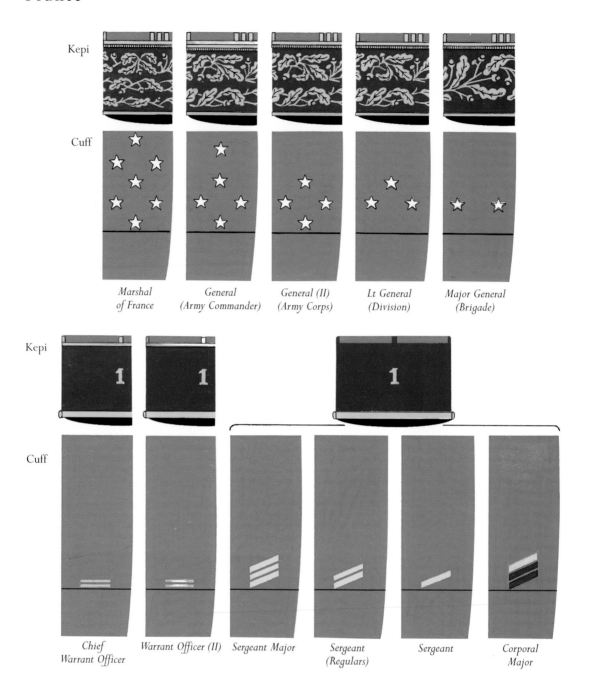

Kepi

Cuff

Marshal of France	*General (Army Commander)*	*General (II) (Army Corps)*	*Lt General (Division)*	*Major General (Brigade)*

Kepi

Cuff

Chief Warrant Officer	*Warrant Officer (II)*	*Sergeant Major*	*Sergeant (Regulars)*	*Sergeant*	*Corporal Major*

French Army

Khaki uniforms, previously only worn by African and colonial troops, became standard for all ranks in 1935. Modifications were introduced steadily thereafter, but had not reached all units by the outbreak of war. Thus, although officers were by then being issued with open pattern jackets, many continued to wear the older closed tunic, with its arm-of-service colour and corps number on the collar patches, and metal regimental badge on the right breast pocket.

Although khaki side caps and berets were issued, the basic head-dress for officers remained the distinctive kepi. Their rank was denoted by insignia on the sleeves of the tunic, greatcoat and forage cap, and by complex embroidery and braid patterns on the kepi,

152

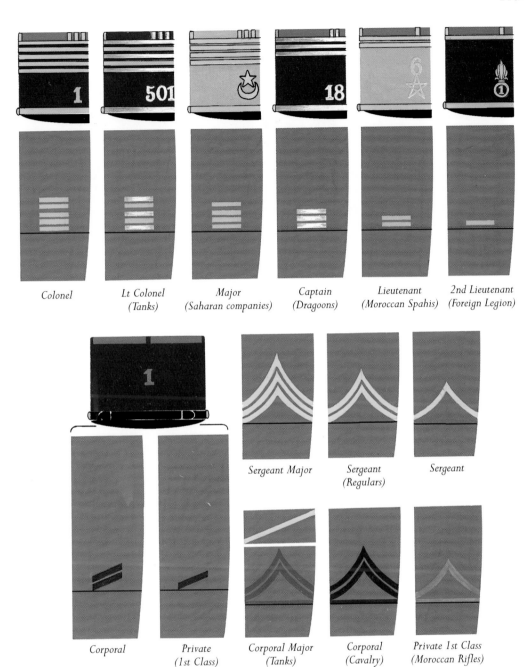

Colonel   Lt Colonel (Tanks)   Major (Saharan companies)   Captain (Dragoons)   Lieutenant (Moroccan Spahis)   2nd Lieutenant (Foreign Legion)

Sergeant Major   Sergeant (Regulars)   Sergeant

Corporal   Private (1st Class)   Corporal Major (Tanks)   Corporal (Cavalry)   Private 1st Class (Moroccan Rifles)

in the form of gold oak leaves for generals and gold and silver lace for field officers and subalterns. However, on active service, generals often wore plain khaki kepis with metal stars on the front according to rank.

When wearing greatcoats or other over-garments, rank was denoted by a series of stripes on tabs affixed to a coat button.

Warrant officers and non-commissioned officers wore chevrons or stripes on the cuff, while corporals and above sported gold or silver chin-straps on their kepis. Officers below general rank wore their regimental number or badge on the front of their kepis; other ranks identified their units by the colour of their chevrons and collar patches. Colonial and African troops wore standard uniform and badges of rank.

France

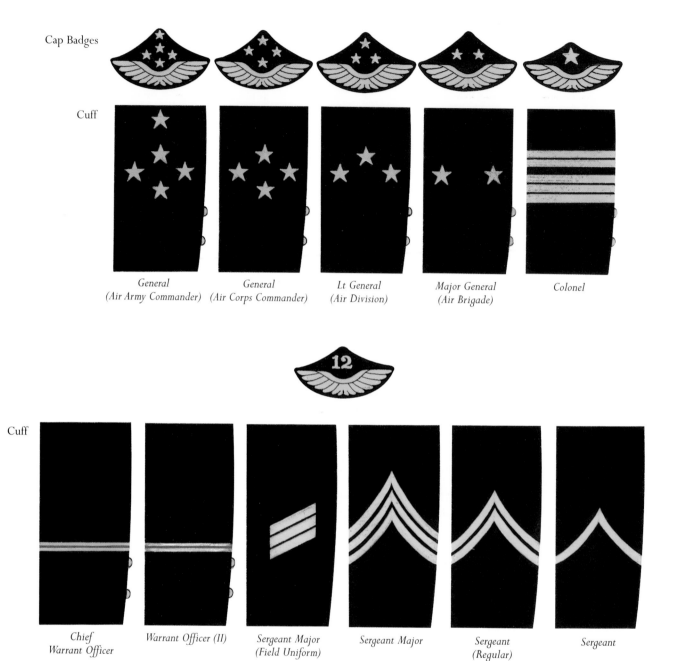

Cap Badges

Cuff

General
(Air Army Commander)

General
(Air Corps Commander)

Lt General
(Air Division)

Major General
(Air Brigade)

Colonel

Cuff

Chief
Warrant Officer

Warrant Officer (II)

Sergeant Major
(Field Uniform)

Sergeant Major

Sergeant
(Regular)

Sergeant

French Air Force

The dark 'Louise-blue' service dress worn by officers and regular non-commissioned officers had its origins in the dark blue uniform worn by the army engineers who, before World War I, had pioneered military aviation. It was supplemented by a double-breasted greatcoat with twin rows of three gilt metal buttons. Head-dress comprised a peaked cap with white cover for summer wear, a black beret as routing working dress and a steel helmet.

Officers' and warrant officers' rank was distinguished by the embroidery or rank distinction lace on the peaked cap and jacket cuffs, or as a simple oval

154

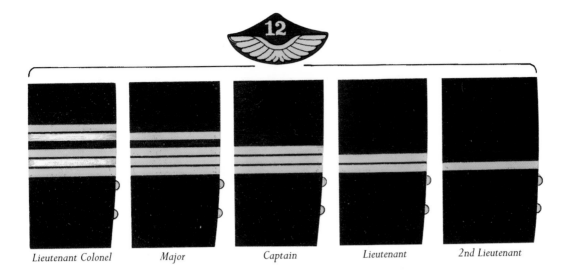

Lieutenant Colonel   Major   Captain   Lieutenant   2nd Lieutenant

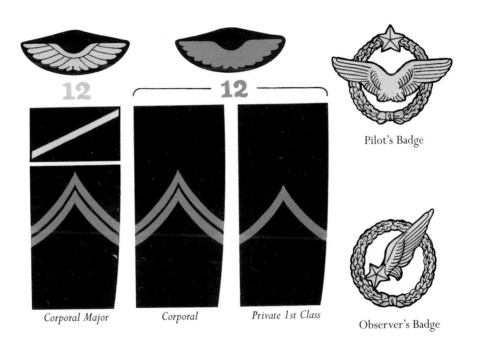

Corporal Major   Corporal   Private 1st Class

Pilot's Badge

Observer's Badge

patch on the front of the working cap. On flying clothing rank was designated on a cloth patch buttoned to the front of the garment. Other ranks wore a dark steel-grey blouse with a round fall collar worn closed over a blue shirt and black tie, matching long trousers, and a 'horizon-blue' greatcoat. Rank was designated on head-dress and cuffs.

The distinction of arm-of-service was identified by an emblem or number incorporated into a winged badge worn on the front of the peaked cap, and on the right breast. Other ranks wore chevrons in branch colours on their collar patches, with the formation number or emblem embroidered in gold for non-commissioned officers and orange for other ranks.

France

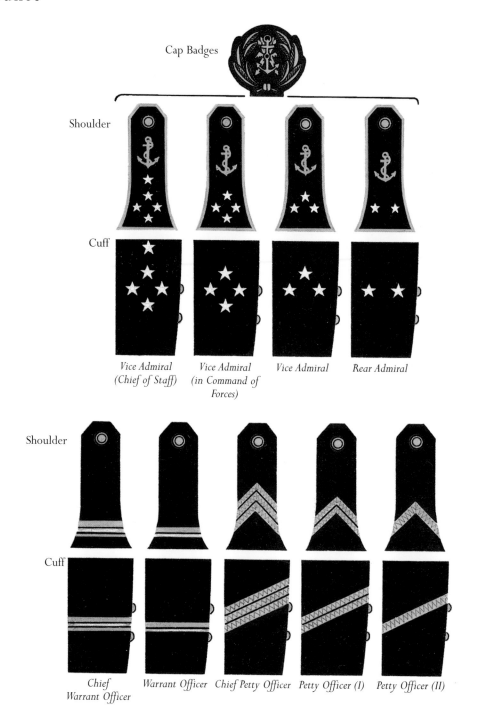

Cap Badges

Shoulder

Cuff

| Vice Admiral (Chief of Staff) | Vice Admiral (in Command of Forces) | Vice Admiral | Rear Admiral |

Shoulder

Cuff

| Chief Warrant Officer | Warrant Officer | Chief Petty Officer | Petty Officer (I) | Petty Officer (II) |

French Navy

Officers' service dress comprised a peaked cap, dark blue double-breasted jacket, matching trousers and black shoes. Their greatcoats and raincoats, the latter worn without insignia, were double-breasted with twin rows of five buttons. During the summer months officers were entitled to wear caps with white covers, white trousers and white canvas shoes with their navy blue reefer jackets, and were also issued with white summer jackets and khaki drill uniforms in hot climates.

Warrant officers and petty officers were issued with officers' uniform for full dress or when walking-

156

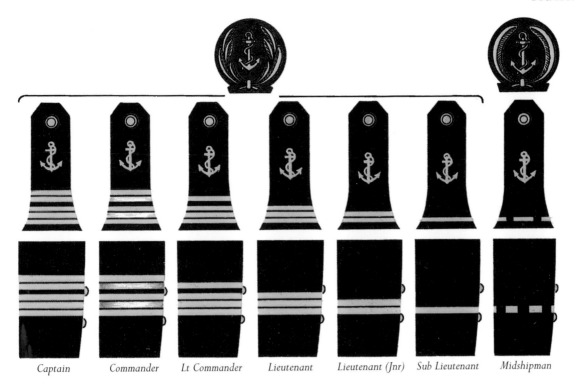

Captain   Commander   Lt Commander   Lieutenant   Lieutenant (Jnr)   Sub Lieutenant   Midshipman

Cap Badge

Tropical Uniform

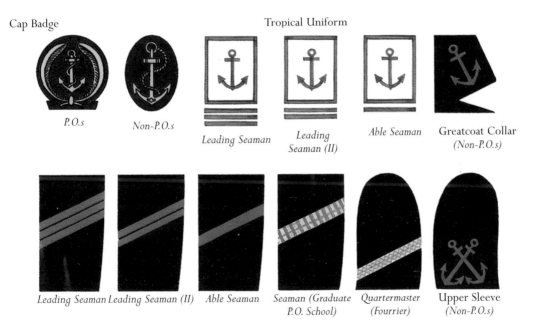

P.O.s   Non-P.O.s

Leading Seaman   Leading Seaman (II)   Able Seaman   Greatcoat Collar (Non-P.O.s)

Leading Seaman   Leading Seaman (II)   Able Seaman   Seaman (Graduate P.O. School)   Quartermaster (Fourrier)   Upper Sleeve (Non-P.O.s)

out, but on board ship most tended to prefer a more practical blue linen working jacket. Officers, warrant officers and petty officers wore their rank insignia on their peaked caps, shoulder straps and cuffs.

Ratings wore a traditional 'square-rig' uniform with its distinctive blue-and-white horizontally striped vest, over which they could wear a double-breasted pea-coat in cold weather. Working dress comprised either blue or undyed denim, with a white

version of the 'square-rig', or alternatively a special white uniform with shorts and a sun helmet, for hot weather. Ratings wore their badges of rank on the cuffs of their jumpers, pea-coats and greatcoats.

Arm-of-service colours were worn on the cuffs, and as 'lights' between the officers' rank distinction lace on the cuffs and shoulder straps. Specialist badges were usually worn on the upper left sleeve, and on the pea-coat and greatcoat collar.

Special Military School

By 1939, the *Ecole Militaire* at Saint-Cyr had gained a reputation as one of the oldest and finest military academies in the world, having produced a succession of famous officers for well over a century, officers who fought in France in 1940 and then with the Free French.

The large grenade of the Special Military School was worn on the traditional light blue shako of the school. Gold badges were worn by the infantry and silver badges by the cavalry branch of the Academy. A black-on-bronze badge of similar design was worn on the helmet.

French officer kepi badges were always worn on the front of the headgear. Those of the officers were embroidered in gold or silver wire, while soldiers' badges were cut out from coloured felt. In most cases the regimental number was worn on its own, in either gold or silver depending on the arm of service of the wearer (scarlet for gunners and engineers, light blue for medical orderlies, and red for others). NCOs wore metal badges.

Badge	*A flaming grenade either 20mm (0.78in) or 30mm (1.2in) in height. Produced in gold and silver and worn on the light blue shake of the school. Larger grenades were worn on the collar.*

Infantry Tank Force

French tank units were drawn from the army's original tank force equipped with infantry tanks, and regiments of former horsed cavalry. In 1936, in line with its essential defensive policy, the army formed two armoured divisions, one as a counterattack unit and the other as a breakthrough force. Even this limited plan was postponed, to the extent that by 1940 the force was at less than half-strength.

Although the French tanks were more heavily armed, and in several other respects better than their German equivalents, the French policy of spreading them thinly along the entire front line proved disastrous. In June 1940, France proved wholly incapable of stemming the German armour-led Blitzkrieg as it forced its way through the Ardennes. Within six weeks the mighty French Army was defeated and France petitioned.

All armoured troops, mountain troops and fortress troops wore berets. Armoured troops wore dark blue berets which sported the badge shown above. Other armoured clothing included a three-quarter length brown leather coat.

Badge	*A crossed cannon and medieval helmet insignia produced in white metal, worn on the front of the beret. Approximately 30mm (1.2in) in height. Worn only by members of armoured divisions.*

British Empire

Tens of thousands of Indians, Australians, South Africans and New Zealanders fought in World War II. For the most part they were organised and equipped in the same way as British forces. British Empire units wore British rank insignia and were awarded British medals for acts of bravery on the battlefield.

First Special Service Force

In June 1942, Lieutenant-Colonel Robert Frederick was authorised to raise a unit able to operate in arctic conditions. Raised from American and Canadian volunteers, it was known as 'the Force'. The recruits were mainly backwoodsmen, trackers and lumberjacks.

Training consisted climbing, demolition and skiing. Though it lacked heavy mortars and machine guns, the First Special Service Force was equipped with submachine guns, light mortars and bazookas. The unit eventually comprised 2400 officers and men divided between six combat and one support battalions. It was disbanded in 1944 at Villeneuve-Loubat after suffering 2300 casualties.

Battle Honours

- *Kiska Island, August 1943*
- *Anzio, January 1944*
- *Rome, June 1944*
- *France, August 1944*

---

2 Squadron, Royal Australian Air Force

No 2 Squadron can trace its origins back to January 1917, when No 68 Squadron, Royal Flying Corps, was formed in Britain from Australian personnel. When World War II broke out it was part of the Australian Air Force and was equipped with Ansons.

No 2 Squadron was a reconnaissance unit. Operating from Darwin, by the time Japan entered the war in December 1941 it was flying Hudsons. As well as reconnaissance duties, the squadron flew bombing sorties against enemy ships and land targets. Later in the war it was operating Mitchells.

Battle Honours

- *Darwin, December 1941*
- *New Guinea, April 1942*
- *Hollandia, April 1944*
- *The Moluccas, September 1944*

2nd Canadian Division

The symbol 'C II', initially in gold or yellow but subsequently in white, superimposed on a Royal blue patch.

The bulk of the Division arrived in Britain in August and September 1940, although two battalions were delayed until December, having spent two months stationed in Iceland. The Division, which formed part of the Canadian Corps based in Surrey and Sussex, formed the bulk of the force which assaulted the beaches of Dieppe, distinguishing itself in the fierce fighting which followed. Canadian made up 298 officers and 4663 men of the 6100 assault force, and nearly 1000 died on the beaches.

As part of the First Canadian Army, 21st Army Group, the Division took part in the Normandy landings, again distinguishing itself in the breakout from Falaise and the sweep up the coast to the channel ports, through Dieppe to the Scheldt. Having fought its way into Holland, the Division advanced to the Waal, and in the final stages of the war assisted in the liberation of the remaining areas of occupied Holland.

44 (Rhodesian) Squadron

No 44 Squadron, Royal Flying Corps, was formed in 1917 and became known for pioneering the Sopwith Camel in night operations. Disbanded in 1919, it reformed in 1937 as a bomber squadron. Its early operations consisted of North Sea sweeps, security patrols and minelaying.

In May 1940, the Squadron began to target enemy lines of communication and invasion barges in the Channel ports. In April 1942, it took part in a daring daylight raid against the MAN diesel engine factory in Augsburg, Bavaria, for which two of its personnel were awarded the Victoria Cross.

Battle Honours

- *Dieppe, 19 August 1942*
- *D-Day, 6 June 1944*
- *Northern France, August 1944*
- *Holland, 1945*

Battle Honours

- *North Sea, April 1940*
- *Channel ports, May 1940*
- *Augsburg, April 1942*
- *Germany, 1945*

464 Squadron, Royal Australian Air Force

No 464 Squadron, RAAF, was formed as a Ventura Squadron at Feltwell, Norfolk in September 1942. In July 1943 it transferred from Bomber Command to 2 Tactical Air Force (TAF), and then converted to Mosquitoes.

It undertook low-level precision bombing raids for the rest of the war, the most famous being the raid on Amiens Prison shortly before the D-Day landings to free captured Resistance fighters who might otherwise have been interrogated and given away secrets of the imminent D-Day landings. The Squadron was

487 Squadron, Royal New Zealand Air Force

No 487 Squadron was formed at Feltwell, Norfolk in September 1942 and carried out daylight raids with Venturas until June 1943.

The unit converted to Mosquitoes in August 1943 and for rest of the war, as part of No 140 Wing, undertook a series of daring low-level precision raids over Occupied Europe and Germany. The most famous of these raids was the attack on the Gestapo headquarters in Aarhus, Denmark.

Battle Honours

- *Northern France, July 1943*
- *Amiens, May 1944*
- *Northern France, June–September 1944*
- *Germany, 1945*

Battle Honours

- *Northern France, July 1943*
- *Normandy, June 1944*
- *Northern France, June–September 1944*
- *The Low Countries, 1944*

Australian Imperial Force

The Australian Imperial Force insignia had a trophy of arms, swords and bayonets, surrounding a crown, the whole above a boomerang. It originated from the badge of the first regiment of the Australian Light Horse, which served with the Imperial Forces in South Africa, and in the Middle East in World War I. Contrary to popular opinion, the insignia does not represent the rising sun.

Most Australian formations adopted as their badges the national animals and birds of their country. With few exceptions they incorporated a boomerang in the design. The badges were used as divisional signs and vehicle markings, and were worn in combination with coloured patches as distinguishing marks for personnel.

Small coloured patches, which were worn on individual soldiers' sleeves, varied in shape according to the branches of service, the colour denoting the brigade or division to which the battalion was attached.

Royal 22nd Regiment (Canada)

The insignia of the regiment sports a brass beaver with a central coat of arms surrounded by the words *Régiment Canadien Français* within a red circle. Above the circle is a crown, and below are the words *Je Me Souviens* ('I remember').

The 22nd (French-Canadian) Regiment was formed on 7 November 1914 for service with the Canadian Expeditionary Force on the Western Front. It was disbanded in May 1919, but because of its outstanding service was reformed as an entirely French-Canadian entity in April 1920. It was renamed the Royal 22nd Regiment in June 1928.

The 'Van Doos', as the Regiment came to be known, fought as part of the 3rd Infantry Brigade, 1st Canadian Division, during World War II. As such, it formed part of the British Expeditionary Forces which fought in the Mediterranean and later in Northwest Europe after the D-Day landings. Like its predecessor in World War I, the Regiment fought well in Europe against the Germans.

Battle Honours

- *North Africa, 1940–43*
- *Middle East, 1941*
- *Burma, 1944*
- *Southwest Pacific, 1945*

Battle Honours

- *Sicily, July 1943*
- *Italy, 1943–44*
- *Normandy, June 1944*
- *Northwest Europe, 1944–45*

1st Canadian Parachute Battalion

On 1 July 1943, the War Committee of the Canadian Cabinet authorised the formation of a parachute battalion, to be used as a mobile reserve in the defence of North America. Te recruits were trained at the élite US Army Parachute Training School at Fort Benning, Georgia.

By 1943 it had become clear that the United States would not be invaded, thus the men of the Battalion were transferred to England to become part of the 6th Airborne Division. Here they received further training, taking part in complex field exercises, progressing from company to battalion and brigade level. One of these exercises simulated a widely dispersed landing and the many associated problems. This was of great value later during the Battalion's first airborne operation.

Dropping to the northeast of Caen on D-Day, the Battalion was scattered over an area 10 times the size of the drop zone. In the three months following the D-Day drop, the battalion suffered 50 per cent casualties, with 25 officers and 332 other ranks killed. The Canadians were withdrawn from the front in February 1945 to begin preparations for the Rhine crossing, which took place in March 1945.

HMAS Sydney

HMAS *Sydney*, formerly HMS *Phacton*, was a modified Lyander-class cruiser. Launched in March 1934, she entered service in August 1935. Armed with eight 15.24cm (6in) guns, four 10.16cm (4in) single-mounted anti-aircraft guns and eight 53.34cm (21in) torpedo tubes, she displaced 6809 tonnes (6701 tons). She was but one of many Royal Navy ships transferred to the navies of British Empire members.

The precise details of her sinking remain a mystery as none of her crew survived the incident. What is known is that she closed with the disguised German raider *Kormoran* in the Southwest Pacific on 19 November 1941. She was taken by surprise when *Kormoran* opened fire. Although she returned fire, sinking the raider, she was herself mortally damaged, and was last seen by the survivors of the *Kormoran* sailing at speed away from the engagement. She probably suffered a large explosion of some sort and sank, taking all hands down with her.

Battle Honours

- *D-Day, 6 June 1944*
- *Northern France, June–August 1944*
- *Ardennes, December 1944*
- *The Rhine, March 1945*

Battle Honours

- *Sinking of the* Kormoran, *19 November 1941*

Other Axis

Countries such as Bulgaria, Hungary, Finland and Romania were willing partners in the Axis alliance, and participated fully in the German invasion of the Soviet Union in June 1941. However, far from sharing in the spoils, the armed forces of these countries suffered heavy losses of men and material in the titanic battles on the Eastern Front.

Collar Patches

Army General

Air Force General

Shoulder

General

Lieutenant General

Major General (Air Force)

Shoulder

Warrant Officer

Sergeant

Corporal

Private 1st Class

Private (Air Force)

Bulgarian Army & Air Force

Despite its German allegiance, the Bulgarian Army took its traditions from Tsarist Russia, a factor which influenced the style of its uniforms throughout the war.

Officers wore a tunic, breeches and black riding boots, or trousers with boots and black puttees. Their double breasted greatcoat had a double row of gold buttons. General officers' greatcoats were adorned with scarlet lapels and piping and their trousers had a red double-strip; those of other officers had arm-of-service colour piping. Other ranks wore a single-breasted tunic with stand collar, trousers and black boots. The greatcoat was double-breasted, but fastened with a single row of buttons.

Army Officers   *Air Force Officers*

Colonel
(Engineers)

Lt Colonel
(Artillery)

Major
(Engineers)

Captain
(Air Force)

Lieutenant
(Infantry)

2nd Lieutenant
(Air Force)

Cadet
(Air Force)

Cap Badge
Air Force General

Cap Badge
Army Officers

Cap Badge
Air Force Officers

Collar Patch
Air Force Cadet

Officers wore khaki peaked caps with coloured bands and piping and an oval metal cockade in national colours at the front. Other ranks tended to wear a side cap with a shield in national colours on the right, and guilt metal or brass Bulgarian lion on the front.

Rank insignia was worn on the shoulders, and for officers in the form of rank distinction lace attached to the left of their side caps. Arm-of-service colouring was worn on the shoulder straps and collar patches.

Air Force personnel wore either Army khaki or Air Force grey uniform. Officers wore German-pattern collar patches embroidered in silver wire, non-commissioned officers rectangular light blue collar patches with silver-grey bars. Their arm-of-service colour, appeared as light blue piping on their blue-grey peaked cap, their collar patches and shoulder straps, and as piping on their trousers, breeches and greatcoat. Pilots wore embroidered wings on the right breast.

Cuff

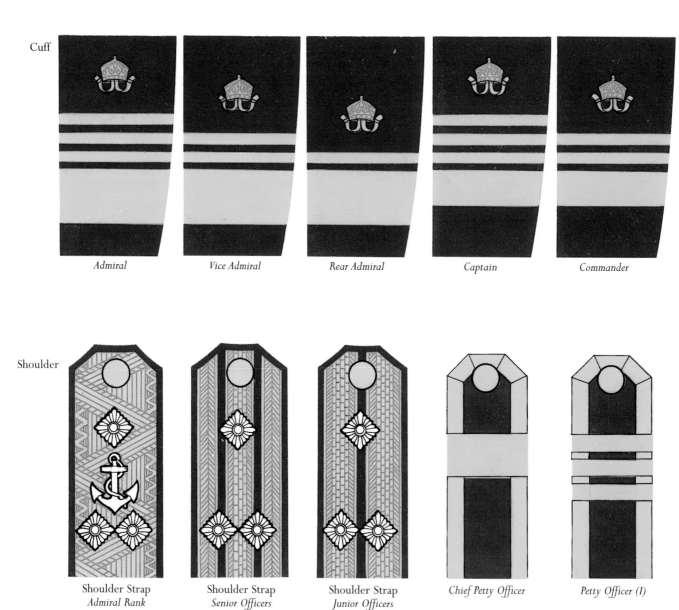

| Admiral | Vice Admiral | Rear Admiral | Captain | Commander |

Shoulder

| Shoulder Strap *Admiral Rank* (here Admiral) | Shoulder Strap *Senior Officers* (here Captain) | Shoulder Strap *Junior Officers* (here Lieutenant) | *Chief Petty Officer* | *Petty Officer (I)* |

Bulgarian Navy

The uniform of the Royal Bulgarian Navy aped that of the Tzarist Russia prior to 1917. Officers and chief petty officers were issued with black peaked caps with white piping, an embroidered cap badge and black leather peak and chin strap. They wore a black double-breasted reefer jacket with two rows of buttons in front, a white shirt, black tie and matching trousers. When required the great-coat was double-breasted. In hot weather officers and chief petty officers wore a white cap cover and tunic.

Ratings wore a Russian-style cap with an oval metal cockade on the front in the national colours, and a Cyrillic inscription on the tally. A blue jumper was worn inside the trousers, as was the blue linen working jumper. Ratings also wore a light blue-and-white striped vest with a blue denim collar sporting three white lines. These were supplemented by a pea-coat for colder winter weather.

168

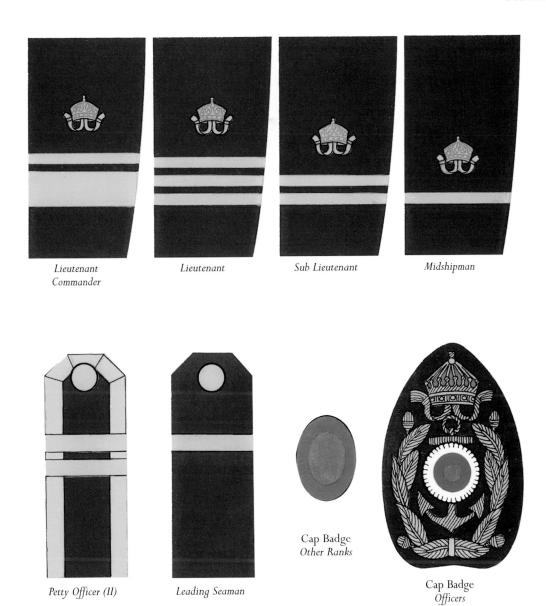

Lieutenant Commander   Lieutenant   Sub Lieutenant   Midshipman

Petty Officer (II)   Leading Seaman

Cap Badge
Other Ranks

Cap Badge
Officers

Rank badges were worn on the shoulder boards or patches by all ranks, and on the cuffs by officers in the executive or line branches. Executive officers wore a distinctive crown above the rank distinction lace on their cuffs.

However, when officers wore their summer white tunic, their rank distinction lace was worn on the outside of the cuffs only.

Officers in the administrative branches did not wear lace on their cuffs, and wore their buttons, badges and shoulder-board lace in silver. It was only the officers in the executive and line branch who were permitted to wear gold badges, buttons and lace.

Arm-of-service was indicated by the colour of the underlay and stripes on the shoulder boards, and by 'lights' on the officers' cuff rank distinction lace.

Germany's influence on Bulgaria, which was partly due to Bulgaria's wariness of Soviet intentions, did not seem to show in the uniform of the Royal Bulgarian Navy, as it had done in her Army.

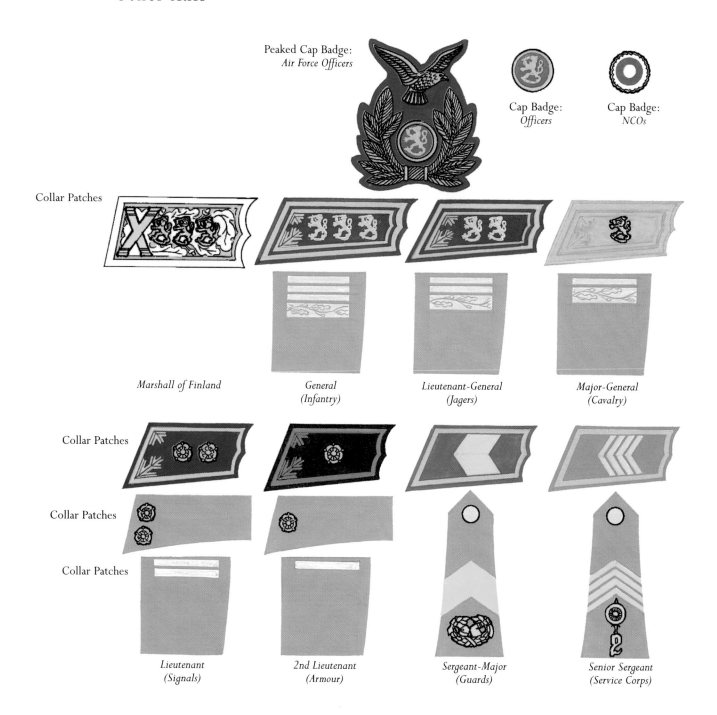

Peaked Cap Badge:
Air Force Officers

Cap Badge:
Officers

Cap Badge:
NCOs

Collar Patches

Marshall of Finland

*General
(Infantry)*

*Lieutenant-General
(Jagers)*

*Major-General
(Cavalry)*

Collar Patches

Collar Patches

Collar Patches

*Lieutenant
(Signals)*

*2nd Lieutenant
(Armour)*

*Sergeant-Major
(Guards)*

*Senior Sergeant
(Service Corps)*

Finnish Army & Army Air Service

The Finnish Air Force was a branch of the Army, and as such did not have an individual uniform of its own. Flying clothing comprised a single-piece overall and flying helmet and gloves made of leather. Fur-lined flying suits and boots were provided for crews of open aircraft and bombers.

A dark blue service dress was introduced for Air Force officers, but was rarely worn during the war; the most common uniform was that of the Army, which was basically similar for all ranks.

Army badges of rank were worn on the cuff, collar and shoulder boards. Arms-of-service were differentiated by colour; black for armour, red for

Cap Badge
ORs

Cap Badge
Officers & NCOs
(worn with other badges)

Pilot's Badge
(Breast Pocket)

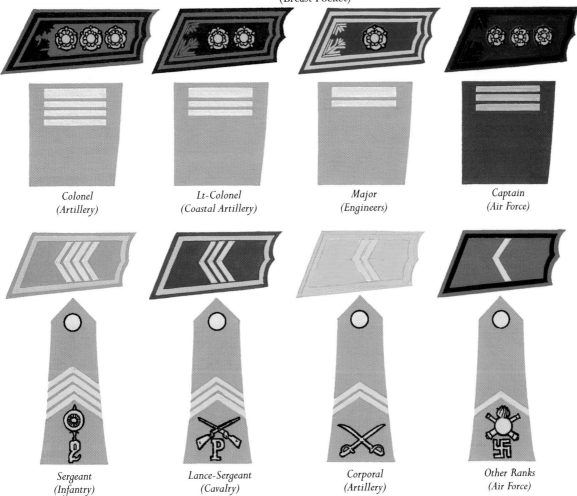

Colonel
(Artillery)

Lt-Colonel
(Coastal Artillery)

Major
(Engineers)

Captain
(Air Force)

Sergeant
(Infantry)

Lance-Sergeant
(Cavalry)

Corporal
(Artillery)

Other Ranks
(Air Force)

artillery, yellow for cavalry, and dark green for the infantry.

Non-commissioned officers wore emblems of service on their lapels: crossed rifles above the monogram 'P' for the infantry; crossed swords for the cavalry; and an exploding cannon superimposed over crossed barrels above a swastika for the artillery.

The Air Force arm-of-service colour was blue, worn above a swastika on shoulder boards. Qualified pilots wore a white metal badge with a black swastika on a blue background at its centre on the left breast pocket.

Regular Army officers wore a small button-shaped cap badge depicting the Finnish eagle at its centre.

Admiral
(Summer)

Capt., Cmdr.,
Lt-Cmdr

Junior Officers

Shoulder

Cuff

Admiral

Vice-Admiral

Rear-Admiral

Captain
(Engineers)

Commander

Lieutenant
Commander

Cuff and Arm

W.O.
1st Class (I)
(Machinist)

W.O.
2nd/3rd Class
(II/III)
(Torpedoes)

W.O.
4th Class (IV)
(Signals)

C.P.O.
(Sergeant Major)

P.O. (I)
(Mines)

P.O. (II)
(Supply)

Finnish Navy

Finnish Navy uniforms were similar in basic design to those of the British Royal Navy. Officers and chief petty officers wore peaked caps, reefer jackets with white shirts, and black ties. However, petty officers and ratings wore square rigs with blue caps bearing the name of the ship or shore installation in gold lettering on long tallies, jumpers with blue denim collars, bell-bottomed trousers and black shoes.

In cold weather, officers and chief petty officers wore double-breasted greatcoats with twin rows of six buttons, and, in extreme cold, black astrakhan caps. Petty officers were issued with double-breasted

Lieutenant (Medical)　*Sub-Lieutenant*　*Ensign (Music)*　*Reserve Ensign*　*'Official' (Lieutenant)*　*Cap Badge: Senior 'Official'*

P.O. (III) (Medical)　*Leading Seaman (Gunnery)*　*P.O. (Radio) Conscript*　*Leading Seaman (Conscript)*　*C.P.O. (Admin.)*　*P.O. (Admin.)*

pea-coats to keep freezing temperatures at bay. In fact, every rank received extreme-weather clothing for hot and cold conditions. The Finnish Navy knew the cold: its greatest problem pre-war had been a lack of ice-free ports in its own territories.

On their uniforms, officers wore rank distinction on the cuffs and on the greatcoat. Insignia also featured tunic shoulder straps, with their branches or corps designated by coloured 'lights' between their gold lace rank-rings. Red denoted the medical, whereas other ranks wore chevrons on their upper left sleeves. Petty officers' branches of service were designated by gold, and junior ranks by red badges above their rank chevrons.

Collar Patches

Greatcoat Cuff

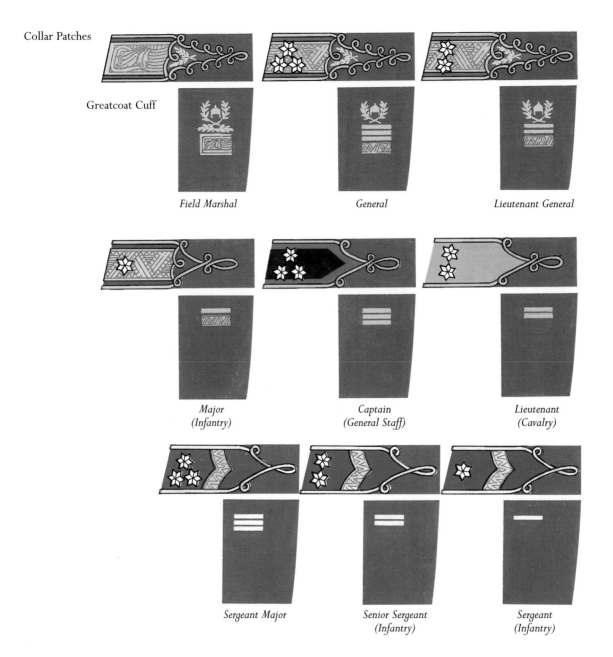

Field Marshal

General

Lieutenant General

*Major
(Infantry)*

*Captain
(General Staff)*

*Lieutenant
(Cavalry)*

Sergeant Major

*Senior Sergeant
(Infantry)*

*Sergeant
(Infantry)*

Hungarian Army

In the Hungarian Royal Army, officers' service dress was distinctly German in influence, although when not wearing the German M1935 helmet the side cap with high pointed crown was uniquely domestic. All ranks were issued with a single-breasted tunic with five buttons and side-pleated patch pockets.

During the early stages of the war tanks crews wore one-piece khaki overalls with a double-breasted leather jacket, but later this was replaced by a short single-breasted jacket. Initially members of the Royal Hungarian Gendarmerie wore a black felt hat with a cockerel feather plume, although this fell into disuse as the war progressed. It was replaced with a side cap with the plume on the left side, but as this was not always recognised by their allies on the Eastern fron, it became necessary to introduce a German-type metal gorget as a duty badge.

Rank insignia was worn on tunic and initially on greatcoat collar patches. Just before the war rank

174

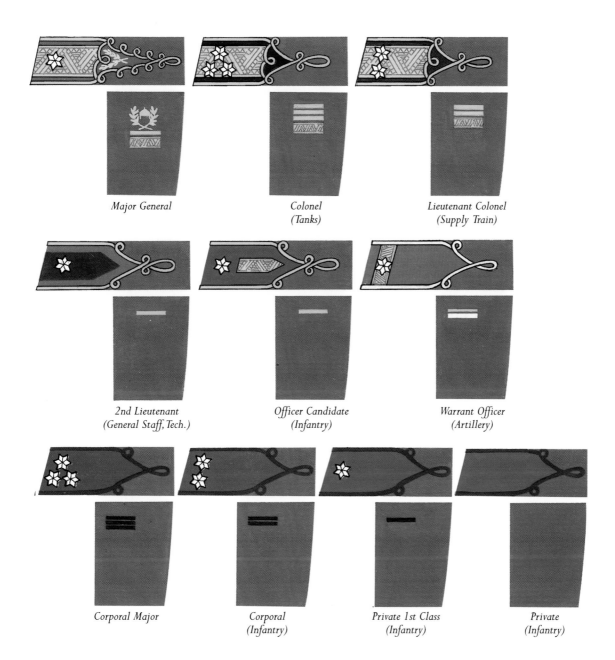

Major General

Colonel
(Tanks)

Lieutenant Colonel
(Supply Train)

2nd Lieutenant
(General Staff, Tech.)

Officer Candidate
(Infantry)

Warrant Officer
(Artillery)

Corporal Major

Corporal
(Infantry)

Private 1st Class
(Infantry)

Private
(Infantry)

badges were worn as shoulder straps on the greatcoat. However, shortly after the commencement of hostilities, these greatcoat patches were moved to the cuffs. All ranks wore lace and braid chevrons on the front of their side cap and field cap according to rank. Regular NCOs were identified by a triangular badge worn on the upper left sleeve.

Arm-of-service colours were demonstrated on the collar patches and on the left side of the cap in the form of a triangle. Other than members of the Gendarmerie who were all professional soldiers, regulars in other units wore a triangular badge on the left sleeve. Parachutists wore embroidered or metal 'wings' on the right breast, other élite units specialist insignia on the left side of the headdress.

Before October 1939, Hungarian troops engaged in securing territories granted by the Vienna Awards and in April 1941, having allied herself with Germany, Hungary was also involved in the invasion of Yugoslavia. As a result the rank-and-file of the Army comprised Hungarians, Romanians, Slovakians, Ukranians and Serbs, and thus presented a force that was far from homogenous both in its appearance and its morale.

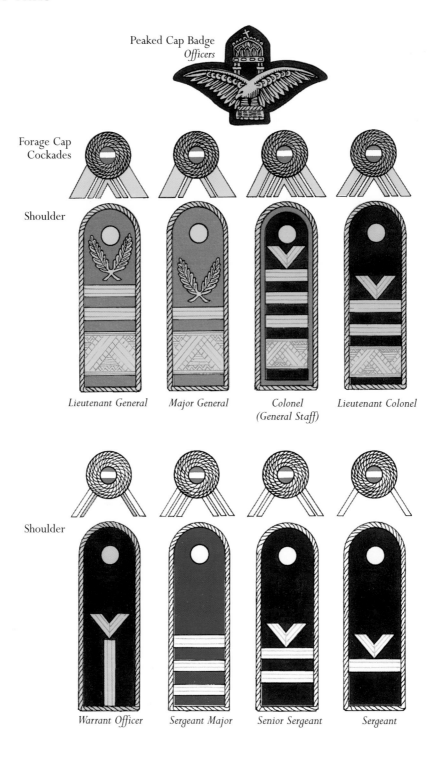

Peaked Cap Badge
Officers

Forage Cap
Cockades

Shoulder

Lieutenant General   *Major General*   *Colonel
(General Staff)*   *Lieutenant Colonel*

Shoulder

Warrant Officer   *Sergeant Major*   *Senior Sergeant*   *Sergeant*

Hungarian Air Force

As a branch of the Army, the Air Force wore a virtually identical uniform. Officers and senior non-commissioned officers were issued with a peaked cap with a brown leather peak, an open khaki service dress jacket, matching trousers and brown shoes. Other ranks wore a naval-style head-dress and army-style jacket, although as the war progressed this was gradually replaced by an open jacket to wear with khaki shirt and black tie.

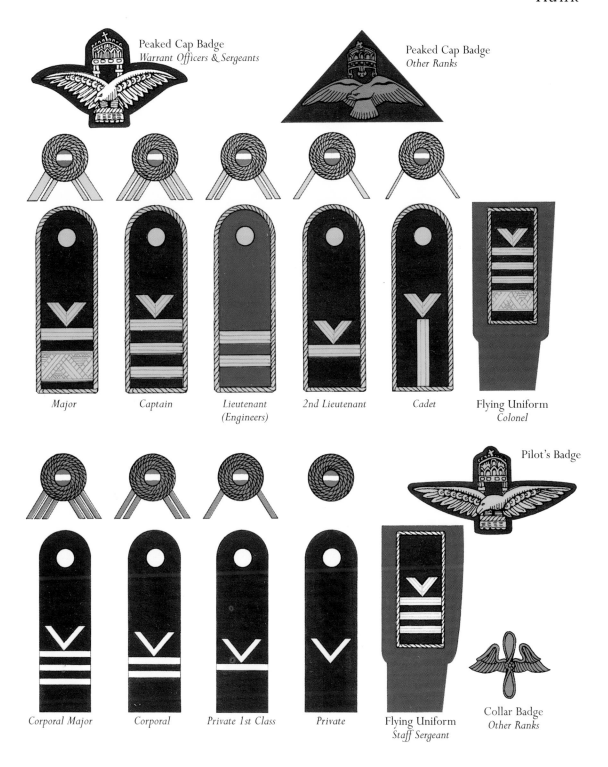

Peaked Cap Badge
Warrant Officers & Sergeants

Peaked Cap Badge
Other Ranks

Major

Captain

*Lieutenant
(Engineers)*

2nd Lieutenant

Cadet

Flying Uniform
Colonel

Pilot's Badge

Corporal Major

Corporal

Private 1st Class

Private

Flying Uniform
Staff Sergeant

Collar Badge
Other Ranks

Flying clothing was varied and included an unlined one-piece leather overall with numerous pockets.

General officers could be identified by two, and field officers by one row of gold beading on the peak of their field caps. Otherwise, rank insignia was worn by all ranks on the shoulder straps of the tunic and greatcoat, on the cuffs of flying gear, and on the front of the field cap. General officers wore scarlet shoulder straps and cuff patches, while the general staff wore scarlet and technical officers cherry velvet piping.

177

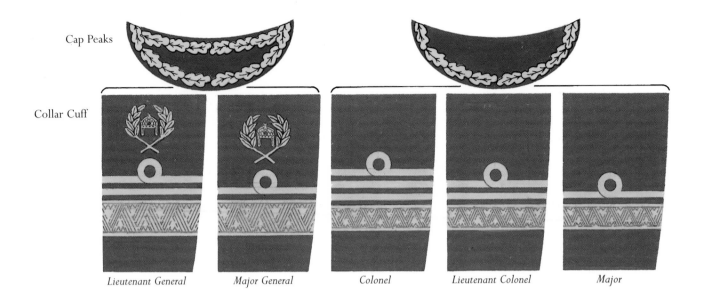

Cap Peaks

Collar Cuff

| Lieutenant General | Major General | Colonel | Lieutenant Colonel | Major |

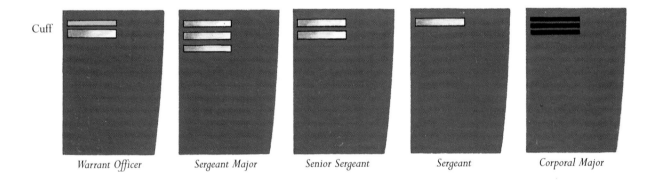

Cuff

| Warrant Officer | Sergeant Major | Senior Sergeant | Sergeant | Corporal Major |

Hungarian River Force

Land-locked Hungary had no coastline and no Navy as such; the Ministry of the Interior maintained the ten old rivercraft of the River Force for police work in Budapest. At the outbreak of war, however, the Danube Flotilla of the Royal Hungarian River Police came under the command of the Ministry of Defence and it was responsible for keeping the river free of mines planted by the Allies.

Personnel wore a khaki uniform; that of the officers and senior non-commissioned officers comprising a peaked cap, single-breasted open service dress jacket – worn with either khaki or white shirt and khaki tie – and matching trousers and black shoes. Their greatcoat was double-breasted with a velvet collar and twin rows of six metal buttons.

Ratings were issued with a khaki cap with a black silk tally bearing the words 'M.Kir.Honred Folyami

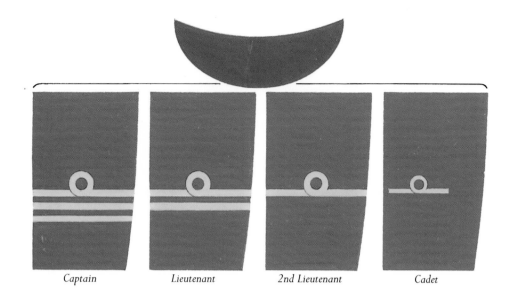

| Captain | Lieutenant | 2nd Lieutenant | Cadet |

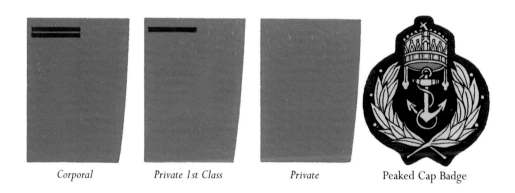

| Corporal | Private 1st Class | Private | Peaked Cap Badge |

erok' in silver. Their tunic could be worn open at the neck, worn with matching trousers and black boots. The greatcoat for other ranks was double-breasted with twin rows of five buttons, and their equipment manufactured from the brown leather of standard Army issue.

Rank insignia was worn on the cuff by all ranks. The rank distinction lace went fully round the cuff in the case of officers' service dress tunics but was in a shortened form on their greatcoats. The three ranks groups were easily identifiable by metal type; officers wore gold buttons, badges and lace, senior non-commissioned officers silver, and junior ranks bronze.

As the war progressed, these ranks played ever-important roles, such as in northern Yugoslavia, where they carried out occupation duties, and in the Battle of Budapest, when they manned riverboats to defend the bridges of the Danube.

Cap Peaks

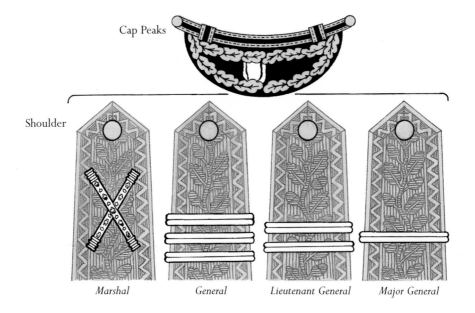

Shoulder

| *Marshal* | *General* | *Lieutenant General* | *Major General* |

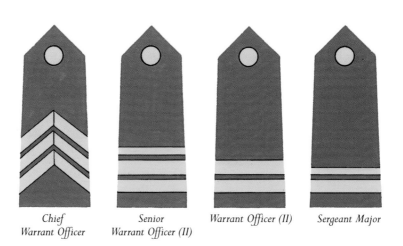

| *Chief Warrant Officer* | *Senior Warrant Officer (II)* | *Warrant Officer (II)* | *Sergeant Major* |

Romanian Army

Romania had the rare distinction of fighting on both sides during the war, annexed as she was in June 1940 by the Soviet Union, and then conferred the status of a German satellite in November 1940 by the Axis Pact. This was a factor which manifested itself in their uniforms. Initially, officers' service dress was very British in its design, the head-dress basically Soviet. Later they were issued with a serge service dress buttoning to the neck.

Generals wore two rows of gold embroidery on the peak of their hats, field officers one. Generals also wore special collar patches with gold embroidery on a red background.

Other ranks wore a plain and very utilitarian khaki uniform, including a short unlined greatcoat carried over the shoulder when not worn. Special units were distinguished by their head-dress: mountain troops wore a green beret and tank crews a black one. The steel helmet was the M1928 licensed from the Dutch

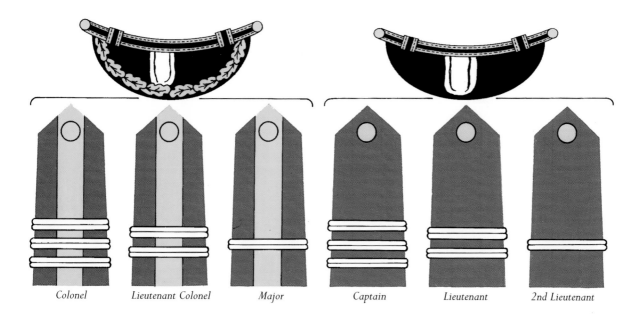

Colonel Lieutenant Colonel Major   Captain   Lieutenant   2nd Lieutenant

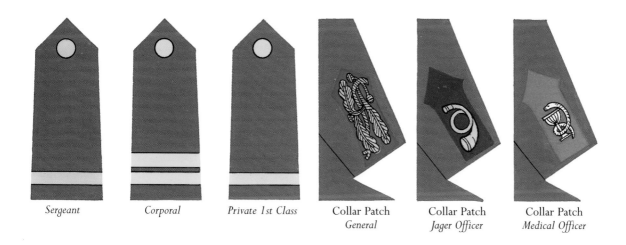

Sergeant Corporal Private 1st Class Collar Patch *General* Collar Patch *Jager Officer* Collar Patch *Medical Officer*

and manufactured either with or without the roman-ian coat of arms on the front.

When available a summer lightweight uniform, which quickly bleached white in the sun, was issued. Winter clothing comprised the short unlined great-coat, lambswool cap (issued with a peak as the war progressed) unpadded trousers, and short lace-up boots, wholly unsuited to winter on the Eastern Front. Many Romanian soldiers suffered through lack of adequate winter clothing.

Rank insignia was worn on the shoulder straps as well as on the front or side of the side- and field cap. Rank was designated by a series of metal bars for offi-cers and cloth stripes for other ranks, worn straight save for chief warrant officers who wore three chevrons peak uppermost.

Hungary's alliance with Germany ended when King Michael overthrew Antonescu and declared war on Germany in 1944. Hungary suffered a final 170,000 Army death-toll before the war's end.

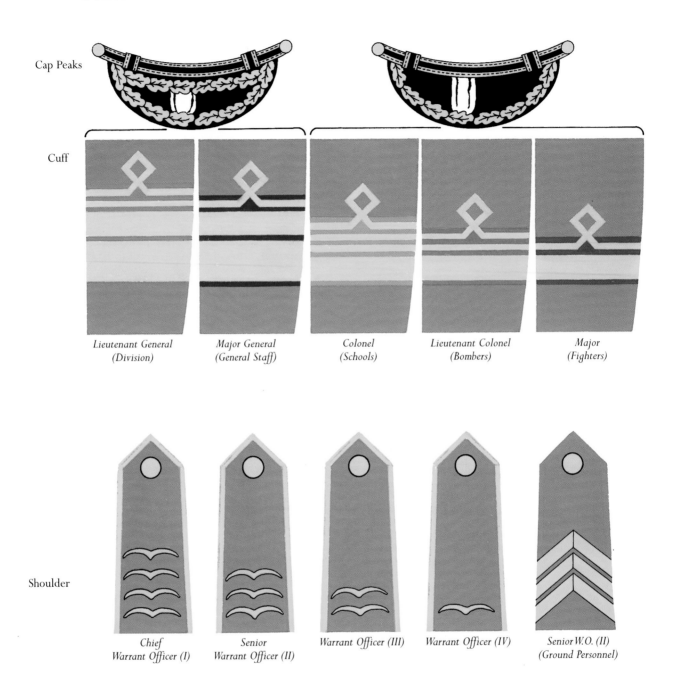

Cap Peaks

Cuff

Lieutenant General
(Division)

Major General
(General Staff)

Colonel
(Schools)

Lieutenant Colonel
(Bombers)

Major
(Fighters)

Shoulder

Chief
Warrant Officer (I)

Senior
Warrant Officer (II)

Warrant Officer (III)

Warrant Officer (IV)

Senior W.O. (II)
(Ground Personnel)

Romanian Air Force

The Romanian Air Force was operating under several different types of aircraft when, in June 1941, she joined her ally Germany in the attack on the Soviet Union. This variety of aircraft reflected the country's shifting diplomacy pre-war and in its earliest stages. Polish, British, German, and French aircraft were used by the Air Force in the advance on Odessa.

Likewise wartime naval uniforms followed an international pattern. Officers and regular non-commissioned officers wore a blue-green service dress with a peaked cap, and double-breasted overcoat and raincoat when required. All officers wore a gold cap badge depicting an eagle surmounted by a crown; general officers wore two rows of gold embroidery on their peaks, and field officers one.

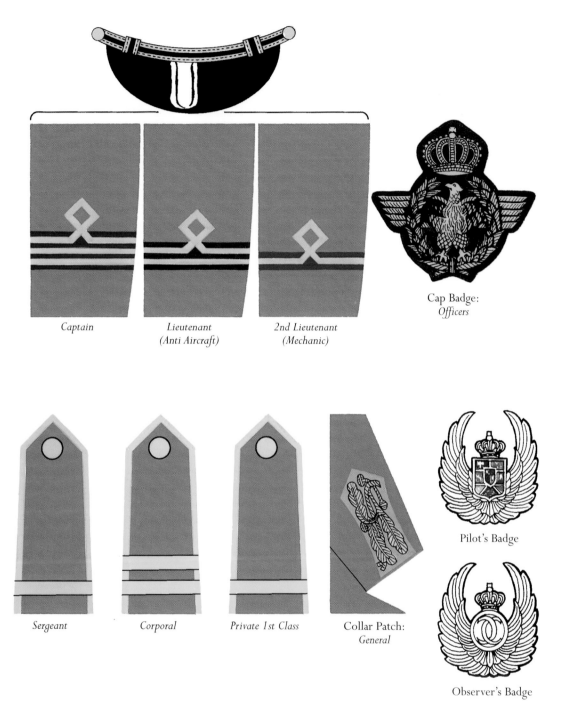

Captain

Lieutenant
(Anti Aircraft)

2nd Lieutenant
(Mechanic)

Cap Badge:
Officers

Sergeant

Corporal

Private 1st Class

Collar Patch:
General

Pilot's Badge

Observer's Badge

On flying uniform, badges of rank were worn in a variety of places including the shoulder strap, side cap, and left breast pocket. Otherwise officers' insignia was officially worn on the cuffs, although informally they were occasionally worn on the upper sleeves of the greatcoat and raincoat. In summer a white cap cover and tunic were worn, the latter with its rank insignia on grey shoulder straps.

Other ranks wore a grey jacket buttoning to the neck, matching trousers and black boots. A soft grey peaked cap was issued, but often discarded when working, in favour of a black beret. Rank insignia was worn at all times on the shoulder.

General officers wore gold lapel badges on a light blue background, and aircrew white metal badges above the left breast pocket.

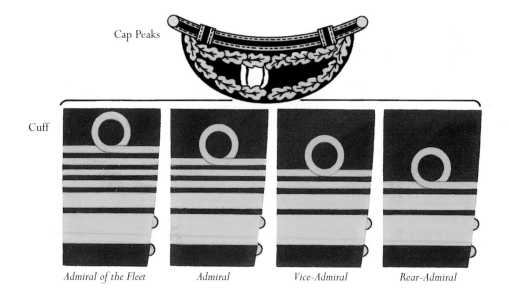

Cap Peaks

Cuff

Admiral of the Fleet   Admiral   Vice-Admiral   Rear-Admiral

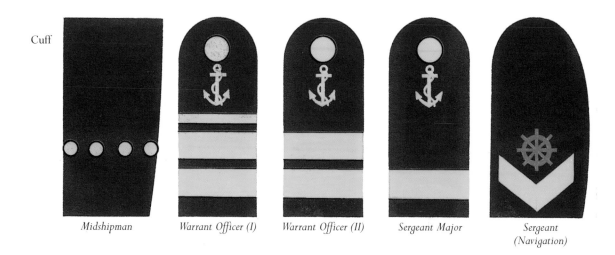

Cuff

Midshipman   Warrant Officer (I)   Warrant Officer (II)   Sergeant Major   Sergeant (Navigation)

Romanian Navy

The Royal Romanian Navy was organised into two parts: the Black Sea Division and the Danube Flotilla. Most of its warships had been designed or built in Italy or Britain. Wartime uniforms were, correspondingly, cosmopolitan in design. The jumper, worn outside the trousers, had a blue denim collar. Petty officers wore a single-breasted tunic, and officers wore a peaked cap, reefer jacket, and white shirt, together with black trousers. Ratings wore a German-style cap with a tally bearing the words 'Marina Regala' in gold. Officers wore a peaked cap in the style of the Royal Navy.

Flag officers could be differentiated by two rows, and other officers by one row, of gold embroidery on the cap peak. Their gold cap badge showed an anchor surrounded by laurel leaves surmounted by a crown.

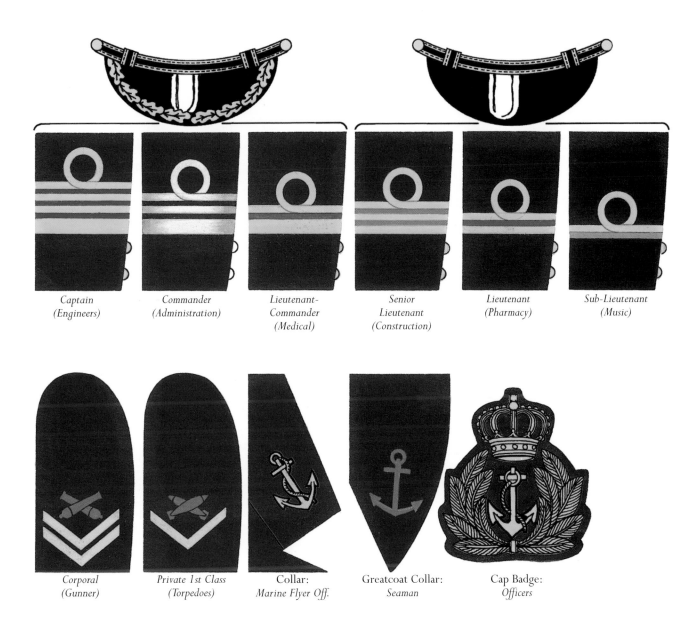

Captain
(Engineers)

Commander
(Administration)

Lieutenant-
Commander
(Medical)

Senior
Lieutenant
(Construction)

Lieutenant
(Pharmacy)

Sub-Lieutenant
(Music)

Corporal
(Gunner)

Private 1st Class
(Torpedoes)

Collar:
Marine Flyer Off.

Greatcoat Collar:
Seaman

Cap Badge:
Officers

Officers and midshipmen wore rank indication lace on their sleeves in all orders of dress including, unusually, greatcoat order. Service specialisations were depicted by coloured 'lights' between the rank distinction lace.

Warrant officers (I), (II), and sergeant majors wore gold rank badges depicting an anchor above a series of three, two and one stripes respectively, on the shoulder. Ratings wore badges of rank in gold, surmounted by red arm-of-service indicators, on the arm.

In June 1943 metal battle badges under German design were introduced for the crews of submarines, torpedo-boats and minelayers, as, after German naval forces arrrived on the Danube, the Romanian vessels were in operation under the command of the German Vice-Admiral Brinkmann; Germany later awarded five dwarf submarines to the Romanian Navy.

Other Allied

Though many Allied countries fell to the German Blitzkrieg in 1939–41, most notably Poland, thousands of Allied soldiers, sailors and airmen managed to escape their homelands and continue the fight from Britain. These servicemen made a valuable contribution to the Allied war effort, fighting with tenacity and courage.

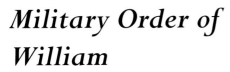

Military Order of William

Introduced by King William I on 30 April 1815, it represents the highest and only award from the kingdom of Holland. Inaugurated to reward military personnel who had rendered to the state deeds of outstanding courage.

Badge	Mounted on an eight-pointed silver convex star. The four arms at the positions of 1, 3, 6 and 9 o'clock comprise seven pencil rays, the others five. The centre is a Maltese cross, at each tip a ball finial. The inner field is white opaque enamel, inscribed VOOR DIOED BELEID TROUW ('For Courage, Leadership, Loyalty'). Crossed Burgundian branches appear between the arms of the cross.

Order of the Grunwald Cross

The Order, which takes its name from a victory gained by the Poles over the Teutonic Knight at Grunwald, was established in December 1943, and confirmed in February 1944 in three classes. Awarded for the organisation of large-scale operations against the enemy, for exceptional leadership, or for personal deeds of bravery carried out on the battlefield, it was first conferred upon 30 recipients in 1943.

It was originally presented in the form of a simple ribbon, there being no way for the partisans fighting in Poland to manufacture the cross.

Badge	A Greek Cross in gilt or silver; all gilt for 1st Class, silver with gilt-edged strip to the face of the cross for 2nd Class, and all silver for 3rd Class. The ends turn slightly outwards. The centre depicts a shield with two ancient swords, hilts uppermost.
Ribbon	Red with centre stripe of white and pale green edges.

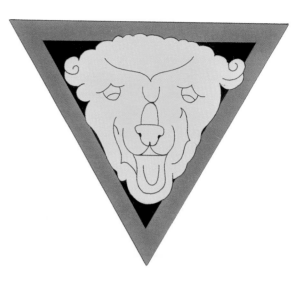

II Polish Corps

The insignia depicted a white, silver or pale grey 'Syrena' or mermaid with shield and upraised sword on a red background. The badge was based on the device of the arms of the City of Warsaw.

The Corps had its origins among the Polish prisoners of war in Russian prison camps. When Hitler invaded the Soviet Union, Stalin agreed to form fighting units from these prisoners. Eventually, around 40,000 Polish military personnel and their families were allowed to transfer to the British-controlled sector of Iran. The Poles then spent a year training up in Iran and Palestine. By the time it was ready for battle the Corps comprised 50,000 men, organised into two divisions: the 5th Kresowa Infantry Division and the 3rd Carpathian Rifle Division. Each division comprised two brigades, each brigade being made up of three battalions. The 2nd Warsaw Armoured Brigade was also attached to the Corps.

Belgian 1st Independent Brigade Group

This formation formed part of the British 21st Army Group and took part in the landings in Normandy and the liberation of its own homeland. The insignia showed a lion's head in yellow, set on a red inverted triangle with a black centre.

Formation badges were adopted by Allied contingents which were raised and equipped in Britain and the Empire. Among the units raised were Belgians, Free French, Dutch, Czechs, Greeks and Poles.

The 21st Army Group was commanded by Field Marshal Montgomery, who accepted the German surrender at Luneberg Heath on 6 June 1945. In August 1945, Headquarters 21st Army Group became Headquarters British Army of the Rhine. As well as the 1st Independent Brigade Group, there was a 2nd Independent Brigade Group.

Battle Honours

- *Monte Cassino, May 1944*
- *Adriatic coast, June–August 1944*
- *Gothic Line, September 1944*
- *Ravenna, December 1944*

Battle Honours

- *D-Day, 6 June 1944*
- *Normandy, June 1944*
- *Northern France, August 1944*
- *Germany, 1945*

1st Netherlands Division

The insignia shows a white sword with a yellow hilt set in the centre of a wreath of green olives. The hilt is flanked with the letters 'E' and 'M' in white, and the whole design is on a scarlet shield in the shape of the native weapon shield of Batavia.

The letters 'E' and 'M' stand for *Expeditionair Macht* (Expeditionary Force). The badge was worn after the liberation of Holland by those who volunteered for service against the Japanese in the Dutch East Indies.

There was also a 2nd Netherlands Division, the insignia for which was a shield divided vertically into five bars, red at the edges and in the centre, and two yellow between the red. This formation was not raised until 1946.

Norwegian Brigade

Following the surrender of Norway to the Germans in June 1940, thousands of her soldiers, sailors and airmen escaped to Britain and France to continue the fight. All Norwegian troops serving with the Allies wore a small replica of their national flag on the upper arm of their sleeves below the shoulder title *Nörge*.

The badge of the Norwegian Brigade depicted the North Cape in white, the midnight sun in yellow, set on a black square background with a khaki border. The Brigade was part of the British 52nd (Lowland) Division. The division saw much fighting after landing in northwest Europe in October 1944, in particular the difficult fighting to the Low Countries in the autumn and winter. The new year saw the Norwegians fighting in Germany.

Battle Honours

- *Dutch East Indies, 1945*

Battle Honours

- *Walcheren, October 1944*
- *Roer, January 1945*
- *Alpon, February 1945*
- *The Rhine, March 1945*

Other Allied

Peaked Cap Bands

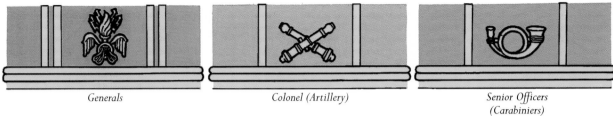

| Generals | Colonel (Artillery) | Senior Officers (Carabiniers) |

Collar Patches

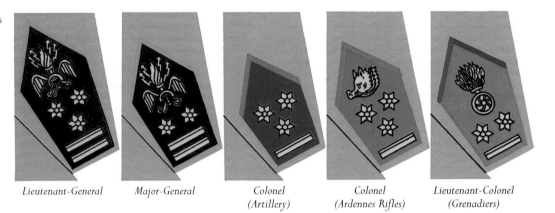

Lieutenant-General   Major-General   Colonel (Artillery)   Colonel (Ardennes Rifles)   Lieutenant-Colonel (Grenadiers)

Collar Patches

W.O. 1st Class (I) (Mtd Chasseurs)   W.O. (II) (Cyclist Carabiniers)   Sergeant-Major   Senior Sergeant   Sergeant

Cuff

Belgian Army

During World War I, the Belgian Army wore khaki uniforms. This was due to the fact that Britain was the only country who could provide enough new uniforms to replace the Belgians' obsolete ones. Officers, with their open tunics collars and ties, looked remarkably British in style. Conversely, by 1939, the other ranks, with their Adrian helmets (adorned with the Belgian lion on the front), closely resembled the French. All ranks wore a black, yellow, and red cockade on their peaked caps.

General officers carried two vertical gold bars and gold piping on their cap bands, field officers a single gold bar. Junior officers carried gold and warrant officers silver piping. Officers' and warrant officers'

190

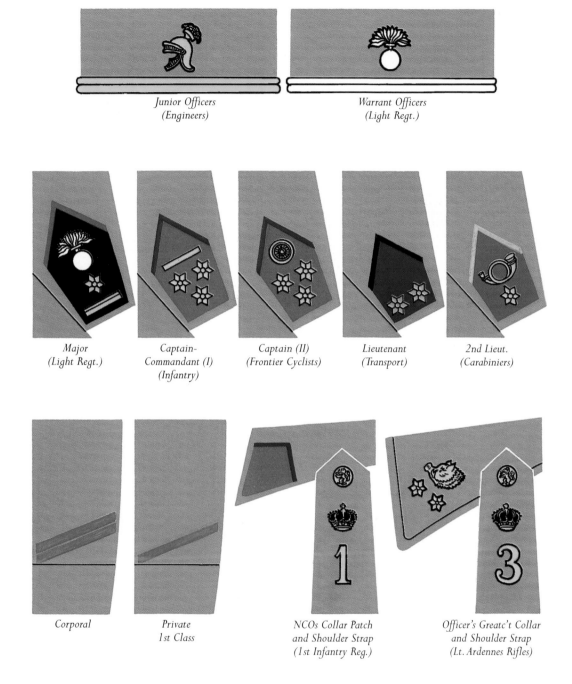

Junior Officers
(Engineers)

Warrant Officers
(Light Regt.)

Major
(Light Regt.)

Captain-
Commandant (I)
(Infantry)

Captain (II)
(Frontier Cyclists)

Lieutenant
(Transport)

2nd Lieut.
(Carabiniers)

Corporal

Private
1st Class

NCOs Collar Patch
and Shoulder Strap
(1st Infantry Reg.)

Officer's Greatc't Collar
and Shoulder Strap
(Lt. Ardennes Rifles)

rank badges were worn on collar patches and shoulder straps and were represented by a combination of bars and six-pointed stars.

Officers' arms-of-service were demonstrated by coloured collar patches and collar patch piping, in addition to an extensive range of yellow metal badges worn on the head-gear, collar patches and shoulder straps.

The insignia displayed on officers' caps, greatcoat collars, and often collar patches, represented their corps or service, whereas those on their shoulder straps represented the units to which they were attached.

The regimental number was worn on the left sleeve, but was often removed on the grounds of security prior to going into action.

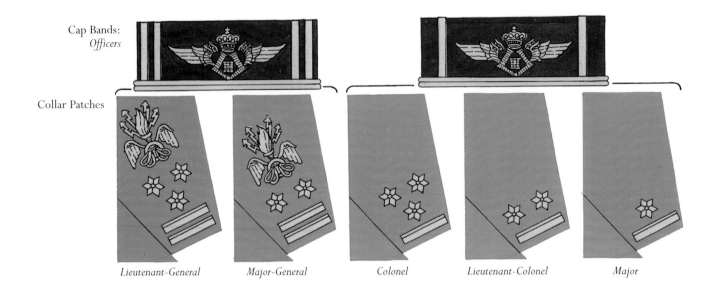

Cap Bands:
Officers

Collar Patches

Lieutenant-General   *Major-General*   *Colonel*   *Lieutenant-Colonel*   *Major*

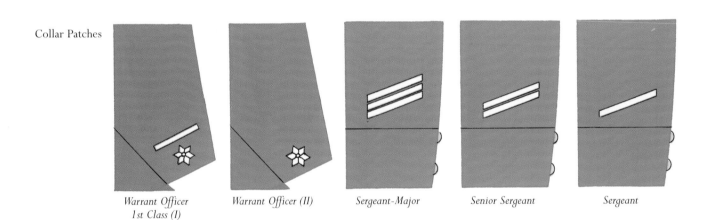

Collar Patches

Warrant Officer 1st Class (I)   *Warrant Officer (II)*   *Sergeant-Major*   *Senior Sergeant*   *Sergeant*

Belgian Air Force

The Belgian Air Force was formed on 1 March 1920 as part of the Army. From its conception until the beginning of World War II, it was always severely hampered by a lack of modern aircraft, which it was often forced to import from England and the USA.

When Germany invaded Belgium, only 180 of the Air Force's 234 craft were operational, most of these being obsolete. Of the few up-to-date Hurricanes present at Schaffen, only one remained intact after the

Belgians managed to disperse. The others had been destroyed outright on the ground.

Although the majority of conscripts to the Air Force wore an Army uniform with Air Force insignia, by 1940 there was another basic blue-grey uniform which the regular cadre of flying personnel had adopted. To further complicate matters, a number of officers continued to wear regimental uniform.

Most flying personnel would wear a peaked cap with a black peak and band, and a double-breasted

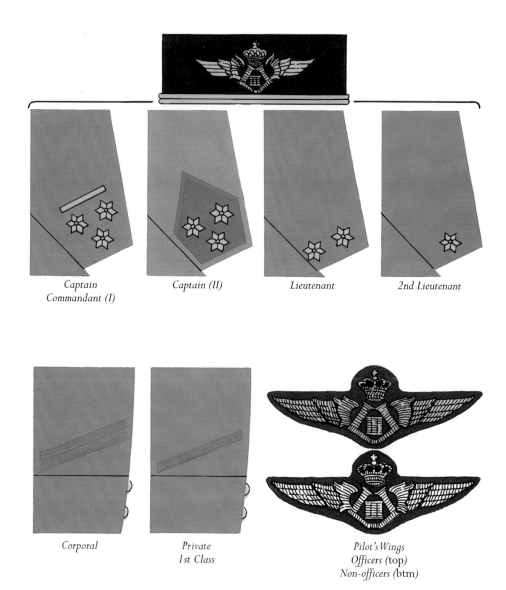

Captain
Commandant (I)   Captain (II)   Lieutenant   2nd Lieutenant

Corporal   Private
1st Class

Pilot's Wings
Officers (top)
Non-officers (btm)

greatcoat of the standard blue-grey colour. Long blue-grey trousers were worn with black shoes. Less common for these personnel were a pair of blue-grey breeches complete with knee-length boots, although these were seen on some officers.

Officers wore rank badges on their collar patches, wings on their left sleeves, and their squadron badges on the right breast pockets.

Cap bands represented wings between two vertical gold bands for field officers, and two pairs of gold bands for general officers. Rank was depicted by a combination of six-pointed gold stars and gold bars for officers. Warrant officers, on the other hand, wore silver stars and bars on the collar to denote their rank, while there were silver bars for sergeant-majors and sergeants, and red bars for junior non-commissioned officers.

Bright blue collar patches with red piping were worn on khaki uniforms, with enamelled squadron badges on the right breast pocket.

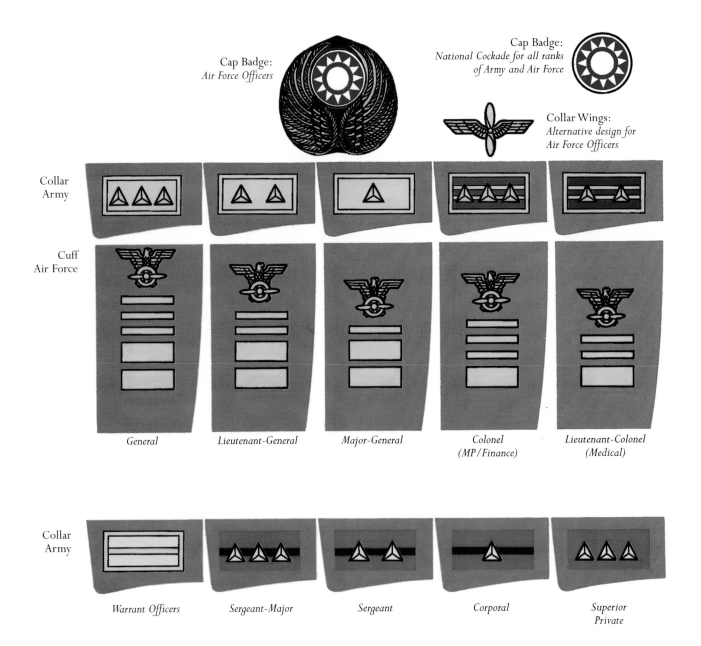

Cap Badge:
Air Force Officers

Cap Badge:
*National Cockade for all ranks
of Army and Air Force*

Collar Wings:
*Alternative design for
Air Force Officers*

Collar
Army

Cuff
Air Force

General

Lieutenant-General

Major-General

Colonel
(MP / Finance)

Lieutenant-Colonel
(Medical)

Collar
Army

Warrant Officers

Sergeant-Major

Sergeant

Corporal

Superior
Private

Chinese Army & Air Force

Both Nationalist and Communist forces wore a wide variety of uniforms throughout the war. Initially Germany had been instrumental in equiping the Chinese Army, to the extent that in the early stages of the war their more elite units would often parade in German helmets over-stamped with the national cockade on the left. On service dress, rank was **indicated by a series of gold triangles on various backgrounds on the collar.**

Collar patches, which varied in colour according to arm of service, were originally made of cloth, but when supplies became exhausted metal and plastic patches became more common. Other ranks wore a cotton label on their left breast with their name and unit stencilled in black.

194

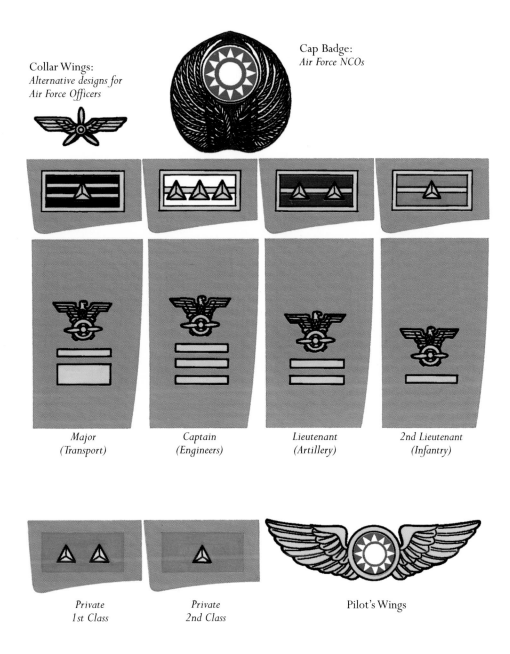

Collar Wings:
*Alternative designs for
Air Force Officers*

Cap Badge:
Air Force NCOs

Major
(Transport)

Captain
(Engineers)

Lieutenant
(Artillery)

2nd Lieutenant
(Infantry)

Private
1st Class

Private
2nd Class

Pilot's Wings

Uniforms in khaki and blue, which tended to fade to grey, became prevalent as the war progressed. Nationalist troops fighting with Stilwell in Northern Burma received a miscellany of United States surplus equipment, and although better catered for than most of their peers, these forces often tended to give a more 'irregular' appearance. Chinese uniforms could vary from region to region and year to year.

Air Force personnel wore khaki. Their cap badges represented the national cockade surrounded by a 'sunburst' of wings, gold for officers and white for other ranks. Rank badges were worn on the sleeves by officers, and on the collar patches by other ranks. Commissioned air crew wore eagle badges on their cuffs and collar patches, and non-flying officers blossoms, instead of eagle badges.

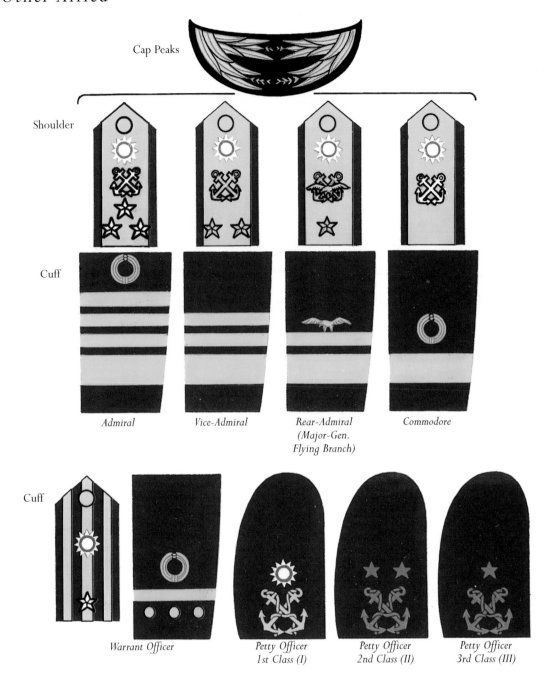

Cap Peaks

Shoulder

Cuff

| Admiral | Vice-Admiral | Rear-Admiral (Major-Gen. Flying Branch) | Commodore |

Cuff

| Warrant Officer | Petty Officer 1st Class (I) | Petty Officer 2nd Class (II) | Petty Officer 3rd Class (III) |

Chinese Navy

Officers were issued with a European-style uniform which had been standardised in 1913. This included a peaked cap and single-breasted tunic with concealed fly fastening trimmed at the edges; ratings wore a traditional square-rig with Royal Navy-style cap. Flag officers and senior officers could be identified by the gold embroidery on their cap peaks. Their greatcoat was double-breasted and worn with shoulder straps. The uniform for the summer months was white and followed the cut of the blue uniform.

Officers' rank badges were worn as rings on the cuff, with arm-of service 'lights' between the rank distinction lace. Shoulder boards were comprised of a series of five-pointed stars, augmented by single and

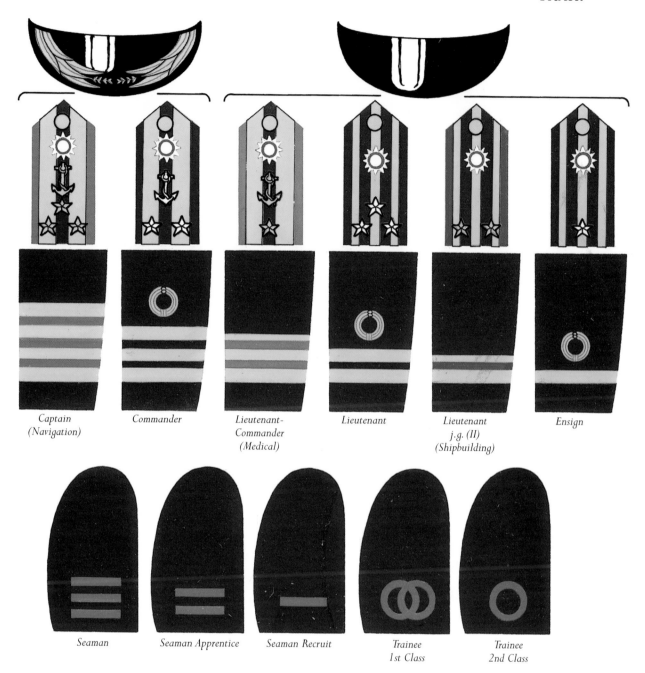

Captain (Navigation)

Commander

Lieutenant-Commander (Medical)

Lieutenant

Lieutenant j.g. (II) (Shipbuilding)

Ensign

Seaman

Seaman Apprentice

Seaman Recruit

Trainee 1st Class

Trainee 2nd Class

crossed anchors for lieutenant-commanders and above, whereas all ranks below these carried the emblem of 'the white sun and blue sky' on their shoulder boards.

Warrant officers were distinguished by a gold bar above three buttons worn on the cuff, and by a shoulder board comprising one thick and two thin parallel gold bars, a single five-pointed silver star, and

'the white sun and blue sky' emblem. Petty officers wore crossed fouled-anchors, or 'killicks', and seamen carried one, two or three bars on the arm.

Communist forces adopted the Nationalist Chinese uniform described above, but once civil war broke out, they often replaced their conventional head-dress with a 'Mao cap' bearing a five-pointed red star.

Other Allied

Cap Badges

Cap Badge:
General Rank

Cap Badge:
Senior Officers

Forage Cap:
Officers and Cornets

Forage Cap:
Officiants and Sergeants

Forage Cap:
Other Ranks

Pilot's Wings

| General | Lieutenant-General | Major-General | Colonel | Lieutenant-Colonel |

| Corps Officiant | Staff Officiant | Senior Officiant | Officiant | Cornet |

Danish Air Force & Army

Danish military uniform was undergoing a fundamental change from black to khaki at the outbreak of World War II. Due to budgetary constraints the change was being undertaken slowly. Thus, when the Germans invaded in April 1940, although most of the officers and regular non-commissioned officers had been re-equipped in khaki, the majority of conscripts still wore grey tunics and greatcoats, light blue trousers and black leather equipment.

Other ranks' uniform consisted of a single-breasted tunic with six bronzed buttons, pleated patch pockets and a stand-and-fall collar. Greatcoats were double-breasted with two rows of six buttons and a large fall collar, while the uniform trousers were worn rolled-up half way up the calf to sit outside the leather field boots.

The new M1923 pattern helmet, forged from steel, bore the Danish coat of arms on the front and had a distinctive shape. When the helmet was not necessary, all ranks wore a khaki side cap.

National Cockade

Cap Badge:
Junior Officers / Officiants

Cap Badge:
NCOs / Cornets

Collar Patches

Captain

Captain (II)

Lieutenant

*Lieutenant
of Reserves*

2nd Lieutenant

Collar Patches

*Sergeant-
Major*

Sergeant

Corporal

*Lance-
Corporal*

Helmet Badge

The Royal Danish Life Guards wore a grey-green field dress which was later adopted by the German-sponsored Schalburg Corps. A small number of Danes fought for the Germans in the Waffen-SS. They were issued with a shield in the Danish national colours which was worn on the left sleeve, or in the form of a Danebrog on the right collar patch.

Rank was indicated by the colour of the lace and braid on the side cap; and by the colour of the shoulder straps; for example, the shoulder straps were blue for officers and brown for other ranks.

Corporals wore yellow lace chevrons on their sleeves. All ranks wore the national cockade on their side hats, the intricacy of the pattern varying with rank. Officers wore a single gold star on the collars of their service dress.

When worn, arm-of-service identification comprised gilt metal badges on the tunic collar for officers, and enamelled badges above the right breast pocket for all other ranks.

Pilots wore their wings above the right hand breast pocket of their service dresses.

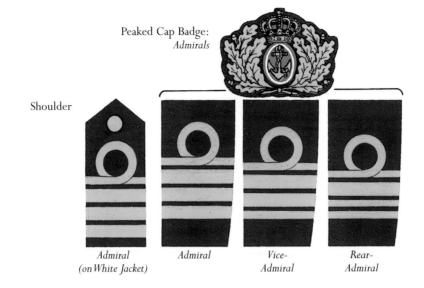

Peaked Cap Badge:
Admirals

Shoulder

| *Admiral (on White Jacket)* | *Admiral* | *Vice-Admiral* | *Rear-Admiral* |

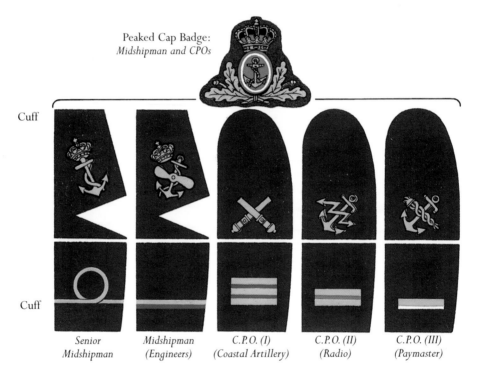

Peaked Cap Badge:
Midshipman and CPOs

Cuff

Cuff

| *Senior Midshipman* | *Midshipman (Engineers)* | *C.P.O. (I) (Coastal Artillery)* | *C.P.O. (II) (Radio)* | *C.P.O. (III) (Paymaster)* |

Danish Navy

The Danish Navy uniform was originally introduced in the 1870s, and altered twice prior to the outbreak of World War II, in 1909 and 1932. Those in the ranks of officers, chief petty officers and petty officers wore a peaked cap, reefer jacket with white shirt and black tie, matching navy-blue trousers, and black shoes.

Ratings in square rig wore a standard sailors' cap with a circular cockade in the national colours on the right side, and a blue jumper outside bell-bottomed trousers. In summer all ranks wore a white cap cover, and officers' and ratings' uniforms were also offered in white versions for hotter weather. Unusually, officers in greatcoat dress exhibited their rank badges on their sleeves rather than their shoulder straps.

Rank

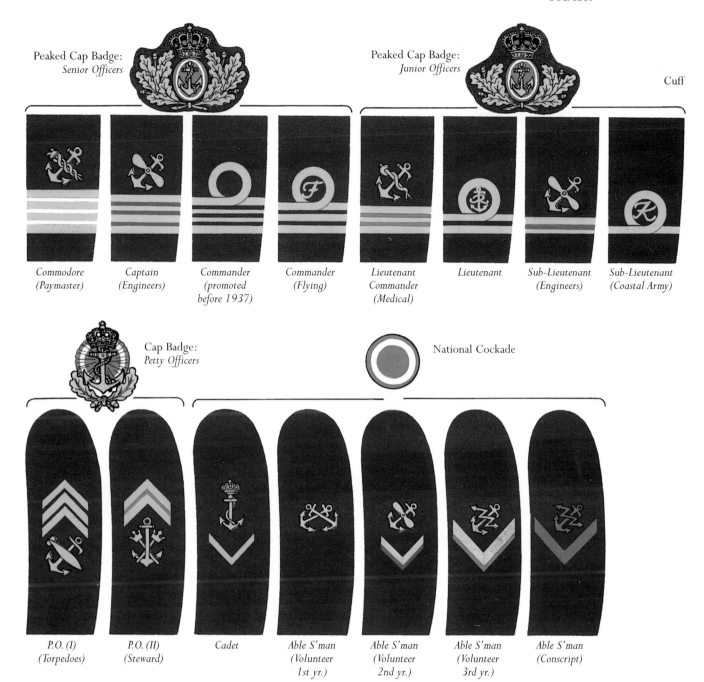

Peaked Cap Badge: *Senior Officers*

Peaked Cap Badge: *Junior Officers*

Cuff

Commodore (Paymaster)

Captain (Engineers)

Commander (promoted before 1937)

Commander (Flying)

Lieutenant Commander (Medical)

Lieutenant

Sub-Lieutenant (Engineers)

Sub-Lieutenant (Coastal Army)

Cap Badge: *Petty Officers*

National Cockade

P.O. (I) (Torpedoes)

P.O. (II) (Steward)

Cadet

Able S'man (Volunteer 1st yr.)

Able S'man (Volunteer 2nd yr.)

Able S'man (Volunteer 3rd yr.)

Able S'man (Conscript)

Rank groups were indicated by the size of the cap badge insignia, rank by the number and width of the silk bands worn on their sleeves by officers and chief petty officers. Petty officers and ratings wore their rank badges and service-of-arm indicators on their upper sleeves.

Officers in certain specialist arms of service wore a letter inside the 'curl' of their rank distinction lace ('K' for Coastal Artillery, 'F' for Air Arm, and 'R' for the Reserve).

Others branches could be identified by the coloured 'lights' that they wore between the rings. For example, the colour red between the rings denoted Medical, and the colour maroon Engineering.

Officers wore gold-embroidered wings above their right breast pockets.

Collar Patches

General

Lieutenant-General

Major-General

*Colonel
(Air Force)*

*Captain (I)
(Grenadiers)*

*Captain-Adjutant (II)
(Air Force)*

*1st Lieutenant (I)
(Cavalry)*

*1st Lieutenant Adjutant (II)
(Air Force)*

Cuff

*Sergeant-Major
(Infantry)*

*Senior Sergeant
(Jagers)*

*Quarterm't'r (top)
& Sergeant
(Air Force)*

Corporal

Dutch Army & Air Force

A grey-green uniform had been introduced for the Army in 1912, but soon the colour was subject to alteration, and by the outbreak of war in 1940, officers, warrant officers and non-commissioned officers wore a field-grey jacket not dissimilar to the German pattern, with matching occasionally piped breeches, ankle or riding boots and leather gaiters. Officers and warrant officers were issued with a brown leather waistbelt with a brass two-pronged buckle and leather cross-strap. Although the side hat was introduced for all ranks in 1937, a few officers continued to wear the kepi until it was finally abolished in the spring of 1940.

Air Force personnel wore Army uniforms but were distinguished by the fact that these were Army uniforms complete with blue piping. The Air Force personnel's embroidered badge comprised a radial engine and twin-bladed propeller and was worn on

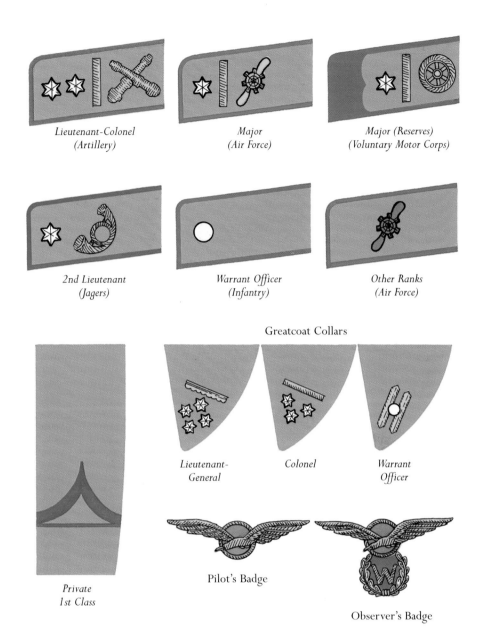

Lieutenant-Colonel
(Artillery)

Major
(Air Force)

Major (Reserves)
(Voluntary Motor Corps)

2nd Lieutenant
(Jagers)

Warrant Officer
(Infantry)

Other Ranks
(Air Force)

Greatcoat Collars

Lieutenant-
General

Colonel

Warrant
Officer

Private
1st Class

Pilot's Badge

Observer's Badge

their collars. Qualified pilots and observers were awarded a guilt metal badge worn on the left breast of the tunic and greatcoat. Flying clothes followed the French pattern.

General officers were distinguished by a special peaked cap, gold embroidered oak leaves on the tunic collar and two rows of crimson piping on the breeches. Officers' side caps were adorned with gold braid piping. Commissioned badges of rank, which took the form of gold and silver six-pointed stars,

with gold bars for officers of field rank, were worn on the tunic and greatcoat collar.

Other ranks wore rank insignia in the form of chevrons, surmounted by a crown for a sergeant-major, on the cuffs.

Piping on the side cap, breeches and tunic collar and cuffs denoted the officers' specialisation; red for artillery, green for Jagers and blue for the Air Force. Other ranks' chevrons were edged in their arm-of-service colours.

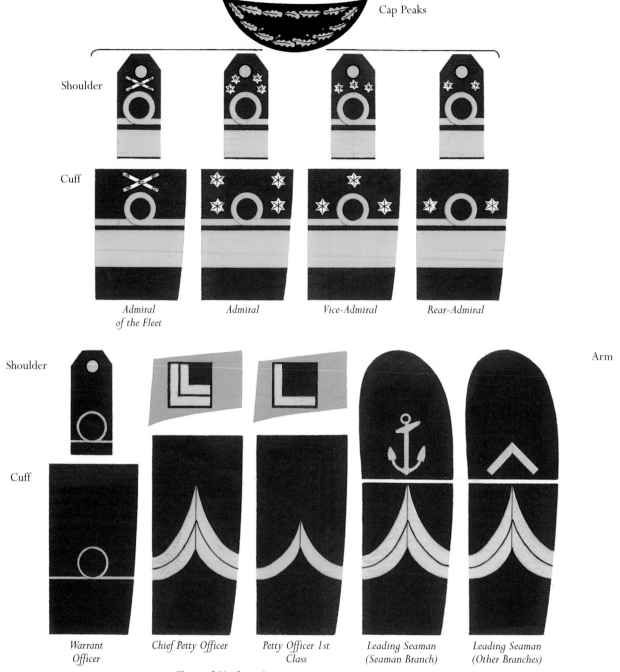

Cap Peaks

Shoulder

Cuff

*Admiral
of the Fleet*   *Admiral*   *Vice-Admiral*   *Rear-Admiral*

Shoulder

Arm

Cuff

*Warrant
Officer*   *Chief Petty Officer*   *Petty Officer 1st
Class*   *Leading Seaman
(Seaman Branch)*   *Leading Seaman
(Other Branches)*

Tropical Uniform Insignia

Royal Dutch Navy

Officers wore a standard uniform introduced in April 1933, with a frock coat issued in lieu of the greatcoat. Ratings wore a standard 'square rig' uniform over a blue and white striped vest. Their cap tally, adorned with the words *Koninklijke Marine* ('Royal Navy') in Gothic lettering, common at the beginning of

hostilities in 1939, had been largely replaced by one in block lettering by the time of Holland's entry into the war nine months later.

All ranks wore white uniforms for summer and tropical wear, including covers for the standard head-dress and a white sun helmet or straw panama hat.

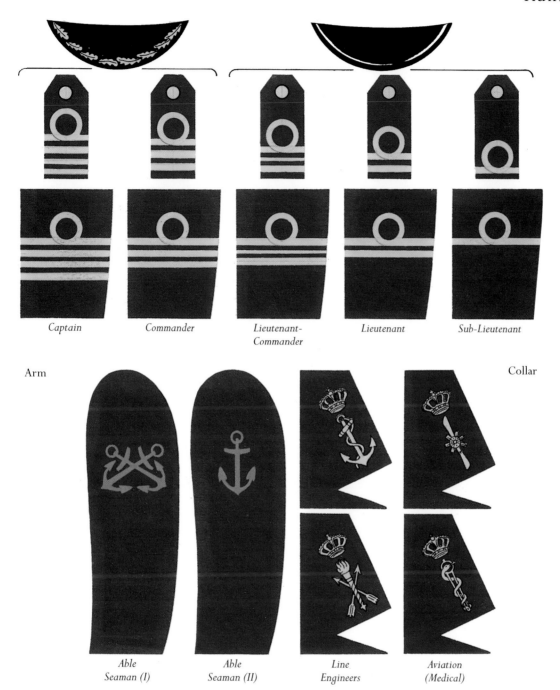

Captain   Commander   Lieutenant-   Lieutenant   Sub-Lieutenant
                        Commander

Arm   Collar

Able   Able   Line   Aviation
Seaman (I)   Seaman (II) Engineers   (Medical)

Officers and warrant officers wore rank distinction lace on the cuffs of their conventional blue uniforms, and on the shoulder straps of their white tunics. Senior petty officers wore their rank badges on the cuffs of their blue uniforms, and on the collar patches of their white (and the Marine Corps' grey-green) uniforms. Ratings wore rank on their cuffs.

Officers wore their arm-of-service emblems in the centre of their cap badges and on the collars of their reefer jackets; ratings' specialist insignia was exhibited on the upper left sleeve. Naval aircrew wore gilt metal wings on the left breast, Marines a painted black helmet with a white metal foul-anchor on the front, and Army badges of rank on Navy uniforms.

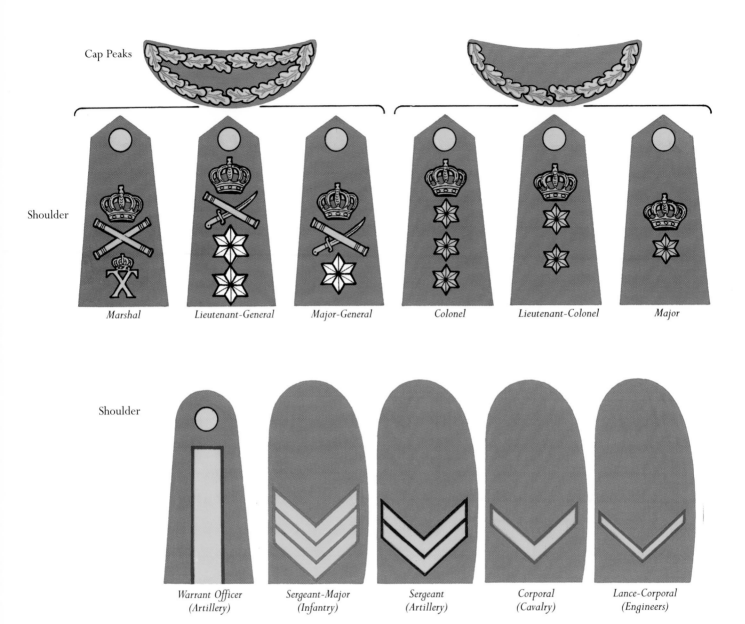

Cap Peaks

Shoulder

Marshal	*Lieutenant-General*	*Major-General*	*Colonel*	*Lieutenant-Colonel*	*Major*

Shoulder

Warrant Officer *(Artillery)*	*Sergeant-Major* *(Infantry)*	*Sergeant* *(Artillery)*	*Corporal* *(Cavalry)*	*Lance-Corporal* *(Engineers)*

Greek Army

The officers' service dress uniforms worn by the Greek Armed Forces were based on the British pattern, often with buttons bearing the British Coat of Arms, with the incorporation of collar patches. Double-breasted greatcoats for officers also bore collar patches and shoulder strap rank badges. Field officers were identified by a single row of gold braid on their cap peaks, whereas the cap peaks of general officers were easily distinguished in contrast by two rows.

Soldiers were issued with side-caps, tunics, single-breasted greatcoats and pantaloons worn with puttees and ankle boots. Mounted personnel wore breeches and riding boots or alternatively, leggings made of leather. Arm-of-service patches were worn on the collars, but often removed prior to going into action.

Evzones, elite highland infantry serving in light regiments and originally formed during the war for

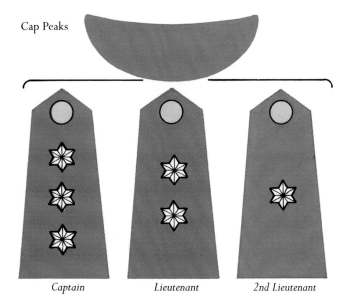

Cap Peaks

Captain   Lieutenant   2nd Lieutenant

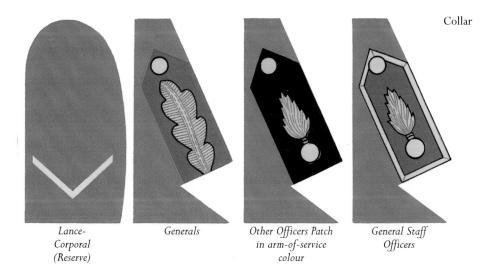

Collar

Lance-
Corporal
(Reserve)

Generals

Other Officers Patch
in arm-of-service
colour

General Staff
Officers

independence at the beginning of the nineteenth century – and which now formed the Royal Guard – wore a distinctive uniform comprising pleated kilts and shoes with woollen pompoms. However, the *Evzones* were invariably forced to abandon their distinctive dress when in combat in favour of the more conventional dress as worn by the other dismounted soldiers.

Officers wore rank badges, comprising crossed barrels for Marshals, and crossed swords and barrels for general officers. Gold crowns and six-pointed stars in gold and silver were worn in a combination for all. These rank badges were worn on their shoulder straps.

Non-commissioned officers wore chevrons on their sleeves, in gold or yellow lace edged with their arm-of-service for regular troops, and in unedged silver for conscripts.

These insignia were distinguishing features on a uniform which had developed along British lines.

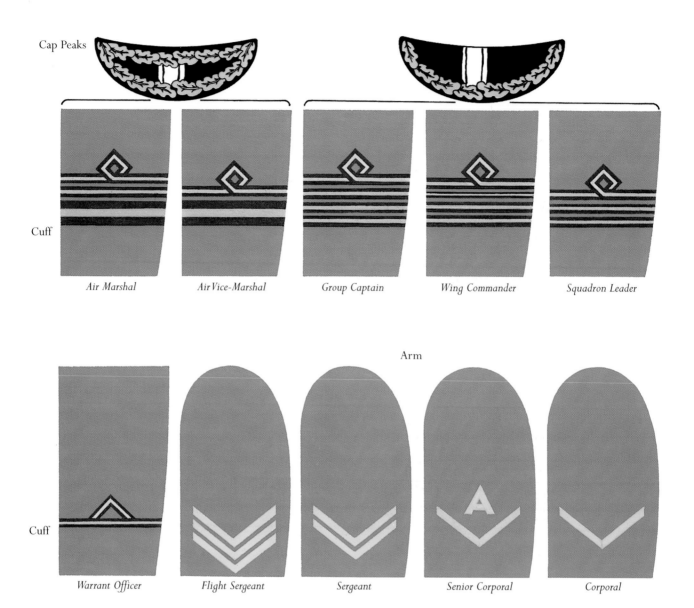

Cap Peaks

Cuff

| *Air Marshal* | *Air Vice-Marshal* | *Group Captain* | *Wing Commander* | *Squadron Leader* |

Arm

Cuff

| *Warrant Officer* | *Flight Sergeant* | *Sergeant* | *Senior Corporal* | *Corporal* |

Greek Air Force

The Greek Air Ministry, directly responsible for the air 'services' to the Greek Army and Navy, was in a position not familiar to every other nation; there was no independent air force as such. The Army air service, in consequence, was small, numbering just 250 officers and 3000 men. However, pilots had often completed their training in England, and proved to be a strong force in the 1941 campaigns.

Officers wore British design service dress, although officers on active service often preferred wearing breeches and high boots. The greatcoat and the side cap were modelled on the RAF pattern of the British. Other ranks wore a grey-blue version of the khaki Army uniform with side caps, single-breasted tunics, pantaloons, puttees and ankle boots. Flying clothing comprised the leather flying helmet, goggles, and a fleece-lined leather flying jacket which was worn over the service dress, or overall.

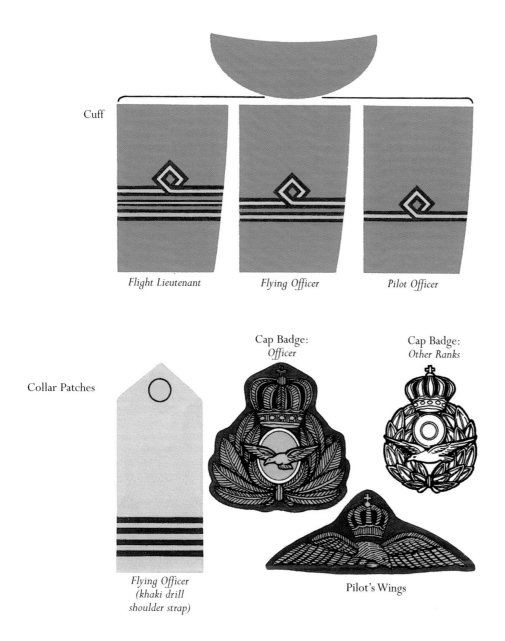

Cuff

Flight Lieutenant *Flying Officer* *Pilot Officer*

Collar Patches

Cap Badge: *Officer*

Cap Badge: *Other Ranks*

Flying Officer (khaki drill shoulder strap)

Pilot's Wings

General officers were distinguished by two – and field officers by one – rows of gold embroidered leaves on the peak of their caps. Their cap badges were embroidered in gold and comprised a crown above an eagle, wings outstretched, on a blue background between two patterns of feathers.

Rank distinctions were designated by thick and thin parallel stripes worn on the cuff, but followed the naval pattern with diamond shaped 'curls' on the upper row. When in summer-issue khaki drill, rank was worn on the shoulder straps and comprised light blue parallel bars, surrounded by a colouring of dark blue.

Warrant officers could be identified by the single light blue stripes that they wore, which were surmounted by an inverted 'v', the whole inset within dark blue surrounds, whereas the ranks of flight sergeant, sergeant, senior corporal and corporal were identified by yellow chevrons worn on the right upper arm.

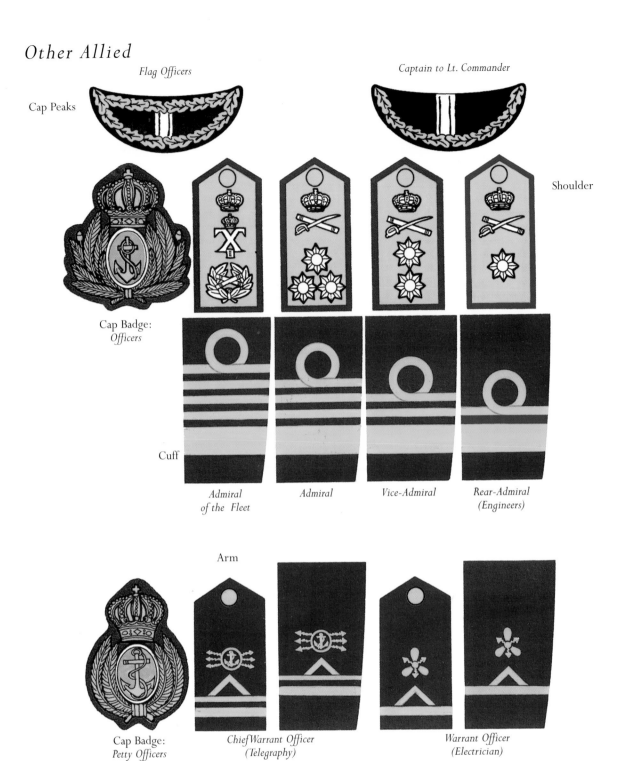

Flag Officers

Cap Peaks

Captain to Lt. Commander

Shoulder

Cap Badge:
Officers

Cuff

*Admiral
of the Fleet*

Admiral

Vice-Admiral

*Rear-Admiral
(Engineers)*

Arm

Cap Badge:
Petty Officers

*Chief Warrant Officer
(Telegraphy)*

*Warrant Officer
(Electrician)*

Greek Navy

Officers wore an international style uniform, following the pattern of the Royal Navy. Lieutenant commanders, commanders and captains were identified by a single row of gold adornment, in a style dependant upon their arm-of-service, on their cap peaks; flag officers wore two rows. All officers wore a cap badge of gold weave depicting a crown above a fouled anchor on a blue background surrounded by a laurel wreath.

Officers were issued with reefer jackets with rank distinction lace on the cuffs, long trousers and black shoes. White tunics with rank distinction lace on the shoulder straps were worn in summer, as were white

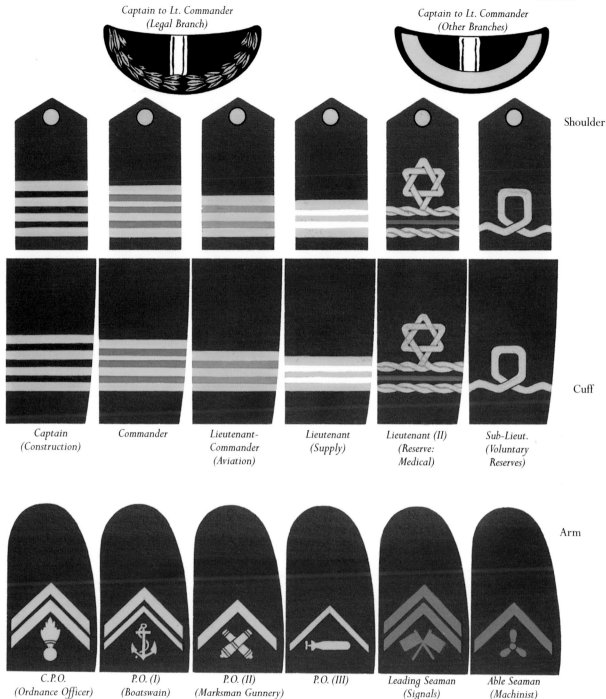

Captain to Lt. Commander
(Legal Branch)

Captain to Lt. Commander
(Other Branches)

Shoulder

Cuff

| Captain (Construction) | Commander | Lieutenant-Commander (Aviation) | Lieutenant (Supply) | Lieutenant (II) (Reserve: Medical) | Sub-Lieut. (Voluntary Reserves) |

Arm

| C.P.O. (Ordnance Officer) | P.O. (I) (Boatswain) | P.O. (II) (Marksman Gunnery) | P.O. (III) | Leading Seaman (Signals) | Able Seaman (Machinist) |

trousers and canvas shoes and white covers over the peaked cap. Rank distinction on the winter greatcoats was also worn on the shoulder straps.

In line with British tradition, officers of the Volunteer Reserve wore 'wavy' rank distinction lace; while officers of the Reserve rank wore distinction lace in which the 'curl' formed a six-pointed star.

Ratings were issued with standard 'square-rig' uniforms, a white version for use in tropical climates, and leggings which followed the British pattern.

Warrant officers and chief warrant officers wore their rank badges and arm-of-service indicators on their sleeves; petty officers and below on their upper right sleeve.

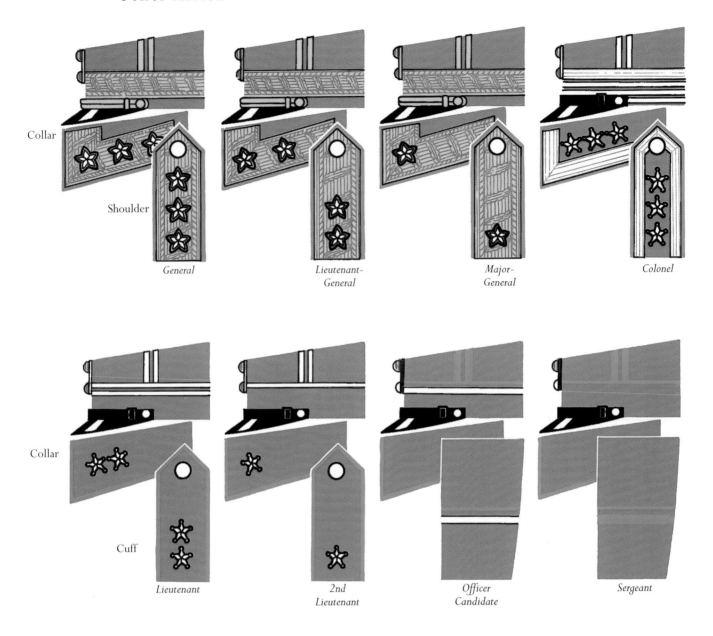

Collar

Shoulder

General

*Lieutenant-
General*

*Major-
General*

Colonel

Collar

Cuff

Lieutenant

*2nd
Lieutenant*

*Officer
Candidate*

Sergeant

Norwegian Army & Air Force

In 1939 Norway's government believed that effective defence of its nation against a major power was impossible due to Norway's small standing army. However, after the shock of the invasion of Finland by the Soviet Union, a force of considerable size was established in northern Norway. The 1912-pattern grey-green uniform continued to be worn by all ranks, either with a kepi or a side cap with a piped flap.

The first helmet to be worn by the men of the Norwegian Army was the British Mark I but this was to be replaced by the Swedish civil defence helmet. This was designated by the Norwegians as M1931. Of course, the helmet could be used as a source of identification and in 1935 an oval badge bearing the stamp of the Norwegian lion was issued to be worn on the front of the helmet.

Rank distinction lace was displayed by the officers on the kepi, tunic collar and greatcoat shoulder straps.

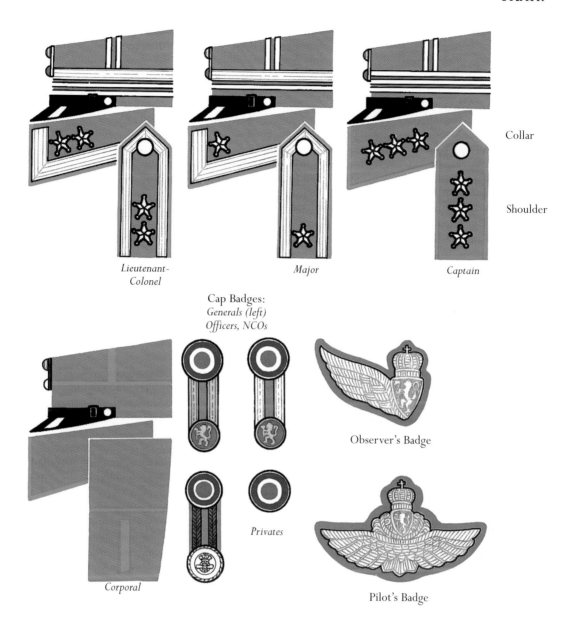

Lieutenant-
Colonel

Major

Captain

Collar

Shoulder

Cap Badges:
Generals (left)
Officers, NCOs

Observer's Badge

Privates

Corporal

Pilot's Badge

General officers wore gold bands on their kepis as well as one, two, or three five-pointed stars on a gold background on their collars and shoulder straps. Field officers were differentiated by one thick, and up to three thin, silver bands on their kepis and from one to three stars silver-edged on their collars and shoulder straps, and junior officers identified by thin stripes on their kepis, and by stars on a plain background.

Non-commissioned officers wore their rank distinctions on their cuffs and as green stripes on their kepis. Arm-of-service distinctions were indicated by the colour and design of the uniform buttons and by the colour of the piping on the kepis, tunic collars, cuffs and trousers.

Despite her size, the Norwegian Air Force was to play a short part in World War II. By early in 1940, nearly all of the airfields south of Narvik were occupied by German forces and most of Norway's newly developed fighters has been destroyed by the Germans on the first day of the Oslo invasion.

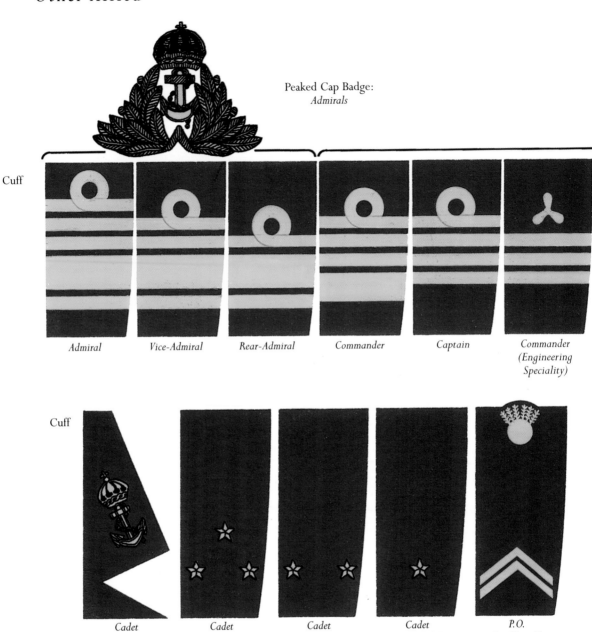

Peaked Cap Badge:
Admirals

Cuff

Admiral   *Vice-Admiral*   *Rear-Admiral*   *Commander*   *Captain*   *Commander (Engineering Speciality)*

Cuff

Cadet (Collar: Anchor)   *Cadet (3rd Grade)*   *Cadet (2nd Grade)*   *Cadet (1st Grade)*   *P.O. 1st Class (I) (Gunnery)*

Norwegian Navy

The Norwegian Navy uniform dated from 1907 and had changed little in over 30 years. Officers, officer-cadets and petty officers wore peaked caps, double-breasted reefer jackets with white shirts and black ties, matching blue trousers, and black shoes. Officers were issued with black astrakhan caps in the winter decorated with a particular pattern of cap badge.

Ratings wore standard 'square rigs' with caps bearing the legend, *Den KGL Norsk Marine* (Royal Norwegian Navy). In winter they were issued with double-breasted pea-coats.

Rank was indicated by the pattern of cap badge for officers, officer-cadets, chief petty officers, quartermasters and petty officers. Officers also wore the conventional rank distinction lace on their reefer cuffs and greatcoat shoulder straps, and as their mark of

Peaked Cap Badge:
Officers

Lieutenant-
Commander

Lieutenant
(Special Service)

Sub-Lieutenant

Commander
(Medical)

Reserve Officers
Lt-Commander
(Supply)

Sub-Lieutenant
(Engineers)

Cockade: *O.R.s*

P.O.
2nd Class (II)
(Radio)

P.O.
3rd Class (III)
(Reserve)

Leading Seaman

Able Seaman

Ordinary Seaman

Peaked
Cap Badge:
P.O.s

distinction, ratings wore their badges of rank on their upper left sleeve.

Officers in certain branches, notably medical and supply, were identified by a flattened top to the 'curl' on their rank distinction lace; others, such as engineers and supply, had the 'curl' removed. Coloured lights, either between or above the rank circles, were also employed to denote a particular arm-of-service.

Chief petty officers were issued with gold trade badges, and petty officers and below them in rank, red badges, which were worn above the rank indicators on the arm. Qualified pilots of the Naval Air Service wore gold-embroidered wings on the right breast of their uniforms. Ratings' special branch and trade badges were designed to incorporate wings and the letter 'A' on the upper left hand sleeve of their uniforms.

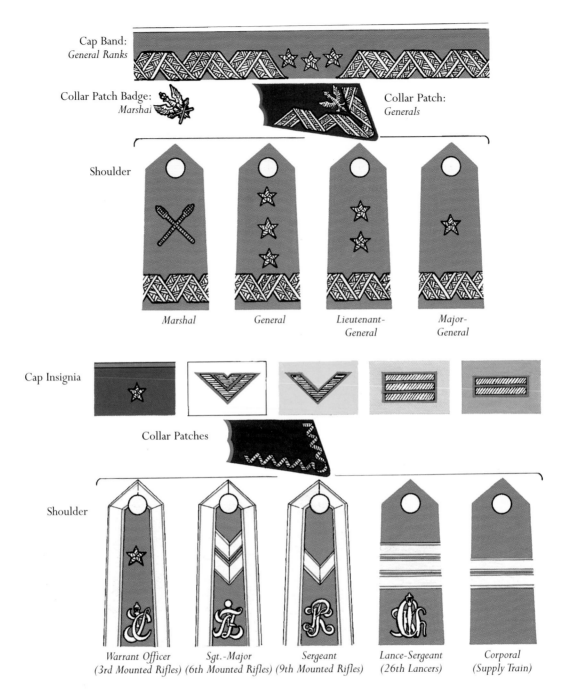

Cap Band:
General Ranks

Collar Patch Badge:
Marshal

Collar Patch:
Generals

Shoulder

Marshal *General* *Lieutenant-General* *Major-General*

Cap Insignia

Collar Patches

Shoulder

Warrant Officer
(3rd Mounted Rifles)

Sgt.-Major
(6th Mounted Rifles)

Sergeant
(9th Mounted Rifles)

Lance-Sergeant
(26th Lancers)

Corporal
(Supply Train)

Polish Army

Rank badges in the Polish Army were worn on the head-dress and shoulder straps. General officers were distinguished by dark blue stripes on their breeches and trousers, by silver braid stripes and rank stars below their cap badges, and by silver zigzag embroidery on the band of their peaked caps, collar patches, shoulder straps and cuffs.

The basic rank badge for all officers was the five-pointed star, embroidered in silver wire and worn on the shoulder straps. Field officers' shoulder straps were further embellished with 5mm (0.19in) double bars embroidered in silver wire, at 15mm (0.59in) from the seam. Regimental numbers and monograms (units were frequently named after famous historical characters) were usually embroidered 7.5mm

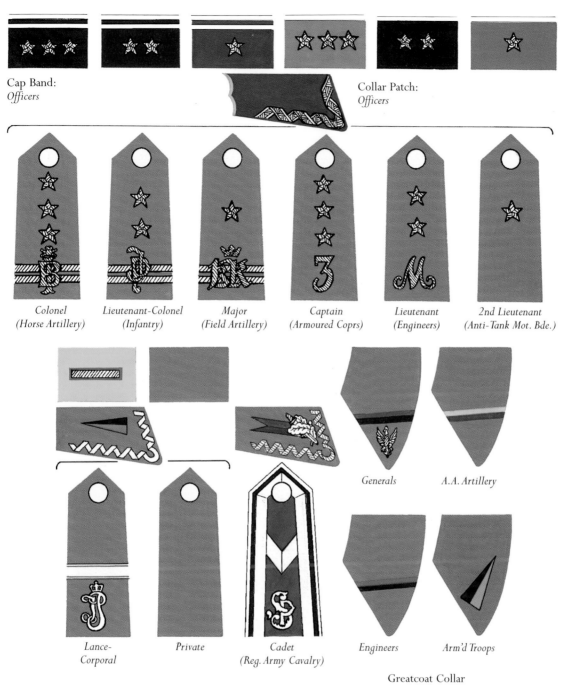

Cap Band:
Officers

Collar Patch:
Officers

Colonel
(Horse Artillery)

Lieutenant-Colonel
(Infantry)

Major
(Field Artillery)

Captain
(Armoured Coprs)

Lieutenant
(Engineers)

2nd Lieutenant
(Anti-Tank Mot. Bde.)

Lance-
Corporal

Private

Cadet
(Reg. Army Cavalry)

Generals

A.A. Artillery

Engineers

Arm'd Troops

Greatcoat Collar
Patches

(0.29in) from the seam, field officers' being evenly positioned across the double bars.

Monograms were worn on the shoulder straps, made in silver wire embroidery for officers and warrant officers, and in white metal for other ranks.

Warrant officers wore single stars at the front of their caps and on shoulder straps. Staff-sergeants and sergeants wore chevrons embroidered in silver on red felt on their caps and on shoulder straps, junior non-commissioned officers straight bars. Warrant officers wore officer-pattern zigzags on the collar, other non-commissioned officers a simpler design embroidered in silver, and junior ranks a zigzag made of silver braid.

Regular army officer cadets were issued with distinctive shoulder straps with silver piping and all-silver braid.

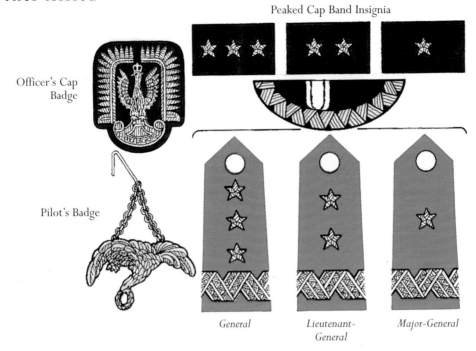

Peaked Cap Band Insignia

Officer's Cap
Badge

Pilot's Badge

| General | Lieutenant-General | Major-General |

Peaked Cap Band Insignia

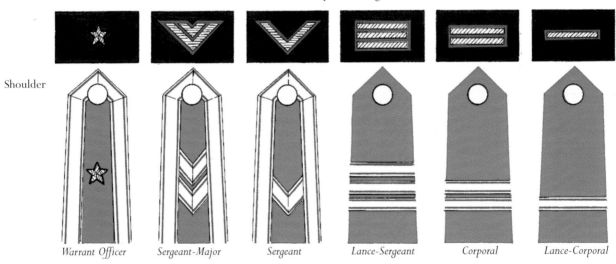

Shoulder

| Warrant Officer | Sergeant-Major | Sergeant | Lance-Sergeant | Corporal | Lance-Corporal |

Polish Air Force

The Polish Air Force dated from the end of World War I – even before Poland gained her independence. In 1936, its uniform was transformed into a blue-grey design, and it was planned that all officers and regular NCOs were to be wearing it by April 1938. Rank badges were worn on peaked caps and berets, on tunic and greatcoat shoulder straps, and on the upper left sleeve of flying suits.

General officers wore silver zigzag embroidery on the peaks of their hats below silver rank stars to denote their status. However, field officers were identified by the much more simple twin stripes, and junior officers wore single stripes around the edges of their peaks.

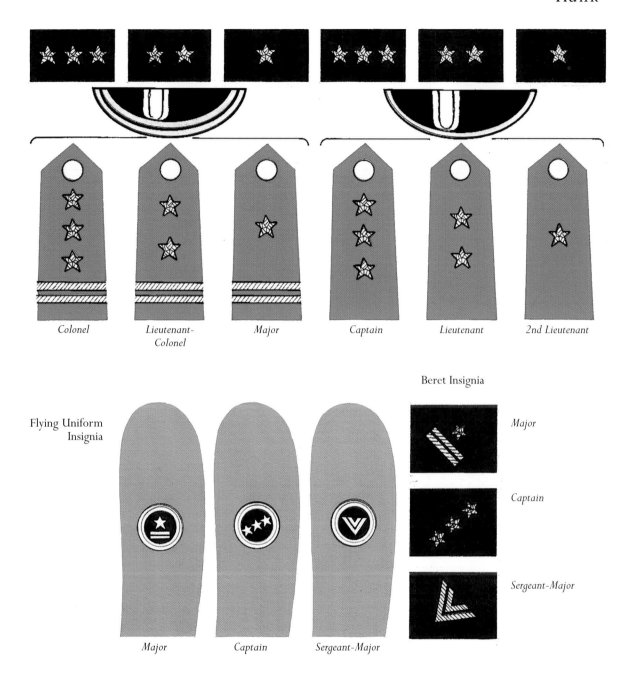

Colonel   Lieutenant-   Major   Captain   Lieutenant   2nd Lieutenant
            Colonel

Flying Uniform
Insignia

Beret Insignia

Major

Captain

Sergeant-Major

Major   Captain   Sergeant-Major

All officers wore five-pointed stars embroidered in silver wire on their shoulder straps. Field officers' shoulder straps were further embellished with 5mm (0.19in) double bars embroidered in silver wire, at 15mm (0.59in) from the seam.

Warrant officers wore single stars at the front of their caps and on their shoulder straps. Sergeant-majors and sergeants wore chevrons embroidered in silver on red felt on their caps and shoulder straps; junior non-commissioned officers wore straight bars.

Specialist officers wore white metal badges on the tunic and greatcoat collars, administrative officials wore royal blue to denote their arm-of-service and medical personnel cherry-coloured cloth as backing to their rank distinction braid on their peaked caps, and as lace on their tunic cuffs and trousers.

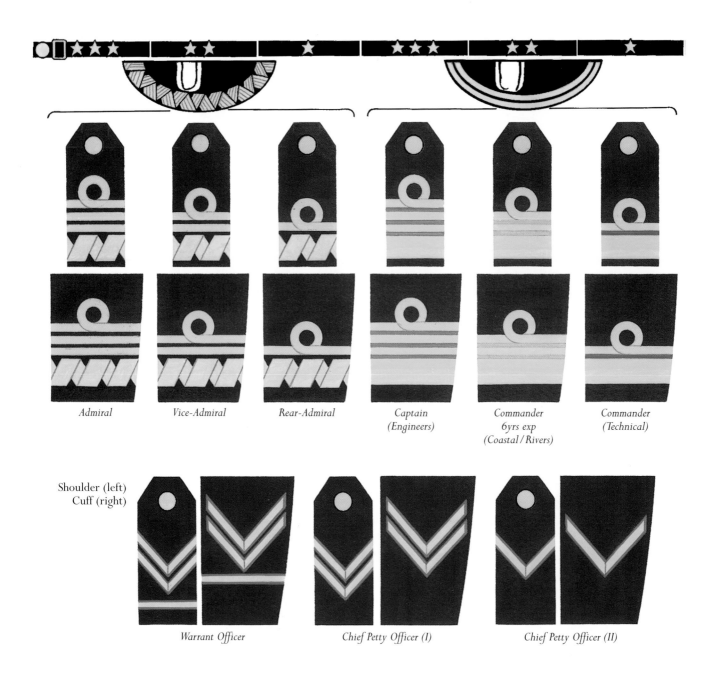

Admiral   Vice-Admiral   Rear-Admiral   Captain (Engineers)   Commander 6yrs exp (Coastal / Rivers)   Commander (Technical)

Shoulder (left) Cuff (right)

Warrant Officer   Chief Petty Officer (I)   Chief Petty Officer (II)

Polish Navy

The Treaty of Versailles had granted Poland 145km (90 miles) of Baltic Coastline and with the acquisition of territory the Poles accordingly constructed a large modern naval complex west of Danzig. The Polish Navy wore uniforms similar to those worn in most other navies. Based on regulations issued between 1920 and 1930, they allowed officers white cap covers, tunics, trousers, and white shoes in hot weather. Rank insignia was indicated by the number and thickness of the gold lace stripes on the cuffs and shoulder straps of the officers, chief petty officers and petty officers. Admirals had zigzag gold braid on the peaks of their caps, senior officers twin rows of braid and junior officers a single row.

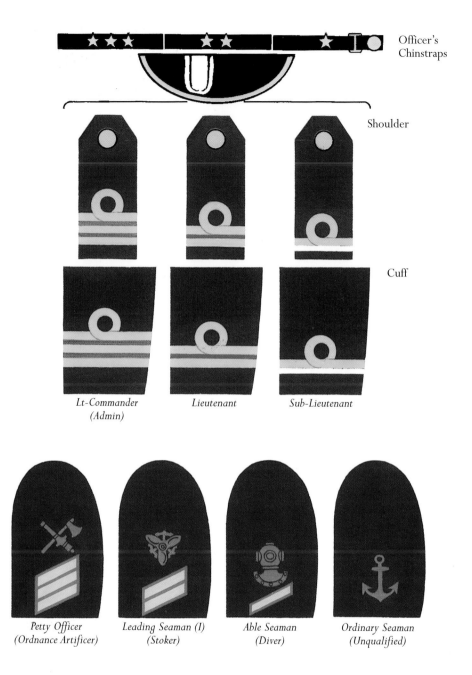

Officer's
Chinstraps

Shoulder

Cuff

Lt-Commander
(Admin)

Lieutenant

Sub-Lieutenant

Petty Officer
(Ordnance Artificer)

Leading Seaman (I)
(Stoker)

Able Seaman
(Diver)

Ordinary Seaman
(Unqualified)

All officers had one, two, or three five-pointed gold stars on their chinstraps which, in conjunction with the marking on the peak, denoted rank when the wearer was donned in protective clothing.

In working order, petty officers could be differentiated by their peaked caps, single-breasted blue tunics, with stand collars, patch pockets, and five buttons.

Ratings wore their badges of rank on the upper left sleeve below their trade or speciality badges, which were yellow for petty officers, and red for seamen. From November 1938 onwards corps and branch colours were worn as backing or 'lights', which was the name given to the coloured cloth positioned between the gold lace stripes located on the cuffs and shoulder straps.

Index

222

Index